The *Bear*
and the *Northland*

The *Bear* and the *Northland*

Legendary Coast Guard Cutters in the Alaskan Ice

ARTHUR G. SHARP

McFarland & Company, Inc., Publishers
Jefferson, North Carolina

ISBN (print) 978-1-4766-9211-1
ISBN (ebook) 978-1-4766-4976-4

Library of Congress and British Library
cataloguing data are available

Library of Congress Control Number 2023026916

© 2023 Arthur G. Sharp. All rights reserved

No part of this book may be reproduced or transmitted in any form or by any means, electronic or mechanical, including photocopying or recording, or by any information storage and retrieval system, without permission in writing from the publisher.

On the cover: The *Bear* at anchor in July 1908 off Alaska (USCG Historian's Office); inset The Coast Guard cutter *Northland* (Alaska State Archives & Alaska State Library)

Printed in the United States of America

*McFarland & Company, Inc., Publishers
Box 611, Jefferson, North Carolina 28640
www.mcfarlandpub.com*

This book is dedicated to my granddaughter, a graduate of the U.S. Coast Guard Academy, her classmates, and all the members of the U.S. Coast Guard, past, present, and future, who have protected our shores faithfully for nearly 250 years and will no doubt continue to do so for centuries to come.
Semper Paratus! (Always ready)

Table of Contents

Preface — 1

Introduction—The Bear *and the* Northland: *The "911s" of the North* — 3

1—*Semper Paratus*, Bert Rankin — 11

2—Captain, My Captain — 15

3—Reindeer Rustlers — 21

4—Do Bears Have Tales? — 33

5—The Bizarre Court-Martial of Captain Healey — 39

6—The *Bear* May Have Been a Ship, but There Was Railroading Afloat — 45

7—Impeach Hamlin and Convict Healey — 53

8—The Fallout Hurts More than Healey — 60

9—Ellsworth P. Bertholf, the Santa Claus of the Coast Guard — 65

10—A Unique Partnership — 73

11—Providing Provisions — 80

12—Relief at Point Barrow — 86

13—1900—A Year of Death, Disease, and Devotion — 92

14—The *Bear* Takes a Hawaiian Vacation — 100

15—The *Bear* Rides the Waves to Bust a Crime Wave — 106

16—The Only Ship the Bering Patrol Lost — 112

17—Judge Not, Lest Ye Be "Thurbered" — 116

18—A Lieutenant Makes a Major Discovery — 121

19—Healey and His Counterparts Share a Conundrum — 126

20—Sailing on the "Inconsistent Sea" — 132

21—Five Killed, a Dozen Captured — 138

22—A Seemingly Hopeless Task	145
23—The *Bear* and the *Karluk*	151
24—The *Bear* and the Explorers	155
25—The *Bear* Goes into Hibernation	162
26—The Great Walrus Hunt	169
27—Routine, but Challenging	174
28—Sailing Toward War	181
29—World War II's Weirdest Battle	186
Epilogue: The Bear *Goes to the Bottom; the* Northland *Ends Life on the Scrap Heap*	192
Appendix A—Technical Specifications/Features (the Northland*)*	195
Appendix B—How The Call *Has Outfitted the* Bear	197
Chapter Notes	199
Bibliography	205
Index	209

Preface

Curiosity may have killed the cat, but it brought the *Bear* alive. In this case the old wooden *Bear* is the legendary United States Coast Guard cutter that served 47 years in Alaska, with occasional side trips to Hawaii and Greenland. The former whaler even served for a while in World War II. It was that longevity that sparked my interest in the *Bear* and its successor, the *Northland*.

When I learned that one of my granddaughters would be graduating from the U.S. Coast Guard Academy in New London, Connecticut, I decided to do a short history of the *Bear* for her as a personalized gift. I am, after all, a historian who writes books. I thought it would give her an insight into the long-serving cutter that has contributed to the academy's cadets the nickname "Bears"; 98,000 words later I had a book completed.

I started the research as a part-time project. Research is my strongpoint. It is also a weak point. I get sidetracked often as I read old newspapers and magazines and forget what I was looking for originally. That is what happened with what was originally intended to be "A short *Bear* story."

There was no shortage of material containing *Bear* stories. I did most of my research by reading old newspapers that documented the activities of the *Bear* and other cutters with which it coordinated assignments, and poring over the ship's logs, which are available on-line. That took me back to 1884. I kept seeing the same names of "Coasties," a nickname associated with members of the service, assigned to the vessel at one point or another, and often together: Captain Michael Healey, Lieutenant Ellsworth Price Bertholf, Lieutenant David H. Jarvis….

I followed their careers as they rose through the ranks, accepted new jobs, completed heroic feats, married, had children … it was almost as if I knew them personally. I had to learn more about them and the men with whom they served. (The Coast Guard comprised only men at the time. It wasn't until 1918 that twin sisters Genevieve and Lucille Baker became the first uniformed women to serve in the Coast Guard.) I read articles about the *Bear* dating from 1884 to 1927, when the technologically updated, steel-framed *Northland* replaced the *Bear* on the Alaskan station. That created a link between the "old" and "new" Coast Guards.

Why end my research there? I continued reading articles and logs about both ships. The *Northland* served from 1927 until 1944, when its Coast Guard career was ended after its propeller was damaged during a sea battle near Greenland. The *Bear* was still afloat at the time, but both cutters' glory days were over. The link between them was not. It will last forever, in this book and the memories of "Coasties" who have served aboard them and assorted cutters since they went to their ignominious endings. (The *Bear* sank at sea while being towed to Philadelphia to be converted into a restaurant; the *Northland* was sold for scrap.)

So, what started out as a short, personalized profile of a U.S. Coast Guard icon morphed into a full-blown history of two of the service's most memorable cutters and the men who served aboard them. I am sure my granddaughter will not mind if I share the book with Coast Guard history aficionados. Maybe that was my goal all along, and I just got sidetracked.

Probably.

Acknowledgments

Thanks go to the many 19th- and 20th-century newspaper and magazine staff members who thought highly enough about the Coast Guard's services in the Alaskan region to write about them. It was largely their efforts that made this book possible, since they reported on the day-to-day events upon which the contents are based. After all, history is always told better through the eyes of the people who lived it.

Caveat

Dates, names, places, etc., relating to different sources' accounts of specific events may not always agree or be spelled correctly. Since communications back in the late 19th and early 20th centuries were not always instantaneous and travel was slow, few publications assigned reporters to distant locations for on-site coverage of significant events. So, at times editors changed information to suit their needs and opinions, avoid time-consuming fact checking with the original sources, or inject local flavor into their reports. The basics of the stories, however, are accurate.

Introduction

The Bear *and the* Northland:
The "911s" of the North

"More than anything there is the sense of scale: you can fly for hours and hours of Alaska and you look down and all you'll see is forests, lakes and snow-capped mountains, with no sign whatsoever of human beings."
—Steve Backshall[1]

If that observation is true today it was even truer in 1867 when the United States purchased Alaska. The vast region was an unknown quantity, one that had to be governed somehow. There was no government per se there at the time, and the native population who lived in the region were so widely dispersed that getting them all together would have been like trying to collect all the stars in one universe in a thimble.

Nevertheless, the U.S. Congress tried to establish an Alaskan government and a means to communicate among the widely scattered—and often lawless—residents. The job was delegated to what was known as the revenue cutter service, to which we will refer as the Coast Guard throughout this book. Due to its efforts, two Coast Guard cutters from different eras, the *Bear* and the *Northland*, became icons in American folklore. That was because they were the links to the old and new Coast Guards between 1884 and 1947, as the *Northland* replaced the *Bear*. Their combined service spanned 63 years, during which Americans followed their paths vicariously. Their collective history was a glorious one.

Between 1884 and 1927 the *Bear* broke ice paths, fought pirates (aka freebooters) and smugglers, escorted vessels carrying copious amounts of gold, rescued explorers, and performed a myriad of less-exciting tasks along its northern patrol route. It was the 19th-century answer to "Who ya' gonna call?"

Captain Charles F. Shoemaker, chief of the Coast Guard in the late 1890s, seemed to have a predilection for the *Bear*. It was the first cutter he thought of when a critical assignment arose. When the president of the North American Transportation Company in Portland, Oregon, requested a cutter to accompany his steamer *Portland*, laden with $2,000,000 worth of gold dust from the Klondike, out of the Bering Sea in 1897, the *Bear* was called upon to do the job.[2]

The Treasury Department decided there was a likelihood the *Portland* would be attacked by bandits intent on stealing the gold. The company president informed the

The *Bear* at anchor in July 1908 off Alaska (USCG Historian's Office).

department that *Portland* would leave St. Michael, Alaska, between September 30 and October 10. Shoemaker immediately telegraphed orders to Captain Hooper, the commander of the Bering Sea patrol fleet, to assign the *Bear* as an escort. The orders were issued and the versatile *Bear* added one more duty to its list. Not many pirates wanted to tangle with the *Bear* and its crew.

Every spring for years the *Bear* was the first vessel to enter the Bering Sea after the winter ice disappeared. Like clockwork the *Bear* left Seattle in April or May. By early June it was at the southern edge of the receding ice floes ready to follow them north. Traditionally it led the parade of passenger and freight vessels that carried the desperately needed fresh supplies for the winter-bound camps.

Throughout the summer the *Bear* patrolled the Bering, leaving it every once in a while to venture up through the Bering Straits into the Arctic Ocean. On those side trips it carried supplies to isolated Eskimo school stations and mission posts, assisted vessels in distress, and visited points off the Siberian coast. People in every Alaskan sea coast point from Point Barrow, at the corner of the continent, down to the Aleutian Islands, and sites in southwestern Alaska, knew the *Bear*. The ship was a traveling public relations campaign for the U.S. government.

The officers and crew did not distinguish among the nationalities of the people they helped. Their job was to help people—all people. Canadians, Russians, Americans... The *Bear* was there for all of them, working alone or with ships of other nations. There were plenty of them as numerous people such as explorers, whalers, military personnel, and curiosity seekers experienced the relatively new far north.

Rear Admiral George S. Melville of the U.S. Navy said that "In many respects the *Bear* is the strongest and best constructed vessel that enters the Arctic Ocean."[3] History bore that out. The coal-burning barkentine *Bear* (a sailing vessel with three or more masts; with a square rigged foremast and fore-and-aft rigged main, mizzen and any other masts) was like a member of a family that people hate to see leave. The Coast Guard just could not bear to take it out of service even after two decades of service. And why would it? The *Bear* had served faithfully since 1884—and it wasn't even a cub then.

The 689-ton vessel was built at Greenock, Scotland, in 1874 by the innovative shipbuilders Alexander Stephens & Son [William]. Owner W. Grieve purchased it for use as an Arctic sealer.[4] The Coast Guard acquired it in 1884 to assist in the mission to rescue the members of the Lady Franklin Bay Expedition party that had been stranded in Greenland for three years.[5] The expedition, led by U.S. Army Lieutenant Adolphus Greely, was assigned to establish a meteorological-observation station as part of the First International Polar Year, and to collect astronomical and magnetic data.

It was a time when numerous scientific expeditions were sent out by different countries and private entities to explore the vast polar regions, much of which were uncharted. Many of the explorers encountered difficulties along the way, which engendered frantic searches for lost members. The *Bear* acquired a reputation for its participation in such ventures. Generally, it was the first cutter or last resort Coast Guard officials thought of when a ship was stranded and sailors, explorers, or local residents were lost. The *Bear* fell into the last resort category with the Greely expedition.

Unfortunately, the explorers became trapped in Greenland and efforts to rescue them in 1882 and 1883 failed. The U.S. government mounted a third attempt in 1884. The government dispatched four ships under the command of U.S. Navy Captain Winfield Scott Schley to rescue Greely's party. The little flotilla included two Coast Guard cutters, the *Bear* and the 723-ton *Thetis* I, built as a sealer and whaler by Stephens & Son in 1881.

The choice of the solidly constructed *Bear* was particularly apropos. Many boat aficionados said that no one ever built a better wooden ship than the *Bear*. It was planked with six-inch oak under a sheathing of ironbark weed and featured a solid prow, valuable assets in Bering operations. Its timbers from side to side had been known to buckle twelve inches under ice pressure and purportedly it had run into everything that floated without noteworthy damage, with one exception. On one occasion $14,000 worth of timber had been knocked off it—without even causing a tiny leak.[6]

If the *Bear* had been a horse it would have been a thoroughbred. As one observer said in 1927 upon the *Bear*'s retirement from Coast Guard operations, "Every year of its service in the Bering it had been nicked in the Arctic ice, but it always returned for more punishment."[7] Significantly, the *Bear* had experienced many narrow escapes before Greely was rescued, and many more after. Not surprisingly, it outlived all the other ships of that expedition.

The other rescue vessels in the rescue fleet were HMS *Alert*, a British Navy survey ship on loan to the U.S. Navy and Canadian government, and the U.S. Navy collier *Loch Garry*, which carried 500 tons of coal. The ships reached Greely's camp on June 22 that year, too late to help many of the explorers. Of the original 25 men on the expedition, only seven returned, and one of them died two weeks later. The *Bear*, however, refused to die.

USS *Thetis* (1884–1899) in the ice off Horse Head Island, Greenland, on 4 June 1884, early in the search for survivors of the Greely polar exploration party; USS *Bear* (1884–1885, later AG-29) is astern (at left) (U.S. Naval History and Heritage Command Photograph).

The ship returned from the Greely rescue mission to begin its normal Coast Guard duties. Exactly how "normal" was defined is hard to say. For the next 43 years the ship carried out whatever task it was assigned. Captains and crews changed, but the ship carried on. It became more than just one of many Coast Guard vessels, though, especially to the people of the "north land," the region for which the cutter was named. The *Bear* became the symbol of the United States as it meandered between ports near the top of the world. Alaskans awaited its arrival every spring with all the excitement of a royal family expecting the birth of a new king or queen.

If ships could multi-task, the *Bear* was a master at it, as would be its successor, the *Northland*. The *Bear*'s second, and long-time, commander, Captain Michael Healey, who was as well-known as the cutter, was charged with several specific duties. (Captain A.A. Fengar was the cutter's first commander.[8]) One was to protect the whalers in the Arctic region. In 1892 alone there were 52 whalers in the Arctic, of which four were lost. The fleet brought back over $2,000,000 worth of whalebone.

It was Healey's duty to make sure none of the ships got caught in the ice and that the crew members and the people on the mainland were safe. By conservative estimates, under Healey's command the *Bear*'s crew rescued at least 300 shipwrecked sailors and aided hundreds of sick and destitute miners and others.[9]

The *Bear* was also assigned to cruise about the seal islands in early summer and drive off the brazen poachers who were raiding the rookeries. Crew members boarded and searched each vessel entering the northern sea, and made sure no one was swindling the natives. Healey was the only U.S. representative in the area and he took his responsibility seriously. He considered the natives his second family and he was not going to let anyone take advantage of them. That was one issue that was resolved by the time the *Northland* assumed the *Bear*'s duties.

When the U.S. purchased Alaska it had to accept the natives, called generically Eskimos or Alaskan Indians, who had no government representation. (They will be referred to as natives throughout this book.) Sadly, unscrupulous traders and whalers in the region took advantage of them. Swindling natives was a recognized industry among the con artists. They bought valuable furs and ivory for the proverbial song and paid for them with cheap whiskey, which started many natives down the road to alcohol abuse. Healey almost eradicated those practices.

Reporter Donald A. Craig described the *Bear*'s functions eloquently in 1922–38 years after it entered Coast Guard service, using the old style of addressing a ship by gender:

"She is a floating court and post office. She enforces revenue, criminal and civil laws, acts as a common carrier for Government officers and shipwrecked mariners, miners and oil prospectors; guardian and adviser of the native Eskimo population; protector of seals; supply boat to Government school stations and reindeer camps. In fact, she performs through her officers every function of Government that is necessary on the mainland and the islands of northern Alaska; acts as a refuge for everyone in need and policeman toward every wrongdoer."[10]

His report contained one glaring omission: it did not mention the crew members whose work made every mission possible. They were then—as they are now—a special breed of human beings, as another writer described them:

> Its officers are specially educated; its men enlisted for from two to three years. They are subjected to discipline more severe than that which exists in either the army or navy. On the other hand, the nature of the life, with its almost constant isolation from the formulae of land, brings a closer relationship between men and officers. So thinly manned are the coast guard cutters that the officers and men know as much of one another as the inmates of a boarding-school dormitory.
>
> Training for the enlisted man begins with an immediate introduction to the sea, and this acquaintanceship is pushed until the time of his discharge. His school of seamanship is perhaps the most thorough in the world. He is not, like the man o'warsman, a specialist. If he knows how to box the compass, whatever that may be, and to haul in a sheet, he must know also how to man the guns and what is trajectory and what is a breech block cover.
>
> If he knows how to man the gasoline stoves in the gallery, he must know how to man the helm. He must know by heart all the idiosyncrasies of every kind of small boat beat imaginable. A coal-passer may find himself coxswain of a tender bound for a sinking ship.
>
> Men of Coast Guard Must be All-Around Sailor men.... He is a "sailor" in a sense not known in the navy nor on liners, nor anywhere else except perhaps on four-masted sailing craft. Beyond this he is a soldier with rifle belt and leggings, who does infantry drill according to the navy formula and tactics, whenever there is time for it.[11]

Without such sailors, neither the *Bear* nor any other Coast Guard cutter could carry out a mission. The cutters were tools; the officers and crew members operated them. The *Bear* and the *Northland* built their reputations on the close working relationship their crew members and officers built. Those relationships were not always perfect. Neither were the cutters. They, like their crews, were subject to breaking

Uniforms were not uniform for these *Bear* crew members coaling the ship circa 1895 (USCG Historian's Office).

down every once in a while. What mattered was how they rebounded and carried out their missions, which they did faithfully for a combined 63 years.

The wooden *Bear* entered Coast Guard service in 1884 to serve a one-time need in Alaska. That one-year period lasted 43 years. The anachronistic cutter was not retired until 1927, when the state-of-the-art (for its time) *Northland* was commissioned to take its place—and the *Bear* still had plenty of service years ahead in civilian capacities.[12]

The *Northland*'s history was short-lived compared to the *Bear*'s, and its history was not as glamorous. That was because the *Bear* served when Alaska was going through its growing pains and the U.S. and other nations were trying to sort out just how far American jurisdiction went in the region.

The United States government claimed it had sole territorial rights in the Bering. The region was rich in hunting and fishing grounds, especially for fur seals, walruses, whales and cold water fish such as cod and halibut. Not surprisingly, other governments such as Russia, Canada, Great Britain, and Japan disputed America's territorial claim and backed its citizens in any disputes—and there were plenty of them.

At times the disputes grew so serious they almost led to war. It was not uncommon to see British, American, and Japanese warships in the Bering at various periods or to read articles and op-eds in newspapers in which jingoistic reporters and

Captain Michael A. Healey aboard USRC *Bear* with a parrot (USCG Historian's Office).

editors encouraged their respective governments to go to war to protect their citizens' commercial interests. It became the Coast Guard's duty to mitigate the disputes, which was not an easy task. The *Bear*, of all the cutters assigned to the north land, became the symbol of the 911 system of the time. "Got trouble? Call *Bear*." Its name was practically the Coast Guard's brand.

If anyone alive during the *Bear*'s heyday were asked to name one Coast Guard cutter they probably would not have said "*Manning*," "*Rush*," "*McCulloch*," "*Thetis*"... Those cutters, and several others, served in the north land with distinction, as did their commanders. But none of them had the cachet of the *Bear* or its legendary commanders, such as Michael Healey (which was more often than not spelled incorrectly as Healy in newspapers of the day), E.P. Bertholf, Frank Tuttle, or C.S. Cochrane, known as the dean of Arctic navigators.[13] Cochrane was the last commander of the *Bear* and former commander of another famous cutter, the *Thetis*, which was sold by the government in 1916 and converted to a whaler operating off the coast of Newfoundland.

Every year like clockwork the fleet's cutters left their winter bases in Seattle, San Francisco, Oakland, or other West Coast harbors to start their six-month voyages north. They toured the Bering and Arctic region in the nastiest weather imaginable, carrying out whatever tasks they were assigned, ranging from transporting crime witnesses and criminals thousands of miles to courts, to rescuing stranded mariners, and delivering food to starving natives. The sailors' lives were hard for those six months, and not all of them were willing to make the trip more than once. On the other hand there were men like Healey and Bertholf who couldn't get enough of the rigors involved.

Reputedly, Healey knew every island in the region, could name all the natives and residents such as teachers, missionaries, doctors and nurses, possessed a knowledge of the flora and fauna, had a deep understanding of the law and diplomacy... In short, he was the "go to guy" when anybody wanted something done in the region. If he wasn't available, anyone he had trained would suffice. After all, Healey was also an excellent mentor, and many of his junior officers went on to become top administrators in the service.

Imagine everyone's surprise, then, when the Coast Guard unceremoniously court-martialed Healey in 1896 for a variety of reasons, convicted him, and sidelined him on an inactive basis for four years, calling him back only when it became desperate for officers. The Coast Guard survived the bad press, as did the *Bear*. Its post–Healey commanders built on his legacy until the *Northland* took over 31 years later.

1

Semper Paratus, Bert Rankin

"The courtesy has become a ceremony and a part of the tradition of the coast guard's mission of service and mercy into the Far North."[1]

Twenty-year-old U.S. Coast Guard member Bert Rankin, from Alameda, California, died of pneumonia in 1906 while serving aboard the cutter *Rush*. He was buried with full military honors at a Coast Guard station named Dutch Harbor, on Unalaska Island, the base of the service's Bering Sea patrol and the population center of the Aleutian Islands. Crew members of two other cutters, the *Bear* and the *Thetis*, attended the ceremony. Rankin's mother, Dora Wright, honored his memory every year after that by sending a wreath 2,748 miles from Oakland, California, to Dutch Harbor to be placed on his grave. Getting it there wasn't easy.

Traveling to Dutch Harbor from practically anywhere outside Alaska was a logistical nightmare. The Coast Guard solved the problem. It transported the wreath aboard the *Bear*. But, by 1927, after twenty years of performing the service the *Bear* was growing old and technologically outdated. Its successor, the modern *Northland*, assumed the tradition. That was no surprise.

There was hardly any task the *Northland* or its crew members could not accomplish at sea or on land, which was also true of the *Bear*'s sailors, who were more restricted by outdated technology. Replacing the *Bear* and its vaunted crew was a daunting task. The *Northland*'s original and succeeding crews were up to the job—including hauling Bert Rankin's wreath.

Rankin was more than just another member of the Coast Guard who served his time and faded into obscurity. He was, in fact, a symbol of the brotherhood that marks the spirit of the service. That explains why a generation of "Coasties" were willing to transport a single wreath to a remote outpost on the Alaskan coast year after year to honor one of their own—someone most of them had never known. They epitomized the Coast Guard motto of *Semper Paratus*, "Always Ready." They were always ready to help people, whether it was a seaman's mother, a stranger, or one of their own. That is the very meaning of *Semper Paratus*.

Rankin had completed three tours to Alaska during his Coast Guard stint. Since Dutch Harbor was not easy to reach, his mother, Dora Wright, opted to commemorate his memory by sending a wreath in his honor each year. Arranging for that was not much easier than visiting the grave in person. A simple request to the Coast Guard solved that problem. The oft-heard cry went out: "Call *Bear*." It assumed the

The *Bear's* frequent traveling companion, the cutter *Rush*, in an undated photograph (USCG Historian's Office).

duty of transporting the wreath on its annual voyage north in the spring, which it did faithfully until the *Northland* took it over.

Why would the Coast Guard so honor an enlisted sailor who had never done anything different than did his fellow crewmen—other than his job? The answer was simple. He was a "Coastie" who had died doing what he loved, and was therefore worthy of the honor. Bert Rankin had loved the sea and ships since his youth. That love was why he had joined the Coast Guard in the first place.

Bert had attended West End School in Alameda and spent a great deal of his free time playing around the local estuary. (Ironically, it was that same estuary from which the *Northland* began its first 2,500-mile voyage north with Rankin's wreath aboard.) Sadly, he was uprooted due to the career demands on his mother.

Dora Wright was a vaudeville actress who moved from place to place as part of her activities. Dora adored Bert but, recognizing that road tours were not the ideal venue for a growing kid, she enrolled him at St. Louis College in Victoria, British Columbia, until they could settle permanently someday in one place. That day never came.

Bert had a thirst for adventure that some folks attributed to his grandfather, Charles Paige. Charles had served as a firefighter in San Francisco when engines were still drawn by horses. In fact, he was the first San Francisco firefighter pensioned by the department. That sense of adventure may have played a role in Bert's enlistment.

Bert wrote a letter to his mother in which he informed her that some of his friends were joining the Coast Guard and he was going with them. "It's a great life," he said. Off he went. She never saw him again.

Bert wrote faithfully to his mother. She saved his letters in anticipation of the day they would meet again in person. Dora stepped up her career and saved her money for a trip to Victoria to meet him when the *Rush* docked. She finally got there, but he didn't. Instead, the *Rush* crew presented her with a note describing the details of his death and the time and place of his burial. Dora was devastated, but she vowed not to let her loss affect her life adversely.

She went back on the stage, but every time she looked out into the audience she saw his face. The anxiety took a toll on her health. As a result she retired. Her life was in turmoil. She remarried twice. Dora became a widow and operated a boarding house. During all that time she never forgot to send the wreath north. The assignment fell to the *Northland* in 1927 for the first time.

That year the care and placement of the wreath was delegated to Ensign F.N. de Otte, with this request from Dora: "Put this wreath on my son's grave at Dutch Harbor. Perhaps you can find a bit of blue bell too. In his letters my boy used to tell about the flowers." A few weeks later, per his mother's request, a flag was raised over Bert Rankin's grave on the shore of Dutch Point and a wreath of Oakland flowers was placed on the ground. The *Northland's* crew completed its mission once again in tribute to one of their own and as a tribute to their reputation as specialists in applying the adage "Adapt, improvise, overcome."[2]

The *Northland*'s crew members, just like their counterparts throughout the Coast Guard, did not know from one day to the next whether they would be rescuing fishermen from an ice floe in danger of breaking up, delivering babies in remote Eskimo villages that could only be reached a few days of the year, preaching morality to their residents, or destroying German weather stations along the coast of Greenland. And, as hard as it was to believe, the *Bear* served in Greenland too.

Just like its mascot, there was no telling where the *Bear*

The *Bear's* mascot aboard the Coast Guard Cutter *Boutwell* in 1928 (USCG Historian's Office).

was going to turn up next or in what capacity. Somehow the mascot got transferred to the cutter *Boutwell* for at least a photo op. Likewise, the *Bear* moved around a lot.

The Navy repurchased the *Bear* on September 11, 1939, and commissioned it the same day as USS *Bear* (AG-29). The *Bear* made two voyages to the Antarctic (November 13, 1939–June 5, 1940, and October 10, 1940–May 18, 1941), and served with the Northeast Greenland Patrol until returning to Boston November 15, 1943, before being decommissioned on May 17, 1944. Finally, the *Bear* was transferred to the Maritime Commission on February 13, 1948.

Despite the "Coasties'" versatility and adaptability, neither they nor the Coast Guard always earned the respect they deserved from the public or members of the other armed services. The Coast Guard was the Rodney Dangerfield of the military services. Its members deserved better. A glance at why it was successful at what it did in the Arctic regions shows why. The Coast Guard's mentoring programs were first rate, due to the quality of its leaders.

2

Captain, My Captain

"O Captain! my Captain! our fearful trip is done, The ship has weather'd every rack, the prize we sought is won, The port is near, the bells I hear, the people all exulting...."[1]

Walt Whitman may have written those words as an elegy for Abraham Lincoln after he was assassinated, but they apply to the captain of any Coast Guard vessel—with one exception. A Coast Guard captain's trip was never done. There was always another one, each one every bit as challenging as the one prior, and the captain had to be a man for all seasons on every one of them. That explains why the Coast Guard maintained its outstanding service in the Arctic region from the arrival of the *Bear*, through the *Northland*'s era, and beyond.

"Part of the training of a coast guard officer is to take things as he finds them, handle them to the best of his ability, tell the truth about them whether it reflects on him personally or not and proceed to the next thing at hand without getting unduly excited over his own part in the matter, whatever it may be," reporter Robert Frothingham wrote.[2] "In other words, he's not looking for bouquets."

Decision maker, diplomat, disciplinarian, health care director, hygienist, leader, linguist, logistician, navigator, politician, provisioner, tactician, mentor … a captain had to be all these and more. The Arctic region captains in particular had to be well-rounded because of the unique obstacles they faced on their voyages, such as sometimes problematic geographical boundaries like that between the U.S. and Russia (Siberia), and ice and frigid weather that could lock them in for hours, days, or an entire winter and remove them from service until conditions improved.

One of the most significant aspects of the *Bear* to *Northland* transition was the mentoring succession. All cutter commanders were highly qualified, highly capable seamen. The *Bear*, however, seemed to enjoy a more notable succession, which carried over to the *Northland*. Its list of commanders was like a Coast Guard All-Star roster:

- Commander Winfield Scott Schley
- Captain Michael Healey
- Lieutenant Albert Buhner
- Captain E.P. Bertholf
- Lieutenant D.H. Jarvis
- Captain Frank Tuttle

Officers of the Bering Sea Patrol fleet gathered for a photo op on September 27, 1908 (USCG Historian's Office).

- Captain J.G. Ballinger
- Captain Leon Claude (L.C.) Covell
- Captain Charles S. Cochrane

There were several possible explanations for the historic handoffs from one outstanding commander to the next aboard both vessels. It may have been because the *Bear* was considered by many seafarers to be the Coast Guard's top-of-the-line Arctic cutter and the *Northland* inherited its cachet, so both cutters demanded the best commanders available. There was, after all, a different skill set required of the Arctic fleet commanders compared to those who served along the East and West Coasts.

The East and West Coast commanders, for the most part, did not have to deal with ice, frigid temperatures, constant blizzards and gales, and the myriad harsh conditions endemic to their Arctic counterparts. The same was true in reverse. The *Northland's* commanders were less suited to deal with the calmer conditions of the southern patrols. That was why the Arctic fleet commanders were more prone to take over for one another. It made sense for the Coast Guard to keep them in the northern regions because they were best qualified to replace one another—and many of them preferred to stay there.

Or, it may have been that the *Bear* was a step above the other cutters performance wise because of its sturdy build and superior seaworthiness and the *Northland* possessed those same characteristics, which were enhanced with new technology. The *Northland* became the *Bear* on steroids. Perhaps command of the *Bear* and later the *Northland* was considered by all executive officers to be the most coveted position in the Arctic fleet and a steppingstone to the top administrative assignments in the service, so they all upped their leadership skills to earn it. That ensured those two cutters always seemed to have the top skippers at the helm.

The cutters' executive officers, in turn, chose their successors wisely through solid mentorship skills, which perpetuated the continuing chain of highly successful commanders who captured the public's attention and brought glory to the Coast Guard. Or, it may have been a combination of all those reasons—and the Coast Guard in general benefited from the stream of notable commanders on the *Bear* and the *Northland*.

The commanders of the other cutters were certainly proficient at their jobs. Many of them had served aboard the *Bear* or the *Northland* and transferred their skills via reassignment to officer positions aboard other vessels. No wonder the Arctic fleet commanders were so willing to praise and mentor their junior officers to keep the chain of command going. That certainly paid off when Captain Healey was unexpectedly court-martialed in 1896.

First in line to replace him was his executive officer, Lieutenant Albert Buhner. Junior officers had to be ready to take the helm when exigencies required. Buhner stepped in seamlessly—for three weeks. Then, he too was threatened with a court-martial. Captain Francis Tuttle, who had served with Healey for many years, replaced Buhner without a hitch.

A year later Tuttle led the *Bear* on one of most publicized missions in its history when the ship was dispatched to Point Barrow to rescue whalers stranded there on eight ships. He had an "all-star" list of officers and crew members aboard, including Lieutenants E.P. Bertholf, Charles S. Cochrane, David Jarvis, and Executive Officer James M. Brown, many of whom had apprenticed with Healey on the *Bear* and would become its commander at different points. Two other second lieutenants, B.H. Camden (who doubled as the San Francisco *Examiner*'s correspondent on the expedition) and H.G. Hamlet, whose father was the commander of the cutter *Chase*, had completed one Arctic tour apiece on the *Bear*. (The Coast Guard has a remarkable history of men—and now women—who have followed their parents' footsteps and served as "Coasties.")

That was a "dream team" put together at a time when such a group was absolutely necessary to effect the timely rescue of the stranded men whose survival was at stake. One newspaper headline demonstrated that Jarvis and Bertholf were almost household names: "Land expedition will be led by Lieutenant Jarvis: Bertholf will go with him."[3] If there was ever a prime example of the need for and benefits of mentoring in the Coast Guard this was it. The line of succession was important if the service was to protect its vessels, maintain a corps of excellent commanders, and fill the needs of its constituents in one of the harshest environments on Earth.

Commanders, crews, and cutters were subject to the whims of the weather. It wasn't unusual for items like this to appear in newspapers: "Cutter *Northland* off Cape Romanzoff, still ice bound. Ice conditions are expected to change with a shifting of the wind to the southeast."[4] To be sure, their counterparts in other service areas shared some of these same problems, but to a lesser extent.

A great part of the *Bear*'s and the *Northland*'s patrol areas lay around the Russian territory of Siberia. There existed constant friction between Siberian authorities and cutter captains, although there were times when the two sides acted in accord to get things done. The friction did not deter cutter commanders from interacting in or near Siberia when American interests were at stake however. And, for some reason, American mariners were attracted to Siberia even knowing the risks. When that happened the Coast Guard had no choice but to bail them out if it was feasible.

The schooner *Teddy Bear* disappeared in October of 1921.[5] It had sailed from Nome in the charge of Captain Joe Bernard, with a crew of five or six men on a hunting and trading trip and had not been heard of since. Speculation was that the ship and its crew had been lost five days after clearing from Nome in a fierce storm which swept over the Bering Sea. Experts suspected that *Teddy Bear* was somewhere near or in Siberia when last seen. That was a problem.

There was a Russian Civil War in progress, part of which extended to Siberia. In fact, Coast Guard crew members of the *Bear* had gone ashore in the midst of it a short while earlier. Finally, reports reached the *Bear*, which was cruising along the Siberian coast, that *Teddy Bear* was frozen in at the Poten River, 12 miles south of Emma Village, on East Cape, Siberia. Captain Cochrane investigated and located the missing schooner.

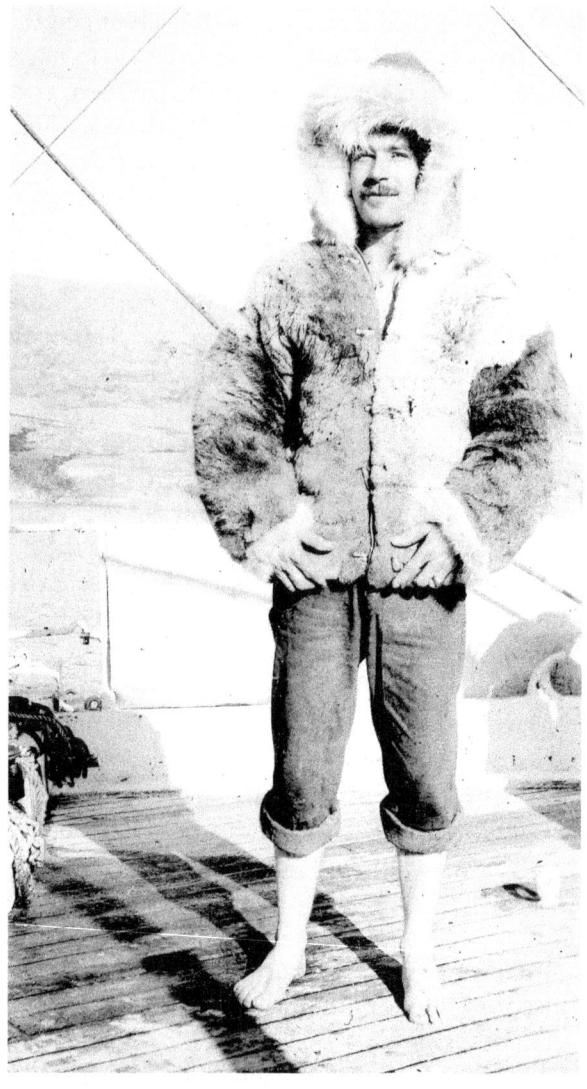

Crew member modeling a fur coat aboard USS *Bear* (AG-29) during a voyage to Greenland in 1941 (Naval History and Heritage Command).

Everyone was relieved when Cochrane telegraphed Captain Ross of the local U.S. Coast Guard Service in Nome to say that the *Bear* had found the schooner and talked with the captain and crew. Cochrane reported that all the men were in good health and waiting for the ice to clear out of the river before returning to Nome. That was one more crisis averted without any undue problems. Generally, though, problems could be resolved without too much difficulty.

Sometimes the conflicts were attributed to language differences. At other times they were due to bellicosity. The two causes merged at times, as Captain Edward Jones discovered on one stop in 1929.

The *Northland* put into St. Lawrence Bay, Siberia while en route to Nome to take aboard a fresh supply of water.[6] Jones also wanted to inquire for the benefit of the Eskimos of Little Diomede Island, which is in American territory, whether the Soviet Eskimos of Big Diomede Island could or could not visit and carry on friendly relations with them. After all, he noted, the islands were within a mile of each other in the Bering Straits.

The Soviet officials declared that under no considerations were the Eskimos of the two islands to visit or communicate with each other. As for the water, the Soviet official in charge at St. Lawrence Bay emphatically said Jones couldn't have any. Fortunately, an interpreter interceded and smoothed over the matter to everybody's satisfaction. The *Northland* received its fresh supply of water. The Eskimos still couldn't visit one another. Such were political matters along the Siberian border for Coast Guard captains. Scientific and humanitarian relationships were different animals.

There were times when the Russians and Americans worked closely together for scientific purposes. On a cruise in 1938, the *Northland*, like a local train, made several stops: Teller, Diomede Island, Wales, Point Hope, St. Lawrence Bay, and East Cape, Siberia. Captain Frederick A. Zeusler, its commanding officer, had the authority to enter Soviet waters after July 1, which he took full advantage of to exchange oceanographic information with Soviet scientists in the region as part of an oceanographic survey of the Bering Sea district which had been carried on from the ship for several years. The survey was scheduled to end that year. It was something in which the versatile Zeusler had great interest, since he was also an instructor in oceanography at the University of Washington.[7]

Coast Guard and Soviet officials often worked together for humanitarian purposes as well. The Jimmy Mattern case showed that.[8] It was a time when pilots such as Mattern, Charles Lindbergh, Wiley Post, and the Soviet aviator Sigismund Levanefsky competed to set new records for endurance flights and perfect the art of aviation. The 23-year-old Mattern attempted a round-the-world solo flight in 1933 to beat the time set by Wiley Post. His attempt in his Lockheed Vega plane named "Century of Progress" came to a premature end in Siberia.

Mattern crash-landed approximately 75 miles outside Anadyr, about 350 miles across the Bering Sea from Nome. No one heard from or about him for two weeks. Then, he walked into Anadyr, from where the news of his safety was sent around the world. His appearance had all the makings of a major political incident between the Soviets and Americans, with the *Northland* in the middle, mainly because U.S. government officials overreacted to the situation.

For some reason they thought the Soviets were not planning to return Mattern to the U.S. without a hassle. Everyone seemed to believe that the *Northland* would be his chariot home. Coast Guard Headquarters said the *Northland* had returned to Nome and was "standing by" for arrival of the American relief plane expected to fly thence to Anadyr to pick up Mattern.[9] Did he need to be rescued or did he simply need a ride home?

Coast Guard administrators sought instructions from the State Department because the United States government did not recognize Soviet Russia as a sovereign nation. Nevertheless, Acting Secretary of State William Phillips said that the department had no objection to *Northland*'s sailing from Nome into Soviet waters to make the pick-up if necessary, and that he expected Soviet courtesy. It was only 400 miles from Nome to Anadyr, and the *Northland* could get there in a little over 24 hours.

Should there be any objection by Soviet officials to the *Northland*'s entrance into their waters, Phillips said, the *Northland*'s commander, S.V. Parker, might arrange with them to send Mattern out to the cutter in a small boat in international waters. The State Department relayed permission to Parker to head for the area and to use his own judgment on how to proceed with the mission. He was caught in the middle of a delicate diplomatic situation.

Consequently, officials at Coast Guard headquarters explained that they did not give Parker peremptory orders for the rescue because there might be complications to the venture unknown in Washington, D.C. Nevertheless, they were pretty sure Parker had analyzed the situation, taken the initiative, and turned the *Northland* toward Siberia to rescue the stranded Mattern, as any aggressive Coast Guard commander would do.

In any case, they were putting Parker in a precarious position. He had no idea what to expect. Meanwhile, the Russians, unaware of the intrigue going on among State Department and Coast Guard officials, were bending over backwards to treat Mattern well and make provisions to get him back to the United States.

The Soviet government dispatched two powerful Arctic-type seaplanes to Anadyr. One of them, piloted by Levanefsky, stopped at Khabarovsk to pick up experienced mechanics to help Mattern repair his plane. The other, flown by an aviator named Buchgoldi, was en route from another point. Prof. Otto Schmidt, chief of Soviet Arctic exploration and travel, revealed that both Russian flyers had long experience in Arctic navigation and their planes were especially equipped for northern conditions. The same government had also ordered four Soviet steamers that had sailed recently from Vladivostok for the Bering Straits to assist Mattern if need be. None of that sounded as nefarious as U.S. government officials had anticipated.

A week after Mattern arrived in Anadyr, Levanefsky flew him back to Nome in a Dornier-Wahl flying boat, where they landed safely. The would-have-been-manufactured international incident never materialized. The *Northland* left its "war footing" and returned to its duties. Mattern went back to the mainland and Levanefsky became a regular and welcome visitor to Nome.

It was just another mission in the Arctic region for Parker and the *Northland* crew, but it showed that they were always one step away from an international incident, real or concocted. No wonder he and his counterparts needed such a diverse range of leadership tools to succeed there.

3

Reindeer Rustlers

"The white men have driven the whales and walruses off the grounds where they once flourished, and the poor Esquimaux are getting in sore straits for some staple article of food." —D.H. Jarvis[1]

The *Bear*'s 1891 and 1892 tours typified the life of a Coast Guard crew towards the end of the 19th century. They were the ultimate multi-taskers on sturdy ships. Contrary to some people's beliefs, the cutters on Bering Sea Patrol were much more than symbols.

Cutter officers carried out numerous governmental functions. Their officers enforced the law, apprehended criminals and transported them to mainland jails after sentencing, and transported floating courts for the Justice Department. They gathered military intelligence for the Navy Department, and carried mail for the Post Office Department. They were efficient at those assignments, especially when it involved poachers and transporting prisoners—or entire ships.

The *Bear* earned a reputation as a "seagoing hoosegow."[2] D.H. Jarvis and Captain J.G. Ballinger were two of the "top cops" on the crew. A report from the crew of the trading schooner *Bonanza* suggested that Jarvis was fast becoming a suitable detective.[3]

The vessel arrived in San Francisco on October 8, 1899, from Point Barrow and Point Hope, Alaska, with a cargo of whalebone, ivory, and furs. Crew members reported they saw the *Bear* at Point Barrow, where Jarvis had two prisoners in irons, a white man and a native, both charged with murder. They had been arrested in the gold mining mecca of Kotzebue Sound.

The white man, an American, was described as a newcomer in the district. Allegedly he had murdered another miner. The Indian, one of the chiefs of his tribe, was charged with a number of murders of white men for the purpose of robbing them of their outfits and supplies. Jarvis was also searching for another white man who had incited a native to shoot at the missionary at St. Lawrence Island.

As if that weren't enough detective work, investigators discovered that the captain of the schooner *Jessie*, who had died near Port Clarence more than a year earlier, apparently from what they thought were natural causes, had actually been murdered. They suspected that a Norwegian who had since laid claim to the *Jessie* and two natives had perpetrated the alleged murder. Jarvis was on the case, while also searching for the murderers of two miners near Point Hope whose sledge was followed by natives who surprised the victims and killed them for their supplies. Jarvis had his hands full with police work, as did Ballinger.

When Ballinger was inducted into the Pioneer Club in Nome in November 1913 people remembered how adept he was at capturing and holding "bad guys." Locals recalled that when he first came to Alaskan waters in 1893 he had a reputation as a tough, but fair, man.

In 1899 he took charge of 20 undesirables rounded up and delivered over to him for shipment to the states by the town marshal, W.M. Eddy. Mr. Eddy, who became acquainted with the bad men and gunmen that followed the western mining camps when he was an express messenger in the employ of the Wells Fargo Company, spotted these men and solicited the aid of the *Bear's* crew in ridding Nome of a vicious and unruly element. It was apropos, then, that on Ballinger's final voyage from Alaska to the states he had on board a group of prisoners.

On that day the *Bear* left Nome at precisely one o'clock, having aboard, in addition to the prisoners and guards, seven destitute men who desired to leave Alaska. Before departing, those seven passengers wrote a letter expressing thanks to Judge Murane, Marshal Powell, Assistant District Attorney Castle and Captain Tom Ross for their efforts in securing them transportation.

In one incident Ballinger was assigned to take the ill-fated 90-foot schooner *General McPherson* under his control. The ship was in danger on August 22, 1899, when the *Bear* encountered it. Then Second Lieutenant Ballinger, who had a penchant for turning any routine assignment into an adventure, and Seaman Rossig were placed on board to take the schooner to St. Michael, a small city in the Nome census area, but it could not get there under its own power.[4]

Another vessel towed the *McPherson* from Ledge Island on the 26th to Norton Sound. There, Ballinger turned the vessel over to Special Deputy United States Marshall D.S. Swift, who had arrested one Jans B. Neilson on a warrant for piracy. Neilson and his entire family were brought on board for transportation to Nome once the *General McPherson* was seaworthy again. Apparently it never was.

Slightly over a year later the schooner was anchored on the east side of the misnamed Safety Harbor when a storm hit around 3:30 a.m. The schooner had departed Nome on September 9 for Point Safety with a crew of eight and $500 worth of lumber weighing ten tons. That was as far as it got. According to a Wreck Report filed September 18, 1900, by the vessel's master, J.S. Morris of Seattle: "Gale, cloudy, heavy sea, dark. Heavy SE Gale and tidal wave ... east side Safety Harbor.... Stranded.... Three anchors out with 60 fathoms best hawser, 45 fathoms second hawser, and 45 fathoms cable on steam anchor.... Left the wreck without assistance.... Total loss."[5]

The ship itself was valued at $7,000, and it was unknown as to whether it or the cargo were insured. That was life in the Bering for ships' crews. They and their vessels might be saved one day but lost the next, despite the Coast Guard's best efforts. All members like Ballinger could do was try their best to help the people under their watch and move on. That is what Ballinger did, reputation fast in hand.

Captain Ballinger's last act before setting sail was to send a note to the local newspaper asking that his thanks be expressed to the people of this city for the kindnesses extended to him.[6] The people were not likely to forget him. On leaving he flew a parting pennant 62 feet long. The only thing missing was poachers aboard, many of whom had headed to trial and imprisonment on the *Bear* in the past.

In 1909 the Treasury Department received notice of the capture of a number of seal poachers by the *Bear* on Walrus Island in the Bering Sea. According to the brief advisory, several of the poachers escaped in their boats. But, the *Bear* transported those taken to Valdez for trial at the next term of court. There were already a number of Japanese poachers at the place awaiting trial. The Japanese sealers never seemed to learn that Coast Guard cutters were usually—but not always—lurking in the fog to apprehend them. They knew that the early bird got the seal sometimes.

There was a report in April 1909 that the largest seal herd seen for years on the Alaskan coast was passing north of Sitka.[7] That was a bonanza for the local Eskimos. They killed more than 200 seals in two days as the herd passed. Experts said they would sell the hides for about $30 apiece, with many more to add. Guesses were that it would probably be another three weeks before the herd passed, during which time the natives would reap a rich harvest.

The natives had competition though. They revealed that several Japanese sealing vessels were following the herd just outside the three-mile limit. Sadly, they said, there was not a cutter in the area to prevent the Japanese from poaching if they were so inclined. Chances were they were so inclined, which was the reason they were there. The cutters couldn't be everywhere at once. And, if they could escape the *Bear*, they would seize every opportunity to do so.

The *Bear* was their particular nemesis, as its persistence in 1908 indicated. Sealing crews could not always wait for their prey to come to them, so they had little choice but to go to them. That meant approaching the islands and slaughtering the animals there. That was never a good idea when the *Bear* was patrolling.

When the weather was bad the seals preferred to stay on land, and the few that were brave enough to go offshore were restless and difficult to approach. They were not easily disturbed on shore either, and they were extremely alert and suspicious while in the water nearby. Moreover, the sealers were in a bind when it came to the condition of the sea.

When it was smooth and the sealing was good, the omnipresent fog prevailed. But, if the sealers tried to shoot their victims in the fog then the sounds of the weapons carried and alerted the patrolling vessels of their presence. For the poachers it was a "damned if you do, damned if you don't" situation. They were no better off when the weather was clear.

During clear weather, the patrol cutters operated offshore among the sealing vessels and boarded and examined virtually every one of them. That was the only way the "Coasties" could determine the nationality of the sealers, which determined their right to take prey in any particular locality.

In 1908 there were 32 foreign sealing vessels operating in the Bering.[8] Thirty of them were Japanese; the other two were Canadian. Cutter crews boarded 28 of them. They were particularly active around the Pribilof Islands, a center of sealing activity. They were so visible there that poachers attempted only one raid that year either on the islands or in the territorial waters. That occurred on July 22 during a heavy fog. Japanese sealers closed in on Northeast Point. Two of them were taking seals within the three-mile limit. The *Bear* captured them both. No wonder jailers and juries were kept so busy with poaching trials in Alaskan courts.

Such apprehensions were heartening to Coast Guard authorities. In fact, they recommended that more cutters be assigned to police the northern waters, with a view of discouraging poachers, although the chances of getting their wish were slim.[9]

One benefit to acquiring additional cutters would have been a reduction in the number of prisoner escort voyages cutters made to U.S. ports. It was not unusual to read in newspapers that prisoners sentenced for varying terms by the floating court in Alaskan waters had been "landed at Seattle by the cutter *Bear* (or other cutters) and will be confined in various prisons to serve their terms."[10] Any such trip took a cutter off line for a short while, which was never ideal for the patrol. A cutter out of action, even for a short time, imperiled natives throughout the region and limited their access to normal services.

The cutters carried teachers to their posts, conducted sanitation inspections, and guarded timber and game for the Interior Department. Crew members surveyed coastlines and regional industries for the Department of Commerce and carried public health service personnel to isolated villages that otherwise had no access to medical service. In short, the cutters and their crews were the lifeline of the Alaska Territory, which may not have thrived without them. That is demonstrated through descriptions of the *Bear*'s annual activities.

In 1891 it arrived at Seattle from Alaska on May 19, none the worse for wear after another lengthy and arduous winter tour of the country's most extreme territory. At least the cutter did: its captain was a bit taxed. The strain of the trip showed on Captain Healey. He checked into a hotel immediately to get some rest. The *Bear*'s Executive Officer, Second Lieutenant David H. Jarvis, filled in reporters on some of the highlights of the voyage and the news of the north that was difficult for them to get due to inefficient communications capabilities between the states and the remote regions of Alaska.[11]

The *Bear*, as was so often the case, returned to the states with more people than it carried when it left. This time it carried among its guests 15 shipwrecked sailors of the unfortunate schooner *Premier*, which had been smashed to pieces April 30 on the rocks at Cape St. John, in western Alaska. They were accompanied by the Honorable Louis H. Tarpley, the United States commissioner at Unalaska, the chief center of population in the Aleutian Islands. He had been in Alaska to take the testimony of witnesses in the murder cases to be heard at Sitka.

Just listening to Jarvis's account was tiring. He was as much a raconteur as a sailor. He brought the events of the tour to life in a way that kept his audience enraptured. Perhaps not enough to entice them to take a trip to Alaska themselves, but excited nonetheless.

"We left Seattle April 9, and thus have been just thirty-nine days out," he said. "During that time we traveled five thousand miles and dropped anchor fifteen times. Our regular cruise is to Bering Sea and the Pribilof and Aleutian islands, but the cruise just ended was a preliminary one, made for the department of justice for Western Alaska."

Part of the reason the *Bear* was sent to Alaska in the first place was to serve as a floating court.[12] If the residents of the far-flung islands couldn't get to the courts the courts would come to them. The government made it "official" in 1922 when it organized a floating court for Alaska and the Treasury Department announced the appointment of five Coast Guard commanders as commissioners: Captain Charles S. Cochran, commander of the cutter *Bear*, in Arctic waters; Captain James Freeman Hottel, commander of the cutter *Haida*, in the Bering Sea; Captain John Boedecker, commander of the *Mojave*, in the Bering Sea; Captain William Stromberg, commander of the cutter *Algonquin*, in the Bering Sea; and Captain Edward D. Jones, commander of the cutter *Unalga*, in southeastern Alaskan waters.

In addition several Coast Guard officers were appointed special deputy marshals: Lieutenants Thomas S. Klinger, Clement J. Todd, Wilfred N. Derby, Frederick J. Birke, and John E. Whitbeck.

And there was no doubt that courts were needed in the north land. The folks living there were entitled to the full benefits of the American legal system. Fortunately for them, Healey and his officers, who often served as judges in local adjudications, were sticklers for the law.

"There have been a number of murders in Western Alaska during the past year and the only court is at Sitka," Jarvis explained. "The murders all happened in the section of the country of which Unalaska is the metropolis, and that place is 1,300 miles from Sitka. There are no regular means of communication between those two points. News and information from Unalaska goes to San Francisco first and then to Sitka."

He provided a salient example. "Last year a murderer was arrested at Unalaska and brought to Sitka for trial. He wanted ten witnesses subpoenaed, and they all lived in Western Alaska, from 1,300 to 1,400 miles away. The man was entitled to them according to law, and to serve the subpoenas and bring the witnesses to Sitka and allow the witnesses for fees and mileage would entail a cost to the government of $7,500. The result was it was concluded that it would be cheaper to detail a revenue cutter for the purpose of bringing in the desired witnesses," he noted.

It might have been easier for the witnesses, but not for Healey and his crew. They were the folks who had to travel from island to island transporting witnesses. That was a clear-cut case of taxing and taxiing at the same time. But that was one of the reasons the *Bear* was in the north.

> "We were in San Francisco when we got orders to go north," Jarvis continued. "We stopped here for coal and sailed again on April 9. Four days later we arrived at Sitka and took aboard Governor Lyman Knapp of the District of Alaska, United States District Attorney O.L. Johnston, and Deputy United States Marshal George Kosterometeroff. They accompanied us to Unalaska.
>
> It was the first time the governor had ever been in Western Alaska. At Unalaska we put ashore a lot of coal that we had taken aboard at Seattle for missions and refuge stations along the Arctic shores. We will take it aboard again on our next cruise north.
>
> From Unalaska we went to Seal or Pribilof Islands, 200 miles away. There we delivered mail and received reports on the condition of the islands.

The reference to mail was significant. It was almost as if the most important function cutters served well into the 1930s was delivering mail.[13] All other services were nice—as long as the mail reached its destination. As late as 1934 mail delivery generated bold headlines and occupied significant space in newspapers:

The *Bear's* coaling crew at Unalaska in July 1918 (USCG Historian's Office).

Cutter *Northland* Arrives at Nome [with] 9 Tons of Mail
   Cutter *Northland* Arrives Nome: First Vessel from States
   The U.S. Coast Guard Cutter *Northland* arrived Nome at 7:50 a.m. today from Unalaska and the States. The cutter left Seattle on May 15th for Dutch Harbor and Unalaska. Arriving with the vessel here were 17,500 pounds of second class mail matter [and four-and-a-half tons of freight] which is now being distributed in the local post office.
   The *Northland* is the second vessel of the 1934 season of navigation to arrive at Nome, but the first boat in here from the States. The *Krassin*, the Russian icebreaker, was the first vessel here, arriving May 21st from the westward.
   The *Northland*, which is in charge of Commander William K. Scammel, will be stationed in the northern Bering Sea waters until next fall, after the last boats leave Nome.
   En route north the cutter encountered only about 70 miles of ice, which was mostly broken up. The *Northland* will remain here for a couple of days and then proceed to St. Michael with the mail.

    The importance of mail was not over-exaggerated, considering the solitude of the far-flung, remote communities in the vast region.
    The Pribilofs comprised two principal islands, Saint Paul and Saint George, and several rocky islets, including two named Otter and Walrus, both near St. Paul. The islands were small and barren during the winter. According to Jarvis's estimates, one was 11 miles long and six miles wide. The other was nine miles long and about eight miles wide. They were devoid of vegetation of any kind in the winter, but there was some present in the summer.
    Saint Paul was named for the Feast of Saints Peter and Paul, which was the day

on which the Russian explorer Gavriil Pribylov first encountered the islands. Saint George may have been named after Pribylov's ship, but no one was really sure of the island name's origin. The islands, which were the only home of fur-bearing seals in the Arctic region, would play a central role in the international unrest over poaching between 1867 and 1911 (the spelling Pribilof is used throughout this book).

The United States considered all fur-seal hunting carried out by foreign enterprises in the Bering Sea to be illegal, ergo it was considered poaching. That opinion, which was not shared by legal experts in foreign governments, led to years of trouble in the region and headaches galore for the cutter commanders. Those headaches were still a few years in the future when Jarvis gave his 1891 report.

When the *Bear* arrived the islands were covered with snow and ice. In fact, Jarvis observed, St. Paul and St. George looked like two big icebergs. That year's winter was very hard, and it snowed every day during the entire month of April, not only on the islands, but in Western Alaska. All that portion of the country was covered with snow. The terrain was so harsh even the seals did not want to be there.

> "The rookeries were deserted," Jarvis recalled. "Not one seal was in sight. That is nothing unusual, however, for they do not come until later in the season. First the bulls appear. They stake out a place for themselves and then the cows come. They gather gradually and it is not until along in the middle of July that all the seals arrive.
>
> The people on the islands did not suffer much, though the winter was severe, and they reported but few deaths. The population on both the islands numbers about 600 persons, nearly all of whom are natives—Russians. There are several Americans there, physician and school teachers and the government agent. The doctor on St. Paul Island is accompanied by his wife.
>
> The ice was very heavy about and around the islands. It presses close down to them, and while we were there floating Arctic ice could be seen.

The *Bear* did not linger in the islands. It departed April 25 and returned to Unalaska, where it stopped for a few hours before resuming its voyage. Its first stop was the Shumagin Islands, about 300 miles south of the Alaska Peninsula. Healey dropped anchor at Unga, where a homicide known as the Hemingway murder had occurred in August 1880. The crew took on board six witnesses there and then visited three other places on the islands to pick up several more. There were many small islands in the neighborhood, and many of them had only a single inhabitant.

The odyssey continued. So did Jarvis, as he told a tale of shipwrecked sailors that had become boilerplate over the years in the region. Shipwrecks were fairly common there. Some sailors survived, some did not. Either way it was the *Bear*'s job to assist them whenever it could.

This time it was the schooner *Premier* that capsized. It had sailed from San Francisco carrying supplies and transferring a cannery for the Arctic Packing Company from Ozernoy to Bristol Bay, a distance of 500 miles. The schooner was wrecked on the mainland, about fifty miles from Berate Cave, which was located on Popoff Island.

> Leaving the Shumagin islands we sailed to Pirate Cove and it was there we picked up the ship-wrecked crew of the schooner *Premier*. The schooner went on the rocks at Cape St. John, April 6, during a snowstorm, and went to pieces. Captain Paulson, with a crew of fifteen men, was on board, but they all escaped (Jarvis explained). They occupied small boats and worked their way across the water to Pirate Cove, fifty miles away.

Pirate Cove contains about fifteen cod fishermen, and when we arrived there the crew had been ten days in the place subsisting on the charity of the fishermen. Though the sailors were not suffering, the fishermen were glad that we arrived and took them on board, for they had eaten them nearly out of house and home.

From there the *Bear* sailed for Sand Point, a fishing station, where it picked up one more passenger, a hardened criminal named Russian Pete for transport to Sitka. He joined the crew of the *Premier* for the ride. Healey was in no hurry to get there. He had one more task to complete, which demonstrated just how diverse his duties were. Jarvis told the story with a sense of amusement.

Sand Point is a great rendezvous for sealers before they enter Bering Sea. They do their trading there. On previous cruises we were given information to the effect that whisky was kept for sale there, and that the sellers had a secret place where they kept it—in the basement of a store house. Captain Healy determined to see if there was such a place and so he set us to watching. We finally located the house—we got an inkling which house it was—and we examined the cellar. "It was the most ingeniously contrived affair imaginable," he declared.

We stepped into the cellar and looked about. It was apparently bare. To the right was a large bulkhead that looked as if it was built solidly against the bank. A match safe and a box holding fire extinguishers were hanging on this bulkhead. We turned up the box and under it were some small bolts and a thumb-piece of iron.

By turning the thumb piece it worked a catch in the floor on the inside of the bulkhead, and the whole half of the bulkhead, which was cut across the center, turned out and up on hinges. The hinges were hidden by cleats that were nailed across, and they certainly looked innocent enough. Nothing was in this place disclosed by the secret bulkhead, but beyond was another bulkhead.

Jarvis made the place sound like the world's most secretive whiskey dispensary.

"About the center of the partition and near the floor was a bolt with a square head, and it ran through one of the rights that seemed to protect the bulkhead," he said. "A piece of gas pipe was lying near the bolt. It looked like a piece of cast away old iron, but the end of it was hammered to fit the bolt head, and served as a key to turn the bolt. As soon as the bolt turned a door a foot thick was opened out of the bulkhead and revealed another secret closet about eleven feet deep by six feet square. To our disappointment the place was empty."

It was newly repaired, but it was evident that it had been in use for several years and the reason it was not filled then was simply because it was too early in the season. We destroyed the place and came away. We were two whole days, but Captain Healy accomplished his purpose and did not regret the delay. No arrests were made because no evidence in the shape of liquor was found on the premises.

There was some irony involved in Healey's willingness to destroy the facility. Some people believed that he had a fondness for alcohol himself, which sometimes caused him to act irrationally. They were right. His predilection for spirits led to his downfall a few years later and caused the Coast Guard to rewrite its alcohol policies. That was not a concern in 1891 though.

"While we were at Sand Point we learned of another shipwreck, the schooner *Dashing Wave* being the unfortunate vessel," Jarvis continued. "The '*Wave*' was owned by Lind & Hough, of San Francisco, and was carrying supplies to fishing stations. She was wrecked on Hair Seal Cape, but her crew of ten men escaped to the mainland in safety. They were near a fishing station and as a small vessel went to their assistance, we knew they were not suffering and so we came away and left them."

3. Reindeer Rustlers

The *Bear* finally got away from Sand Point, but its voyage was far from over. Healey had picked up all the witnesses on his list but one. The ship headed 200 miles to the west, to Cape Pankoff, to get him. The remaining witness was there when the *Bear* arrived, but he did not want to join the growing crowd aboard the cutter. The man told Healey that he had never heard of the murder before. That did not impress the no-nonsense Healey. He took the recalcitrant witness aboard all the same.

Jarvis understood the witness's reluctance to undertake the 1,300-mile journey from Cape Pankoff to Sitka. The trip was a great hardship on witnesses, for it would be nearly a year before they could return to their homes and businesses. The *Bear* wasn't in the region all year to provide taxi services, nor were any other cutters. That wasn't Healey's concern.

The *Bear* got underway again and visited Cape Faukoff. There Healey learned that two men had been lost during the winter. He could not learn their names, but they were white men who went out to the mainland in a dory to hunt. A snowstorm came up and they were never seen again. Realizing that there was nothing he could do, Healey finally pointed the *Bear* to Sitka.

Jarvis's post-cruise analysis was illuminating. He considered the cruise just ended one of the most successful ever made by the *Bear*. It accomplished everything for which it was assigned in a much shorter space of time than anticipated. The *Bear* was not expected to return to Seattle until June 1, almost two weeks later than it docked. He attributed the successful cruise and speedy time to Captain Healey's driving energy, cool management, and his knowledge of the waters, in which he had cruised ever since the Alaskan territory was annexed.

"There are no light houses, no buoys and no government surveys up there," Jarvis said. "Our maps, though not perfectly correct, were made by mariners who studied the coast from the deck of a ship, and are good enough to go by. The thousands of small islands, which are nothing more than reefs of rock, make navigation a very dangerous matter. During our entire cruise we lost only one day and a part of another day. The first day we laid to for a gale of wind, and the other day we encountered dense fog."

At times Jarvis sounded as much a tourist as he did an officer.

"We had a grand view of the Alaskan volcanos, returning from the Pribilof Islands to Unalaska," as he described it. "One day the weather was as clear as only Arctic weather can be, and one could see miles. The mainland stretched before and no sound broke the stillness save the swish of the water, caused by the driving of the vessel. To the south of us, over our bows, we could plainly see Volcanos Bogoslow, Makushin, Akutan and Shivhaidin, covered with snow, as was the whole country."

All four mounts were smoking hard—Bogoslow was puffing. The peak, and for a considerable distance down the mountain side, was blackened and marred, caused by the lava running from the crater and melting away the snow. The view was over our bows. To the north the vision faded where the horizon kissed the sea. All the volcanos are in the Aleutian Islands.

Jarvis would be seeing them again in a short time. No sooner had the *Bear* reached Seattle than Healey received orders to make immediate preparations for sea. The crew began taking on coal the day after it arrived. There was no definite departure date, but there was no doubt it would be leaving for the Bering Sea just a few days after arriving. It would be gone until the first of December.

That was life for the *Bear*. It was even more exciting than Jarvis imagined in his review of the 1891 trip, perhaps because he was unaware of the connection, however tenuous it might have been, between the wrecked *Premier* and a whaler named *Napoleon*, and the introduction of reindeer into Alaska. That was a story that only Healey knew.

The captain shared a few high points of the 1891 voyage too. Before he retired to his hotel upon the *Bear*'s return to Seattle he spoke with a reporter for a few minutes. He said:

> We left here on May 3d last, for Alaska. From there we went to Cape Navarina and distributed the presents awarded by Congress to the Indians who saved the crew of the bark *Napoleon*, in 1885. The Indians were very much delighted with the gifts, and acted as American children act over toys on a Christmas morning.
>
> Then we called at a great many Indian settlements on the American and Siberian shores, and took the census at places where others found it too difficult to go. We built schoolhouses at Cape Prince of Wales and Point Hope, and commenced the erection of another building at Point Barrow. We patrolled the coast until September 1st, when we relieved the *Rush* and continued her cruise around the sealing islands until our departure for this port. The weather has been very stormy in Bering Sea and we had plenty to do frequently in weathering the gales.[14]

He mentioned the "Indians" and the bark *Napoleon* in passing without revealing the importance of his stop. The story was truly one of the most significant of his years in the Arctic.

Among the 15 rescued sailors from the *Premier* was one who was acquainted with the lone survivor of the bark *Napoleon* which had been wrecked on the shores of Arctic Siberia six years earlier. The lone survivor's name was Vincent, and he could easily have served as the role model for the protagonist in the 2000 movie *Cast Away* that starred Tom Hanks.[15]

In 1885 the *Napoleon*, while cruising in the Arctic Ocean, 3,000 miles from Sitka, Alaska, went on the ice off Cape Navarin, on the Siberian coast. Twenty-two crew members, including Vincent, got into a dory and headed for shore. After days of privation and suffering they reached a settlement named Indian Point—300 miles from the site where the *Napoleon* went on the ice.

Sadly, when the Eskimos at the settlement pulled the boat ashore 19 of the sailors were dead. Two of the three still breathing succumbed to their frozen limbs a few days later. Vincent was left alone in a strange, ice-bound land, where the people had queer ways and spoke a foreign tongue.

Indian Point was, like most Eskimo settlements, isolated. Vessels of any kind visiting there were extremely rare. After living in isolation for six months Vincent became convinced he would never see his native land again or even get to let people know what happened to him. There were no writing materials available, so he cut his name in a piece of wreckage from his dory and detailed on it the story of his fate and where he was.

He wrote the story in the natives' language, which he had learned to speak in his six months ashore. Eskimos in villages along the coast passed the piece of wreckage from place to place during their hunting expeditions. It was transferred from camp to camp until finally it reached a northern limit and the hunters told the story as it went.

One day whalers from a ship in distress on the ice near the Siberian coast engaged in a conversation with several Eskimos. The ship got out of the ice without damage and the crew took the natives on board. They did some trading and the Eskimos gave the board with Vincent's name carved on it to the whaler's captain. He listened closely to the Eskimos' story of how it came into their possession.

After the two groups parted the whaler continued north on its hunt. Two years later, at the close of the whaling season, the vessel, returning south, stopped at Port Clarence, which was nearly opposite Indian Point, on the Alaskan coast. The captain left the tell-tale piece of wreckage and the carving on it with the government agent and sailed away. By that time Vincent had become almost a savage man.

A few weeks later the *Bear*, on its annual northern trip, stopped at Port Clarence for a visit. Since the place was the most extreme northerly station it was a great rendezvous location for whalers entering and returning from the hunting grounds. The government agent gave Captain Healey the wreckage and the name carved upon it and told him Vincent's story. That piqued Healey's interest.

When the *Bear* left Port Clarence Healey changed his course to west instead of south and sailed to Indian Point, 350 miles away. He took Vincent aboard and continued on his way.

Vincent was adamant about where he wanted to go. He had become thoroughly acclimated to the region and would not return farther south than Sitka. In fact, he made up his mind to remain in Arctic waters the rest of his life, which he did. The shipwrecked sailor of the *Premier* revealed to Healey in 1891 that Vincent was at that moment en route to the whaling grounds as mate on a first-class whaler.

In 1887, when Healey had rescued Vincent, he wrote the stranded sailor's story in his post-voyage report to the Treasury Department in Washington, D.C. As a result, the government appropriated $1,000 to buy presents for the wealthy old Eskimo chief at Indian Point as a reward for his kindness in caring for and fostering Vincent. Of course, the government officials had an ulterior motive. They wanted to encourage the chief to treat other American sailors kindly if they should fall into his hands in a similar manner.

The government bought many presents for the chief and his Eskimos, and designated Healey and the *Bear* to deliver them. So, in 1890 the *Bear* made a special trip from Point Barrow to Indian Point, where Healey gave the presents to the chief on behalf of the United States. The chief was delighted to accept them.

Healey went ashore as the chief's guest and toured the village. He discovered that the chief owned immense herds of reindeer. In fact, he was the wealthiest Eskimo in that portion of Siberia. The sight of the reindeer inspired Healey with ideas of a new and previously unconsidered enterprise, which he speculated might pay dividends for the Eskimos in the near future.

It was a trying time food wise for the Eskimos of Western Alaska in 1890. Food sources such as walruses, polar bears, and whales that had once flourished in great numbers were no longer to be found. Walruses had all but disappeared and the bears had retreated into the impassable interior. The few that were left were so shy that even the wily Eskimo hunters could not capture them. The whales had migrated away from the shores up to the high seas hundreds of miles north. In short, food was a scarce commodity for the Eskimos.

Healey commiserated with them. In 1890 the Eskimos were in a worse condition than ever before. That was when he began considering the importation of reindeer into the territory to reduce the natives' wants and eventually make the animals as nourishing to them as they were to their relatives of the Siberian coast. That became part of Healey's plan for his 1891 voyage.

That year he intended to sail to Indian Point and take on a cargo of reindeer and transfer them to Western Alaska. He believed that the reindeer could be introduced successfully into Alaska, for they certainly flourished in Siberia and would make a splendid article of food for the natives there. So it was that the visionary Captain Michael Healey became a reindeer rustler and added one more specialty to his crew members' resumes.

True to his word, in 1892 Healey began his life-saving reindeer transportation in between his regular activities. That year *Bear* fans learned from the steamer *St. Paul* that as late as July 11 all on board were well and were performing their duties in their usual steadfast fashion.

On June 4, Captain Healey rescued Peter Viani, sole survivor of three men who were placed on St. Matthew's Island the preceding season to spend the winter in hunting white bears.[16] The fate of Viani's two companions was unknown. They had left the island a month before the *Bear* reached the island. Speculation was that they had drowned.

Later that month the crew rescued Captain Brown, U.S.A., and a party of miners, who were out of provisions on the Fish River. It might have seemed strange that U.S. Army troops were in the region, but their introduction was connected to the *Bear*'s role as a floating police station. At St. Michael alone at one point during the gold rush, where 2,000 "tenderfeet" mingled with hardened miners and gamblers, the *Bear*'s crew replaced the rule of rifle and harpoon and kept the peace in a riotous town until the Army infantry took over. Even with such distractions Healey had not forgotten his reindeer wrangling.

While waiting for a coal ship at Port Clarence, Captain Healey made two hurried trips to Siberia, where Dr. Sheldon Jackson purchased 65 domesticated reindeer. The critters were landed safely at Port Clarence and placed in charge of Miner W. Bruce, superintendent of the reindeer station. The first lot was landed and the herd established July 4. And, on a happy note, it was reported that provisions landed at King's Island in September 1891 by Healey kept the inhabitants there from starving during the winter. The *Bear* and its crew were truly lifesavers.

The diverse assignments were routine for Healey and his crew. The dates of the annual voyage did not change much from year to year. People could almost change the year in Jarvis's account and get a good picture of life aboard the *Bear*. That deviated as the end of the 19th century approached, poaching became a bigger and bigger problem, and "*Bear*" stories became legion.

4

Do Bears Have Tales?

"The reports of my death have been greatly exaggerated."—Mark Twain[1]

*Bear*s certainly had tales when the cutter was mentioned in polite society. People soaked up stories about the fabled vessel and its exploits. They followed the exploits of crew members as if they were family members, especially where Captain Michael Healey was concerned. He was a good man in the public's eye, one many people would love to have a beer with.

An early story showed how willing Healey and his crew were to help the people they met under different circumstances. In 1892 a man from Montana named J.T. Healey (no relation to Captain Mike Healey), who was new to the territory, arrived at Unalaska.[2] He was accompanied by the president of the company for which he worked. They were aboard a steamer loaded with merchandise which they planned to use in trading and mining

Unfortunately, the company's steamer had run out of coal. Representatives of the Alaska Commercial Company refused to sell him any. Residents referred the Montanans to a local dealer, Mister Tingle, who had a contract with the American government to supply the natives with coal. Tingle had about 10,000 tons on hand. He supplied the steamer with coal and provisions and sent the Montanans on their way. That did not end their problems with the Alaska Commercial Company.

Healey's steamer carried a small boat that had been torn down in pieces to save space and be reassembled later. When the Montana crew started to rebuild the boat the Alaska Company hired some of its best crew members away from J.T. Healey. That put him in a bind. The *Bear* to the rescue.

The *Bear* arrived about that time. Captain Mike Healey heard what was happening and put his ship's carpenters to work to help the Montana man. The Montanans quickly finished their project, loaded their supplies on the reassembled boat, and headed up the Yukon to start their business, thanks to the *Bear* and its carpentry crew. They were not only building a boat, but a legacy based on their adventures. Who could resist a story about crew members capturing a feared pirate?

Captain J.W. Spencer of the Standard Oil steamer *Asuncion*, which had been at Cordova, Alaska, offloading oil for the railroad and steamboats, related a story about the *Bear* crew members' bravado in 1891 when they captured one of the most wanted men in Alaska, a bandit named "Russian Pete."[3] He knew the story well as he had been aboard the *Bear* in 1891 and a participant in the operation. Remarkably,

Spencer was only 17 years old at the time. He had plenty of reliable witnesses to back him up.

The *Bear* was patrolling the region en route to the Pribilofs that year. There were several distinguished passengers aboard, including District of Alaska Governor Lyman Knapp, Judge Johnson, and Marshal Shoup. One of the principal goals of the voyage was to capture Pete, whose deeds of rapine and plunder had made him a terror to the inhabitants of a wide section of the coast.

The *Bear* stopped at almost every inlet and village in search of the bandit. Finally, he was located on a small island near Unga, so Healey started making preparations for his capture. He did not have any idea of how much resistance Pete would offer, but the captain was not taking any chances. The outcome was anti-climactic, to say the least.

He dispatched two boatloads of men armed with guns and cutlasses from the cutter. The fearless Second Lieutenant Jarvis, one of the most heralded officers in Coast Guard history, and later an official of the Northwestern Fisheries Company, who was well known to all Alaskans, commanded one of the boats. The operation was well planned.

As Spencer recalled, the boats landed on opposite sides of the island to prevent Pete from making his escape. As the boat Spencer was in approached the shore, a stout, well-preserved man of about 60 years of age strolled down to the beach and helped the raiders land. The man was Russian Pete!

The so-called "terror of the Alaskan coast" did not offer even the slightest resistance. "We sailed for Sand Point, a fishing station, and there arrested Russian Pete, a half-breed who murdered a white man named Miller, last year. Miller and Russian Pete had a row over a squaw, and Pete shot and killed him," Lieutenant Jarvis told a reporter. "Pete took his arrest very coolly, not experiencing the slightest concern."[4] The crew members took the resigned Russian Pete into custody, all for naught.

Pete was placed on trial later at Sitka to answer for the murder. The charges were dismissed on September 11, 1891, because of a lack of evidence and witnesses. The United States Attorney prosecuting the case had run into a dead end. At least the court found out what "Pete's" real name was: it was Lawrence Kalugen. That was small consolation to *Bear*'s crew, however, since they had worked so hard to apprehend him.

Jarvis was almost as legendary in Coast Guard lore as Healey. Stories abounded about his achievements. The captain had great faith in him, as one story in particular about a pirate chase revealed.[5] It came to light after Jarvis was selected by President Theodore Roosevelt as the proper man to untangle the complex condition of federal affairs at Nome, Alaska, and to effect reform there. Roosevelt appointed Jarvis to a position as Collector of Customs for the District of Alaska to get the job done. A writer described him as a man who could get any job done, whether it required tact and diplomacy, physical persuasion, or something in between. "Captain Jarvis is a remarkable man," the writer acknowledged. "He has more power personally over the natives of Alaska than has the United States government."

Additionally, Jarvis was trustworthy in the writer's estimation. He recalled as evidence Jarvis's role in buying reindeer in 1898:

On his thousand-mile journey over the ice-wilderness, where he faced blizzards before which even hardened Aleuts and Eskimos recoiled, it became necessary to purchase three hundred reindeer as a food reserve for the ice-bound men in the far desolation of Point Barrow. Charlie Artisall, an Eskimo of prominence, declined to part with his herd though promised that the United States would liberally repay him, but he said that if Jarvis would take them on his own responsibility he was more than welcome to them. And the Eskimo's faith in Jarvis was such that he refused utterly to accept a written acknowledgment or receipt.

Such trust was not unusual. Frequently, when the civil authorities in Alaska couldn't manage ill-behaved natives they called upon Jarvis for help. More often than not he was able to pacify and disperse unruly men as if they were children. And, he generally did it without arms or a guard.

"In his adventures in Alaska, whether on relief expeditions or in turning back plague-stricken vessels from northern ports, Captain Jarvis has not gone armed," one of his unnamed colleagues said. "His mastery over men is due altogether to his wonderful self-command and his moral force. Although beloved by the rough frontiersmen and feared by the outlaw element, Jarvis has none of the rough characteristics which might be supposed to win leadership among these classes. He is modest and reticent, never enters a liar, never makes any sort of burly demonstration, and is not a 'mixer.'"[6]

People described Jarvis as a man who belied his rugged nature. They said he had a boyish build and a shy manner. Yet, when he was in action those traits deemed to disappear. Witnesses who once saw him single-handedly march half a hundred cutthroats of Nome to his launch and embark with them for the *Bear* said he was like a man transformed. Perhaps his victims underestimated him, which accounted in part for his success in disarming them.

In one adventure there was a pirate cruising in Arctic waters who was terrorizing the coast. Healey assigned Jarvis, then a lieutenant, to capture him. The captain learned that the pirate had taken refuge in a certain cove, and dispatched Jarvis there with instructions not to return without him. On entering the cove Jarvis learned from friendly natives that the pirate craft had gone a hundred miles down the coast. That did not faze him.

Undaunted, and keenly aware of Healey's instructions, Jarvis followed the pirate doggedly. Ten days later he returned with his quarry in charge and his ship in tow. As always, he had acted coolly and resourcefully in an emergency. In this case he might have taken Healey and his threat at face value, whether the captain meant what he said or not. But, Jarvis was not taking any chances, and Healey knew he would get the job done.[7]

Another story demonstrated Healey's belief that nothing untoward would befall Jarvis. On one occasion Jarvis was sent with a small boat and crew to carry provisions to stranded miners. The timing was bad. There was a terrible storm in progress. The boat overturned in the surf, but Jarvis remained cool and saved his crew. Sadly, a boat sent to his rescue perished with all on board.

When the storm abated, Jarvis started back to the *Bear* in rough water. One of the ship's officers watched the struggling boat through his telescope. He said to Healey, "'Lieutenant Jarvis' boat is returning, sir, but the lieutenant, I am sorry to report, is not on her."

"You're a liar," the captain bellowed. "If the lieutenant's boat is coming I'll bet a thousand dollars he is aboard!"[8]

He was—and everybody had another story to tell. Stories about the *Bear* appeared in virtually every section of newspapers, from the society ages to the classified section. They sometimes demonstrated how Healey in particular used the *Bear* as his personal vessel rather than a U.S. Coast Guard cutter.

"There were many callers at the Occidental Hotel yesterday to bid Mr. and Mrs. Sands W. Forman and daughter good-by prior to their departure for China," one item disclosed.[9] Forman was for thirty years one of the best known figures on the streets and in the clubs of San Francisco. The family was sailing on the steamer *Gaelic*, and Mr. Forman said just prior to leaving that they would probably be absent three or four months.

"Captain Healey took a large party of guests aboard the revenue cutter *Bear* and accompanied the outgoing steamer down the bay quite a distance to give the departing couple a hearty god speed on their journey," the story revealed. No doubt the Formans were honored. How Coast Guard officials felt about the *Bear* being used as an escort ship for a private citizen was another matter. But, there was not much they could say. The government offered it as a wedding limo too.

On a cruise in 1891 the *Bear* had aboard a distinguished wedding party.[10] The Honorable Louis H. Tarpley, the United States commissioner at Unalaska, had been ordered by the Department of Justice to go along on the *Bear*'s cruise to take the testimony of witnesses in murder cases to be heard at Sitka. Tarpley left Seattle aboard the *Bear* and made the trip to the Bering Sea. When the cutter returned to Sitka he was married to Miss Bessie E. Bugby, a very accomplished lady in her own right, and the daughter of the Honorable John S. Bugby, the United States district judge for the District of Alaska. The wedding was a brilliant affair for the far-off territory.

"It was a swell affair, and all of the officers attended in full uniform," Lieutenant Jarvis recalled. "We left Sitka the next day." Mr. and Mrs. Tarpley came to Seattle on their honeymoon and were then taken to Unalaska, on the far-off Aleutian Islands. Nobody could ever say there wasn't some romance involved in the *Bear*'s life.

Stories about the Healey family were big news as well, even after the captain had been court martialed and relegated to virtual retirement. About a year after that happened information surfaced that Violette Van Ness, the young woman who was known in private life as Mrs. Fred Healey, was saying "good-bye" to San Francisco. Fred Healey was Mike Healey's son.[11] Apparently reporters knew as much about the couple's marital status and itinerary as they did.

Violette was set to sail on the barkentine *S.G. Wilder* for Honolulu, where it was understood she would join her "youthful husband," from whom she was separated on March 30 last, after a brief period of married life. That was according to the San Francisco *Examiner* of June 5, 1896, and picked up by a Hawaiian newspaper. If anyone wanted to know where he was or how he had gotten there reporters were happy to let them know.

"Young Healey was shipped to Tahiti on the barkentine *Tropic Bird* by his father," they said. "The *Tropic Bird* sailed April 1st last, and arrived in Tahiti after a passage of twenty-six days. Young Healey took passage to Honolulu on one of the cocoanut schooners and has been in communication with his wife." No wonder: they were preparing to sail around the world, albeit without letting the world know.

"Violette Van Ness does not deny that she will sail on the *S.G. Wilder*, but wants to get away from San Francisco as quickly as possible, which is her reason for not taking passage on the steamer," the account continued. "She is very reticent about the meeting with her husband, which she wants to be kept as quiet as possible. Their future residence place will be Japan, and a tour of the world is contemplated."

The community had a need to know what the Healeys were up to. "Inquiry on the waterfront fails to bring forth any light on the above item. Cocoanut vessels are new in this trade, and not so common but what track may be kept of them," the reporter let out. "The *Morning Star* and *Norma* are the only sailing vessels from Tahiti that have arrived here within the past sixty days, and Mr. Healey was not a passenger on either of them."

Everyone expected the couple to do what the newspapers published. "After the romance of the Healey–Van Ness nuptials, either of the high contracting parties could be expected to do the opposite to that which they would give out for publication," the writer concluded.[12] There were no secrets among the members of the Healey family, or about the *Bear* and its encounters. That was partly because the loquacious Captain Healey was almost always willing to share his stories with reporters about what happened in the widespread north land.

The Arctic region was vast and its population was small. Based on those facts people might have believed that very little of moment occurred. That was not the case. The sealers, whalers, fishermen, and cargo carriers operating in the area had numerous encounters with Healey and his counterparts. That alone led to some bizarre stories, such as the strange case of Captain Mariano Mayo, a California-based whaler who went north, was declared legally dead, and returned home alive and well.[13]

Supposedly Mayo died on a little island in the Arctic sometime in late 1895. Then rumors started circulating in his home town of San Leandro that reports of his death were greatly exaggerated. His friends grew excited over the news. Other people there might not have been as happy as the strange story and Captain Healey's role in it unraveled.

It was another whaler returning from the north who brought the information that Mayo was still alive. That piqued the interest of the members of the Lodge of Workmen and of the Portuguese Union of San Leandro. They didn't put much faith in the story, but they were anxious to clear up a mystery for monetary reasons. Mayo had been a member of both organizations, and both had paid insurance on his life.

Mayo was an old-time career whaler who had settled in San Leandro. As such he made a trip every year to the northern waters. He wasn't the most skilled whaler in the industry. Luck was against him and he made little money. He was at least lucky in love. Mayo married a young lady of San Leandro. They produced two children who were still alive when the sordid story of Mayo's resurrection broke.

In 1892 Mayo arrived in the Arctic regions as usual. This time he was successful. When the captain returned to San Leandro he built a fine home and announced that he was quitting the whaling business soon. He promised his wife that he would only make one more trip, which would be his last one.

Buoyed by his 1892 success Mayo left San Leandro in 1893 expecting to make enough money to last him for the rest of his life. He vowed to remain in the Arctic region during the winter months or as long as it took to accomplish his goal. The captain said he would remain there for three years. His plan was to secure his provisions from a supply ship which sailed north annually. That was the last anyone heard from him.

Mayo had been gone almost a year, during which no one had heard a word from or about him. Then, Healey returned from patrol with the information that Mayo was dead. His widow refused to believe the captain, as did the members of the lodges that held his life insurance. Healey's word wasn't good enough for them. They wanted some proof.

Healey was happy to tell what he knew. Mayo had broken his leg during his trip. The *Bear* encountered Mayo's vessel and found him in a bad condition. The crew took him aboard the cutter and gave him surgical treatment. Healey transported him to a small island in the far north and left him there after hiring a nurse to care for him. Mayo suffered for several days before he died of blood poisoning. Healey made an affidavit of his knowledge of the case. So did a man who claimed that he buried Mayo.

The two affidavits were the evidence of his death. Subsequently Mayo's estate was probated and the lodges paid his life insurance to his widow. She remarried and remained in San Leandro. That created a legal conundrum. In the eye of the law Mayo was dead. The story caused no end of gossip in San Leandro as the residents awaited Mayo's return and the ensuing legal wrangling.

He had said that he would be absent three years, and that time was nearly up. That, however, was none of Healey's concern. He and the *Bear* moved on as the public waited for more stories of their escapades. There was no shortage of them as the contents of these pages attest.

Incidentally, real bears do have tails, but they might not be recognizable. Scientists are not sure if they always did, as the size of their tails has decreased over time. Maybe they had long tails millions of years ago. They now have tiny tails compared to their large body size.

Conversely, the cutter *Bear* had a small body size compared to its peers, but it generated huge "tales"—and its "tales" continue to grow with time. None of them were as strange as the story about its beloved Captain Healey's court-martial.

5

The Bizarre Court-Martial of Captain Healey

> *"Captain Healey of the revenue cutter Bear has been placed upon waiting orders pending the investigation of charges that have been made against him."*[1]

The December 1895 news that Captain Healey was under investigation came as a shock to people in Alaska and elsewhere. He was a legend in the north land. "Hell Roaring Mike" Healey and his cutter, "Healey's Fire Canoe," were synonymous.

"What could he possibly have done to warrant an investigation?" people asked. The answer caught a lot of folks by surprise—including Captain Healey.

Under Healey's command the *Bear* became legendary. To many people the *Bear* represented the U.S. Coast Guard in its heyday—which was a long one. Newspapers printed stories of its whereabouts, activities, captains, and crew members for public consumption. Followers formed a romantic view of life aboard the cutter. In truth, life there was anything but romantic. That showed in the court-martial of Captain Michael A. Healey, the Coast Guard's first African American captain.

Healey and the *Bear* were a perfect match, a marriage of vessel capability and unrivaled ice seamanship. A January 1894 article in the *New York Sun* described the captain in glowing terms[2]:

> Capt. Mike Healey is a good deal more distinguished person in the waters of the far northwest than any president of the United States or any potentate of Europe has yet become. He stands for law and order in many thousand [acres] of land and water, and if you should ask in the Arctic Sea, "Who is the greatest man in America?" the instant answer would be "Why, Mike Healey."
>
> When an innocent citizen of the Atlantic coast once asked on the Pacific who Mike Healey was, the answer came, "Why, he's the United States. He holds in these parts a power of attorney for the whole country."

By late 1895 he needed the power of several attorneys to defend himself.

At the time the charges were placed against Healey he was the commanding officer of the *Bear*. (He also commanded the cutters *Chandler*, *Corwin*, *McCulloch*, and *Thetis* at one time or another.) Healey was best known for his enforcement of federal law along Alaska's 20,000-mile coastline. Along the line he had become a friend to missionaries and scientists—some of them—and a rescuer of whalers, natives, shipwrecked sailors, destitute miners, and reindeer. (One eminent scientist in particular would testify happily against him at his court-martial.) The natives regarded him as a benefactor and reacted jubilantly when the *Bear* started breaking the ice to enter their communities.

Not everyone was fond of him. Many of his crew members thought of Healey as a tyrant. His word, which he often made known vociferously, was law aboard the *Bear*. Healey was not averse to administering physical punishment to misbehaving seamen when he warranted it necessary. Yet, Alaskans in general treated him as an idol at times.

Why did the people of Alaska even care? After all, it was just a barren waste that a U.S. Secretary of State named William Seward had purchased from Russia in 1867 for $7.2 million. (That would be about $133 million in 2023.) The purchase added 586,412 square miles of new territory to the U.S., at a bargain price of about 47 cents an acre. The price didn't matter to some critics, who labeled the purchase as "Seward's Folly" or "Seward's Icebox." Regardless of what it was called, someone had to police the new territory after it was formally transferred to the United States on October 18, 1867, through a treaty ratified by the United States Senate.

The Russians didn't seem to be interested in the job. If they were they would not have sold Alaska in the first place. Russia had established a presence in North America during the first half of the 18th century, but few Russians ever settled in Alaska. Most of those who were there after the American Civil War (1861–65) departed and left the territory to the natives.

The natives had no centralized government, limited access to medical service, few schools… Many of their settlements were so isolated the natives rarely, if ever,

Captain Healey's next-to-last command, the *McCulloch*, on which he exhibited dementia (USCG Historian's Office).

saw outsiders. The U.S. government had a monumental task trying to organize such services in what was known as the Department of Alaska until 1884, when it was renamed the District of Alaska.

There was only one government agency that could provide the service required to bring Alaskans together: the Revenue Cutter Service. The *Thomas Corwin* initiated the service when it became the first revenue cutter to patrol the Bering Sea, starting in 1877 under Captain J.W. White. Healey made his debut in the department eight years later when he assumed command of the *Corwin*.

Healey was an anomaly in the Coast Guard.[3] He was the first mixed-race Coast Guard captain, although that never seemed to bother anyone or affect his rise to the highest rank in the service. He was born near Macon, Georgia, in 1839, the fifth of ten children born to Michael Morris Healey, an Irish plantation owner, and his wife Mary Elisa Smith, a former slave.

The highly religious family included several distinguished individuals besides Michael. Three brothers entered the priesthood. One of them, James, became the first black bishop in North America. He served as the bishop in Portland, Maine, in the mid–1880s. Patrick, also a priest, served as the president of Georgetown University in Washington, D.C., and Sherwood became an expert in canon law. Three sisters became nuns. One of them earned a position as a mother superior.

James and Patrick maintained close ties, as they sailed together from Le Havre to New York on May 29, 1886, and continued to Portland, where they were expected to arrive June 11. That was about the same time the Coast Guard announced that Michael would continue to serve in Alaska and take command of the *Bear*.[4] The twin announcements highlighted the fact that the brothers were all immersed in service to others, although there was a stark difference in the paths they chose.

Michael was not interested in academic pursuits. He turned to the sea. Michael began his seagoing career as a cabin boy aboard the American East Indian clipper *Jumna* in 1854. He became an expert seaman and rose quickly to the rank of officer on merchant vessels. In 1864, during the American Civil War, he applied for a commission in the U.S. Revenue Marine and was accepted as a Third Lieutenant. Notably, President Abraham Lincoln signed his commission. That launched his long Coast Guard career.

His early years in the service comprised tours on several cutters along the East Coast. But, there was a growing need for Coast Guard officers on the West Coast as more and more explorers, miners, and business people developed a new interest in the new frontier. He was transferred to Alaska in 1875 as the second officer on the cutter *Rush*. That began his lengthy and honorable service in Alaskan waters. To many people it was a shame that it was tarnished by his ignominious 1896 court-martial.

Healey earned his first command when he was named skipper of the *Chandler* in 1877. He was promoted to captain in March 1883 and assumed command of the *Corwin*. That led to a blemish on his record. In October 1882 he and *Corwin* participated in a controversial bombardment of the Tlingit native village of Angoon on the sparsely populated Admiralty Island. The incident resulted from a dispute over Tlingit customs, which could be expected in a region where Americans were unfamiliar with the natives' way of life.

The Tlingits had a custom of asking for compensation from supposedly negligent parties for accidental deaths. White settlers in the area agreed with the practice; Alaskan government authorities did not. The 1882 confrontation began on October 22 when a Tlingit Indian named Ti'Len was killed by a prematurely exploding harpoon while he was whaling near the village with two white men. All three were employed by the Northwest Trading Company. The villagers stopped work to mourn the shaman's death and asked the company for 200 blankets as compensation for his demise. The company's superintendent, J.M. Vanderbilt, denied the request and ordered the Tlingits to return to work. They refused and continued mourning.

The superintendent was incensed. He traveled fifty miles south to Navy headquarters at Sitka and told the commanding officer of the screw frigate U.S.S. *Adams*, E.C. Merriman, who was the senior U.S. authority in Alaska at the time, that the Tlingits were rebelling and holding two white men hostage. That did not please Merriman, who overreacted.

Commander Merriman visited the Tlingits personally to investigate the matter, but the *Adams* drew too much water to get in close to the village. Karma was kind to Merriman. Healey and the *Corwin* happened to be in Sitka at the time to take on coal. Merriman invited him to join the expedition to participate in what came to be known as the one-sided "Battle of Angoon" on October 26, 1882. Healey took Merriman, 50 sailors, and 20 Marines on board and headed for Angoon, towing the Northwest Trading Company's tug named *Fugitive* and the *Adams's* launch.

When the American force reached Angoon the leaders discovered that either the Tlingits had never actually held the two white men against their will or had released them. Nevertheless, the Americans demanded that the Tlingits fork over 400 blankets to them "under the penalty of having their canoes destroyed and principal village shelled and burnt." There was a lot lost in the translation, since the Tlingits spoke very little English.

Consequently, Merriman ordered that the village be bombarded to teach the natives a lesson. They were, after all, as described in a report by U.S. Customs Collector William Morris, "a rich and warlike tribe, very insolent and saucy toward the whites."[5]

The battle did not catch the Tlingits by surprise. They took the Americans at their word and evacuated the village on the night of October 25 in anticipation of the shelling. As a result, no one was killed or injured the next day as the Americans shelled the village and set it afire, although one account says six children suffocated when houses in the village burned.[6] Then, the American party boarded the *Corwin* and returned to Sitka to resume their normal duties.

According to all accounts, the supposedly "warlike" Tlingits did not return any fire.[7] More important, they survived the bombardment and rebuilt the village even though they lost everything they had.[8] Decades later a survivor of the attack described it as "the day we suffered for a crime that was not committed."[9]

The U.S. Indian Claims Commission paid the villagers an out-of-pocket

5. The Bizarre Court-Martial of Captain Healey

settlement of $90,000 in 1973—almost 100 years after the bombardment occurred. That did little to help the people who lived in Angoon in 1882 or remove the stain from Healey's record. But, blemishes of that ilk were a risk that Coast Guard officers had to take. Not everybody, including Healey, was immune to them or proposed monetary settlements at times.

In 1886 seaman George Ford placed a $10,000 lawsuit against Healey for rescuing him. The *Corwin* had picked up the shipwrecked sailor who apparently was not happy with the way he was treated. As a result, he was charged with insubordination, even if he wasn't a crew member. He retaliated by filing his lawsuit. A judge dismissed it, though, after Ford disappeared.[10]

Bizarre results like that were one of the hazards of Healey's job. So were court-martials, as unusual as they were. Certainly it wasn't something Healey envisioned as a virtual career ender when he took command of the *Bear* in 1886. That was when he hit his stride as a commanding officer and started attracting attention from the public.

During the last two decades of the 19th century, Healey was in essence the U.S. government in most of Alaska. Mention the Coast Guard and most people thought of Michael Healey. In his twenty years of service between San Francisco and Point Barrow, he acted as judge, doctor, and policeman to Alaskan natives, merchant seamen, and whaling crews. According to biographical information:

> He operated in an eerie echo of what would become the mission of his Coast Guard successors a century later: protecting the natural resources of the region, suppressing illegal trade, resupply of remote outposts, enforcement of the law, and search and rescue. Even in the early days of Arctic operations, science was an important part of the mission. Renowned naturalist John Muir made a number of voyages with Healey during the 1880s as part of an ambitious scientific program. With the reduction in the seal and whale populations, he introduced reindeer from Siberia to Alaska to provide food, clothing and other necessities for the native peoples.[11]

All of that fell into the "But what did you do for me today?" category in 1895 as U.S. Treasury Department authorities, under whose responsibility the Coast Guard fell, announced the charges against Healey. Healey's prior accomplishments were all but forgotten as the service prepared its case against the venerable captain. The question was what motivated them.[12]

Speculation was rife. Some people believed it was an effort by the Treasury Department to force Healey out of the service because he was a dinosaur whose old methods of discipline and seamanship were outdated. Another theory was that the department wanted to replace all its older captains and Healey was just the first to go. A third idea suggested that the move was a conspiracy among younger officers to oust the senior commanders so they could move up the career ladder. Nobody knew for sure, but the theories provided grist for the rumor mill as the trial approached.

Rumors aside, none of the speculations deterred the authorities from going ahead with the court-martial. The nation tuned in to find out what would happen to Healey. The Treasury Department tried to keep the proceedings quiet. That did not work.

Inquisitive reporters were able to feed eager followers with detailed accounts of the testimony and the participants' reactions. It was an exciting time for court-martial "groupies," but not particularly so for the Treasury Department as the trial morphed into a scandal and media circus. Many people seemed to forget that underneath all the hype a man's career and reputation were at stake. Captain Healey could only hope that everything turned out well for him. It didn't.

6

The *Bear* May Have Been a Ship, but There Was Railroading Afloat

> "The 1896 court-martial of Captain Michael A. Healey is a cautionary tale for all Coast Guard officers. Indeed, for officers of all branches of the armed services and business as well. It proved that the enlisted men and women make the officers; the officers do not make the enlisted men and women. The same concepts hold true in any facet of life where there are leaders and those who are led."[1]

The reason for the investigation was revealed early in December 1895 when Captain Shoemaker, commandant of the revenue cutter service, announced that he had received full and specific charges against Healey signed by three officers of the Bering Sea patrol fleet, whose names he did not disclose immediately.[2] Like everything else about the proceedings, their names were made public eventually.

Shoemaker merely said that general charges had been received earlier and made known to Healey, who steadfastly denied them. In fact, he believed he was being railroaded. That was a possibility. But, there may have been some merit to the charges. An unidentified veteran of the Pacific Coast service, with whom Healey had sailed since he was a lieutenant, hinted at that. He justified Healey's drinking habit, while seeming to condemn it[3]:

> For the last 10 or 15 years Healy has had the hardest cruise of any officer in the service. Year after year he was detailed to accompany the whaler fleet into the Arctic Ocean, and there he was vested with the powers of an ex-officio justice of the peace and commissioned to try petty cases or charges of insubordination. That was where he acquired a hard name.
>
> He was severe, believing that severe punishment was necessary in that latitude to prevent the repetition of minor crimes. It was not uncommon, even in late years, for him, after adjudging a person guilty, to sentence the accused to be flogged, and he generally saw to it that those sentences were emphatically carried out. He often said such treatment was absolutely necessary to enforce anything like law and order in those seas. Evil-doers, therefore, had always a wholesome dread of the approach of the *Bear*, knowing full well that if their crimes and misdemeanors were reported and found to be true, after a fair trial they were sure to suffer severely.
>
> Then, again, Healy was the only man the government ever sent into the Arctic who thoroughly understood the currents and knack of ice navigation. He was known to stand aloft, lashed to the frozen rigging, for 40 hours on a stretch, plowing a way through the ice packs. No man without a constitution of steel could have stood such service as Healy underwent. To keep up his strength and withstand the rigors of icy gales he consumed large quantities of stimulants, and that was where he began to acquaint the habit of drinking.

After a number of years of this sort of service, naturally he acquired the habit of being a stern, unrelenting disciplinarian, and in many instances, instead of treating his young officers as members of refined society, as they had been on the east coast, where the service was a continual picnic compared with Arctic cruising, he talked gruffly, more perhaps, than was necessary, dispensed with the refined politeness of an Annapolis graduate, and ran his ship much on the same principle as a merchant marine vessel. With all his gruffness, overbearing, and severe treatment, he was a tenderhearted man.

Many instances have come under my personal supervision where he has assisted young officers to become proficient in such duties, such as Arctic navigation and routine work. That is the principal reason for the old-time officers standing by the man. To those who knew him personally he was a jovial companion, but it was a mistake for any young, inexperienced officer to try and tell him what his duties were as laid down by the department.

Like every other man, Healy had his faults. "When his wife did not accompany him on his cruises he was apt to drink to excess, but he never incapacitated himself from duty. His present disposition is due wholly to the severe, dangerous, soul-thrilling service in the Arctic seas. Many other men, whose occupations were much less hazardous than his, have failed completely, and I think it is to Healy's credit that he has performed his duty as well as he has."

Nevertheless, Shoemaker relieved Healey of his command and replaced him with the ship's executive officer, German-born Civil War hero Lieutenant Albert Buhner. Oddly enough, Buhner was next in line to be accused of specious charges. Life was not all copacetic aboard the *Bear*.

It was common knowledge that there was strife on the ship well before the Treasury Department's top leaders got involved.[4] The *Bear* returned to San Francisco from its annual cruise on November 14, 1895. Rumors of the infighting among officers and crew members preceded the ship. No one aboard was eager to discuss them though. The one thing that was clear was that Captain Healey seemed to be at the center of the dissension. Interested parties suggested that he did not have too many friends among the crew, officers or enlisted. That seemed strange, based on his record.

There was no one in the Coast Guard who was better known than Captain Healey. He had been making trips north for over a decade, and he was the best-liked man in the United States among the whalers. He was a skillful navigator, and during all the years he had been at sea his ship had never been involved in an accident, other than being grounded temporarily once or twice, which was a matter of course for cutters. Yet, none of these factors seemed to impress his own crew.

The perceptible coolness between Captain Healey and his officers manifested itself soon after the *Bear* reached the Bering Sea.[5] Many of the officers aboard would be witnesses at the upcoming court-martial, which was not on anyone's radar at the time. The officers included First Lieutenant/Executive Officer Albert Buhner; First Lieutenant/Navigator Howard Emery; Second Lieutenants Chester M. White and George M. Daniels; Chief Engineers John K. Daily and Charles F. Coffin; First Assistant Engineer J.E. Dorry, and Surgeon Thomas Bodkin.

Anonymous insiders who reported on the unpleasantness said that only two of them, whom they did not name, supported Healey. The rest only obeyed orders because they had to. This state of affairs had lasted for several months, they said, so the *Bear* did not carry a particularly happy group in the officers' quarters, which had to have affected the enlisted men adversely.

By the time the *Bear* reached San Francisco the disgruntled officers had already forwarded a complaint to the Secretary of the Treasury. The gist of it was that Captain Healey had been under the influence of liquor on several occasions, and had been guilty of conduct unbecoming an officer and a gentleman. There was also some suspicion that he was suffering from a head injury, although that was not part of the complaint. Healey refused to talk about it, other than to say he tripped over a rope in the dark.[6]

There were two incidents in particular that allegedly prompted the drunkenness charge. One was attributed to Lieutenant White:

> Captain M.A. Healy and Lieutenant Chester White were "at outs" from the start and so there was trouble.
>
> White was disrated and sent to his cabin. He then accused the commander of drunkenness and conduct unbecoming an officer and a gentleman. Some of the other officers of the revenue fleet sympathized with White, and charges against the captain were formulated and forwarded to Washington from Alaska.
>
> For a time that was the last heard of the matter and the *Bear* came to San Francisco. A few days later Chester White ran away with Mabel Howe, alias Mabel Charming, of "The Passing Show" Company and left his wife in this City lamenting.[7]

The second, according to eyewitnesses, had occurred in Sausalito, California, on Thanksgiving Day 1895. Allegedly, not only had Healey been a bit tipsy, but he had abused a lieutenant. The incident was described at the ensuing court-martial. It began with a dispute between Healey and the lieutenant in question, according to the account in the San Francisco *Call*, which covered the court-martial closely. Its report on the first day of the trial provides a credible backdrop of the charges.[8]

> In the Cabin of the *Bear*.
> "A Liar, Sir." Was What the Captain Called His Subordinate, According to the Evidence.
> "What do you mean by spitting in my face?"
> "If you say I spat in your face you're a liar, sir."
> This brief but spirited conversation and the events said to have called it forth formed the subject matter for yesterday's proceedings in the Healey investigation.
> George M. Daniels, second lieutenant of the *Bear*, was first examined. He said that on Thanksgiving Day, 1895, he saw Captain Healey in an advanced stage of intoxication on the ferry wharf at Sausalito.
> The *Bear* was lying in the stream, not far from the wharf. He and the captain went aboard in a small boat, and in a few minutes the captain called him into his cabin.
> As soon as the witness was inside the cabin Captain Healey closed the door and commenced to insult him, making use of many outrageous expressions, and ended by the insult already alluded to.
> At this stage in his testimony the witness appeared to be overcome by the recollection of events described, and burst out into a prolonged giggle.
> "Funny, wasn't it?" queried one of the captain's attorneys, imitating the Daniels giggle as best he could.
> "Well, yes, it was rather funny," responded the lieutenant, and he giggled again.
> "By the way, Mr. Daniels, when the captain spat in your face what did you do?" asked the attorney.
> "I wiped off my face," was the witness's answer, whereat a smile circulated about the judicial chamber.
> "Did you say anything? Any bad words, for instance?"
> "I asked the captain what he meant," answered Daniels, "and he said that if I accused him of such an insult I was a liar."
> "That was all there was to the little affair, was it?" inquired the captain's representative.
> "Yes," answered Daniels, "that was all."
> "And the captain was really drunk?"

"Oh, yes," was the lieutenant's answer, "very drunk."

The morning session here closed, the reading of the charges against the captain having taken up a considerable portion of the time. These charges were drawn up by Lieutenants Daniels and Emery, and accuse the captain of drunkenness and conduct unbecoming an officer on Thanksgiving Day, 1895, at Sausalito. The latter charge is based upon the assertion of Daniels that the captain spat in his face and tried to pick a quarrel with him on that day.

During the recess the officers, having taken lunch, congregated in little groups about the corridors and conversed upon the affair at issue.

As the afternoon session opened a man attempted to enter the room in which the investigation was going on. His entry was, however, barred by an individual in uniform, who after flourishing a bayonet in midair drew with it an imaginary line on the floor in front of the door, remarking grimly as he did so: "'That's the dead line."

H. E. Emery, first lieutenant of the *Bear*, was the first witness of the afternoon. He said Daniels had requested him to go with him aboard the *Bear* on Thanksgiving morning, as he expected to have a row with the captain. The witness listened at the door while the captain and Daniels were within the cabin.

He heard Daniels exclaim, "What do you mean by spitting in my face?" To which Captain Healey answered, "If you say I spat in your face you're a liar." He knew the voices, and said he could not be misled in this particular. He had seen the captain shortly before the encounter, and he was then "'disgracefully drunk.'" Immediately after the cabin scene, the witness, at the suggestion of Daniels, telegraphed his version of it to the Secretary of the Treasury at Washington.

Mr. Emery's testimony consumed a long time and all present exhaled a sigh of relief as he left the stand. When asked a question, the lieutenant, before answering, spent from two to five minutes "in rumination deep and long." When asked his reasons for that, he said he wanted to be sure of what he was saying. When his answers told against the captain, however, they came without delay, a circumstance which caused the old man to glare more than once in indignation.

Albert Buhner, temporarily in command of the *Bear* pending the outcome of the investigation, was next called upon to testify. He said he had conversed with Captain Healey on the wharf at Sausalito on the morning of Thanksgiving Day, and that the captain was perfectly sober. This was perhaps fifteen minutes before the alleged spirited interview between the captain and Daniels in the cabin.

Chief Engineer Coffin of the *Bear* testified that he had heard Daniels' question and that he had also heard the Captain's answer without being able to distinguish the words. He was on deck at the time and got a glimpse of the captain through the skylight. The old man appeared to be much excited, but sober.

This closed the case for the prosecution.

H. B. Vogel, steward of the San Francisco Yacht Club's establishment at Sausalito, said he saw Captain Healey between 9 and 10 o'clock on Thanksgiving morning at the clubhouse. The captain was sober and conversed with the witness for several minutes.

William Boundy, a gunner on the *Bear*; Thomas Powers, quartermaster; Herman Dunberg, coxswain, and J.P. Peterson and Joseph Byrnes, seamen, all of the *Bear*, were in the boat which conveyed Captain Healey to the cutter from the wharf at Sausalito on Thanksgiving morning immediately before the little affair with Daniels. All testified that the captain was perfectly sober at the time. At this point an adjournment was taken for the day.

In the evening Captain Healey was seen, and on being asked his views in reference to the probable outcome of the investigation replied: "My attorneys will not permit me to speak for publication, so I can say but little. They would wish me to keep my mouth shut tight as a clam, as they do, but, hang it! A man must speak sometimes or he'll burst! This whole thing is a job put up by a few young fellows who don't want to work and hate to obey. And then I suppose the boys think the old men ought to get out of the way and give them a chance. Perhaps they're right, but even though I am old I don't relish being run out by men whom I have made. After all I'm not quite a fossil, even if I'm not so young as I might be.

"By the way, before I forget it, I must acknowledge the deep obligation under which The *Call* has placed me by publishing its long and accurate reports of the investigation, though it's a wonder to everybody where it gets the information. The *Call's* treatment of me has been most respectful, and I am deeply grateful for it.

"As for the publicity, I have nothing to fear from it, but I am mortally afraid of mysterious, Star Chamber proceedings."

On being asked how he thought the trial would end the captain answered: "I can only conjecture, and conjectures are not worth much, but I am not afraid to entrust my official honor to the action of the heads of that service in which I have won a name that no power on earth can take from me."

Whichever incident it was, if either, that precipitated the charges against Captain Healey, they both involved the excessive use of alcohol. They, combined with stories such as the one about an earlier head injury that might have been caused by inebriation, suggested that the captain had a drinking problem. The injury had occurred two months earlier. On September 19, 1895, Healey had fallen overboard from the wharf while boarding his ship at Unalaska.[9] He struck his head on one of the piles and sustained a serious injury.

Two months had passed and Healey still had not recovered thoroughly from the effects. He checked into the Occidental Hotel in San Francisco when the ship arrived, where reporters tried to interview him. Healey adamantly refused to discuss the situation, but he did say he expected to be as hale and hearty as ever in a few weeks.

"If I am to be the subject of an investigation," said he, "well and good. Then I will be able to talk. If I am not, the least said the soonest mended. I am known on the Arctic Coast from San Diego to Cape Flattery and from Cape Flattery to Herschel Island. If you can find any one ready to throw a stone at me outside of these men who are said to have signed the communication to the department bring him along. I'll stand all he can give me."

He had a foreboding though. When the ship arrived back at San Francisco he gathered the crew and told them he was going to leave them. "It may be for years and it may be forever," he said. "But no matter what comes or goes you have all a warm spot in my heart. Every man has done his duty, and if I ever go out as commander of the *Bear* again I hope every one of you will be with me."[10]

A reporter for *The Call* noted, "The men cheered and cheered again, because, no matter how many rows Captain Healy may have had with his officers, a more popular commander with his crew never sailed in an American revenue cutter."[11]

The *Bear's* crew members may have been sanguine toward Healey, but they were less so regarding the other officers aboard. One of them, who acted as their "sea lawyer," an old Navy term for an idle, litigious "longshorer," more given to questioning orders than obeying them, reported: "We never had such a mean trip. The officers and the old man were at outs and they had a regular parrot and monkey time (a period of quarreling). Captain Healey is getting along in years and the youngsters seem to think he should retire and give them a chance. We have some queer sub-officers in this ship and to my mind they are the ones that should be investigated."[12]

There was no question about whose side the crew was on. But, when the officers were asked about the situation they refused point blank to be interviewed. More important, they would not reveal the names of any of the officers who had grievances against the captain. They said that whatever information they possessed they were saving for Secretary of the Treasury John G. Carlisle. They were sure he would order an investigation based on their allegations and the facts of the case would come out then. They were correct.

Officers serving under Buhner charged him with unbecoming conduct toward them. The department had a scandal on its hands, much to its chagrin, and the rancor displayed by certain participants at the court-martial did little to make it disappear.[13] The trial was significant to its leaders and the officers of the fleet, because it was the first one on the Pacific Coast to be conducted according to the new regulations of the Treasury Department, which had gone into effect only two years earlier. Thus, it was a showcase court of inquiry.

The new regulations prescribed the form of hearing and allowed the accused to be represented by counsel, who were permitted to cross examine the witnesses for the prosecution and introduce evidence in rebuttal. Civilians could be called as witnesses, but they could not be compelled by any process of the court to testify, and evidence so given by request had to be considered. Any officer who refused to testify when called as a witness was liable to be punished by revocation of his commission. Department authorities were afraid that their showcase was turning into an empty shelf.

Nobody was happy with the shadow being cast over the proceedings almost before they started, especially Healey.[14] He was not taking the charges against him well. Reportedly, after Healey learned he was relieved of his command he tried to drown his troubles by drinking himself into delirium. Even his son, also a Coast Guard member, could not calm him down. Finally, Healey passed out and his son was able to transport him to the local Home of the Inebriates, to be detained for two weeks.[15] Ironically, excessive use of liquor was at the heart of the charges placed against the captain.

Just three weeks after that event occurred, Buhner was relieved of the command of the *Bear*.[16] Captain Francis Tuttle received instructions to relieve Buhner while recent charges made against him were looked into. Officers serving under Buhner charged him with unbecoming conduct toward them. Charges around the *Bear*'s officers were flying faster than bats at a mosquito convention.

One reporter suggested that "The revenue service cutter *Bear* seems determined to remain before the public and to conduct herself in manner unbecoming a respectable vessel of the Treasury Department."[17] That was after the vessel's crew members accused two of the original complainants against Healey, Lieutenants Daniels and Dorry, with sleeping on watch and neglect of duty. Apparently, the Treasury Department was so incensed at the developments on the *Bear* that it began a game of musical chairs in which it implemented a general shifting of officers and men to the other cutters.

While all this was going on Shoemaker announced that a trial board comprising three or five officers of equal rank with Healey would be convened at San Francisco early in January 1896, during which a large number of officers and men would testify. The announcement piqued the nation's interest since it involved the *Bear* and Healey. They eagerly awaited what became the time's "Trial of the Century" for their long-time favorite captain, who had a lot at stake.

Healey's history and reputation apparently did not matter to the officers who filed the complaints against him. They did more than just threaten to ruin his career, though: they set in motion an atmosphere of distrust and disharmony among the western Coast Guard officers that was detrimental to the service as a whole.

People inside and outside the Coast Guard speculated as to who "they" were. The three names ultimately uncovered were lieutenants who served aboard the *Bear*:

George M. Daniels, Howard Emery, and Chester White. White vehemently denied that he was one of them. (He was right. The third accuser was Lieutenant J.E. Dorry.) In fact, White alleged, his name was associated with the others as part of a conspiracy to dismiss him from the service. Healey's friends could believe that; they suggested that the Coast Guard was trying to do the same to the captain.

Actually, Healey's defense team used that point during the trial. They claimed, based on the testimony of Lieutenant Daniels and Engineer Jones, that Healey was the victim of a conspiracy among the younger officers. The witnesses, of course, denied any knowledge of a conspiracy. The defense did not get very far with its argument as it exercised strong efforts to have the charges against the veteran captain dismissed.

White went on the offensive when his name was mentioned as one of the complainants. He gave a lengthy statement to newspapers denying his status as one of them. That was a bold move, which most likely did not endear him to the authorities overseeing the court-martial: "In the first place," he said, "I did not prefer charges against Capt. Healey and would not now desire to say anything except in praise of him. I do not think that the captain had a firmer friend in the service than I have been and still am. I left San Francisco on account of him, principally, because I did not desire to testify at any hearing that may be held on the charges."

Part of the reason may have been that he did not want to draw any more attention to himself or the Coast Guard. White's wife had just begun divorce proceedings against him on the grounds of desertion.[18] She claimed that White told her he was leaving their marriage to go east with an actress. That was not going to reflect well on White or, by association, the Coast Guard.

White may have thought he was doing the right thing to help Healey, but Coast Guard authorities did not. They embarked on a campaign against the lieutenant that lent credence to the theory that the whole episode was a set-up, as White explained.

"The first charges were made by Lieutenant Daniels and in them he alleged drunkenness, tyranny and abusive conduct on the cruise. I have learned that Lieutenant Emery, the senior lieutenant, made charges based upon the captain's actions at San Francisco. In neither case did I have anything to do with the charges," he stated emphatically.

White noted that Daniels and Emery had not known Healey long, whereas he had. They had been aboard the *Bear* for only one year, while White had put in four years, one more than the normal tour of duty. "I have been on the cutter on the Pacific station four years," he noted. "I was the navigating officer and I was not transferred at the end of my three years' service, but assigned again on the *Bear* as special duty as a navigating officer, because Captain Healey wrote to have me retained."

Reasonable people might have inferred based on that disclosure that Healey and White worked well together, and unless the captain had broken their bond through some sort of egregious action the lieutenant would not have remained loyal. Moreover, White would not have been willing to risk his career to protect the captain. Shoemaker and Assistant Secretary of the Treasury Charles Sumner Hamlin seemed unwilling to let White do that when he threatened to resign, at least not until the court-martial was over.

White intimated that he knew well before official charges were made that they were coming.[19] "I left San Francisco November 15th within twenty-four hours after the *Bear* got into port," he said. "I did not care to testify against the captain and I supposed that my evidence would be important to the man who made the charges against the captain because I had been under him so long and knew more about him than they did. The only way I saw out of it was to resign from the service."

That was a significant "Semper Paratus" sacrifice for one Coast Guard member to make for another, especially one who had been treated so badly by the press when it blamed him for filing the original charges against him. It did not impress Shoemaker and Hamlin though.

"I had received an offer from a large Chicago house to enter commercial life and do business for them in Alaska," White explained. "I thought it a good opportunity and coming at this time it made my decision to resign on account of the charge against Capt. Healey more easily arrived at."

The decision, apparently, was not up to him. Before he left San Francisco for Chicago White submitted his resignation via telegram to Coast Guard headquarters in Washington. Normally, resignation requests were honored pro forma. Not this time. He waited for four days in Chicago for news about his request. He heard nothing, but he had no intention of letting the matter drop.

White traveled to Washington to confront Shoemaker and Hamlin personally. They informed him that his request had been denied. Instead, they transferred him to the cutter *Dallas*, based in Boston. White reluctantly accepted the assignment, although he suspected that soon after he reported for duty he would receive orders to report to San Francisco as a witness in the Healey court-martial. "As I feel an injustice has been done me in the statement that I preferred charges against Captain Healey and the whole affair looks to me like an attempt to drive me out of the service, I will go on duty on board the *Dallas*," he announced. He was not happy about it, but not too many people were enthralled about the entire episode. It was taking on all the aspects of a vendetta and giving the Coast Guard a black eye.

Finally, Shoemaker and Hamlin recognized that they might be opening a can of worms if they forced White to testify. They shuffled the witness line-up and let White go on his way.[20] They announced early in December that since he was no longer a member of the service he would not appear at the trial. That meant it was probable that only two officers now on the Pacific Coast would be designated as members of the board, since so many others would be called as witnesses. The other members would be sent from the East. That settled, everybody sat back and waited for the trial to start, which was scheduled for January 10, 1896.

7

Impeach Hamlin and Convict Healey

> "Quite a number of changes are anticipated in the revenue cutter service, but it is not expected that any will be made until the court-martialing of Captain Healy, late of the Bear. Several of the older officers may be retired, as the last Congress passed an act fixing an age limit and retiring officers over 65 years of age. Heretofore superannuated officers were simply placed on 'waiting orders' at three fourths pay; but those who are to go on the retired list will receive only half pay. Captain Healy was a visitor to the Custom-house yesterday."[1]

No court-martial in recent memory had aroused as much interest in naval or civilian circles. The numerous charges were headlined as drunkenness, incivility to officers and laymen, and the old stand-by in military trials of conduct unbefitting an officer. They were compelling. Nevertheless, Healey's many friends expected he would be vindicated. They conceded, however, that the case against him was said to be strong.

In total, there were about twenty-five specifications. Twice as many witnesses for the prosecution and the defense were scheduled to testify. The principal witnesses included the *Bear*'s subordinate officers. Anticipation ran high as the board settled in to listen to the testimony.[2]

Notably, the five officers comprising the board included only three of equal rank to Healey: Captain D.B. Hodgson, of the revenue cutter *Fessenlen*, at Detroit, president: Captain L.N. Stodder, supervisor of anchorages at New York; Captain W.C. Coulson, assistant inspector of life saving station, San Francisco; First Lieutenant H.B. Rogers, commanding revenue steamer *Hartley*, San Francisco, recorder; and First Lieutenant W.E. Reynolds, revenue cutter *Grant*, Port Townsend, Washington, prosecuting officer.

The trial began on at 10 a.m. on January 23, 1896, behind closed doors. That set the tone for the proceedings, as the greatest secrecy was enjoined on the members of the court, counsel and witnesses. Twenty officers in undress uniform were in attendance that first day, awaiting the pleasure of the court. Most of them had been called as witnesses for the prosecution.

The first matter of business was the defense's almost pro forma objection for Captain Healey that the charges were not sufficiently set forth. The court overruled the objections quickly and started calling witnesses. Untrained observers might have thought the speed with which the court began portended that the trial would be over quickly. They would have been wrong. It took almost a month, ending on Friday, February 21, 1896. That was due in part to the large number of witnesses.

Engineer Jones of the cutter *Grant* had the honor of being the first witness called. Lieutenants Daniels and Emery of the *Bear* followed. Since they were all witnesses for the prosecution they adhered to the charges promulgated. But, the defense counsel offered them a robust challenge. It was too early to tell to what extent the cross-examination weakened the force of direct testimony.

In general, it was the outside opinion of officers that the force of direct testimony could not be broken. That was significant, considering there was a theory among observers that a conspiracy existed among the officers to deprive Captain Healey of his command and drive him from the service. The officers denied that it did, as reporters noted. One officer remarked to a reporter:

> Look there at that group of a dozen officers. Do they look like men who would conspire against an old officer to bring him into trouble? No; they are honorable, upright men, who have at heart the good of the service, and in this affair many of them have been misrepresented and maligned. One officer, against whom charges were preferred by the crew, was the subject of inquiry and acquitted. It was alleged and so published that he was drunk for three days, but when the inquiry established the fact that he was sober and on duty and he was acquitted and vindicated, only a line or two announced the result.

Speculators suggested that the officers suspected of the alleged conspiracy were Healey's supporters, rather than detractors. Many of the officers present at the trial were from the cutters *Grant*, *Corwin*, *Rush* and *Bear*. They included Captain Buhner (*Bear*); Captain Tozier (*Grant*); Captain H.D. Smith (*Perry*); Captain Munger (*Corwin*); Captain Phillips (*Wolcott*); and Captain Wadsworth (*Rush*). These vessels had been in the Bering Sea the previous summer when the *Bear* was in the Arctic, and all were familiar, more or less, with the occurrences of the summer cruise and could empathize with Healey's situation. The speculation would have to wait until another day.

At 4 p.m., with due formality, the court adjourned until 10 a.m. the next day. "Thereupon the officers in waiting donned the attire of ordinary mortals and vanished," a reporter noted. The next day was more of the same.

Three early witnesses, Captain D.F. Tozier, Lieutenant Berry, and Engineer Frederich, all of the cutter *Grant*, berthed at Port Townsend, were called.[3] Captain Tozier testified that Captain Healey was a competent and efficient officer and that he had never seen Healey intoxicated while on duty.[4] But, Tozier acknowledged, he was a man who enjoyed a good time. That was no secret throughout the Coast Guard. That penchant for a "good time" was a trait that many of Healey's counterparts shared, which future orders from the Treasury Department to all officers regarding alcohol aboard cutters proved.

Ironically, Tozier did not have the best reputation in the northwest.[5] Some folks called him an unscrupulous man who, according to reports, amassed a large collection of Northwest Coast artifacts, often by stealing the things he coveted or intimidating reluctant sellers. No one knew just how Tozier laid hands on them—including a hunter's hat that is now in the collection of the National Museum of the American Indian in Washington, D.C.

Lieutenant Berry testified that he did not think Captain Healey was a fit officer for the cutter service, although he had never seen the captain drunk while on duty. He said that Captain Healey liked to have a good time, and had many of them. Berry admitted on cross examination that all the officers of the cutter had similar tastes. Like Tozier, Frederich testified that he had never seen Captain Healey intoxicated while on duty.[6]

On and on the testimony went as the promised parade of witnesses told their stories. There was a significant development on January 24 in the way the trial was conducted. Everyone participating was sworn to secrecy. Nevertheless, details of testimonies continued to leak out—starting with the day everyone was sworn to secrecy. That was the day the story of the *Pheasant* surfaced.

Lieutenant Ross of the cutter *Corwin* told about a "whiskey and tobacco" festival aboard the British ship HMS *Pheasant* to which the crews of all the cutters then at Unalaska were invited.[7] There was often more than one cutter there at a time. Ross said that as Healey was walking away later he was so overcome by alcohol that he mistook the edge of the wharf for his bunk. His mistake was made known throughout the fleet, which created a lot of rejoicing. That did not help anyone's positive image of Healey.

A string of witnesses discussed the *Pheasant* affair. One, Patrick Hutton, former master-at-arms of the cutter *Grant*, even claimed that it was not the first time Healey had been unable to distinguish a wharf from the water. In fact, Hutton said, he had rescued the captain from a watery grave at Unalaska.

The *Grant* was casting off and Captain Healey and numerous officers and civilians were standing on the edge of the wharf waving farewell to friends on the departing vessel. Healey was on the bulwark and lost his balance. Hutton saw him fall and jumped into the water after him. A boat was let down from the *Grant* and the captain and Hutton were taken aboard the cutter.

Cutters of the 1908 Bering Sea Patrol tied up in Unalaska, June 1908; the *Bear* is at the right (USCG Historian's Office).

Healey complained of a severe strain in his back, but sat upright in the boat and walked up the cutter's gangplank without assistance. Hutton could not be sure if there had been any alcohol involved in Healey's fall. He noted that, "If he was drunk when he fell off the wharf, the cold water had evidently sobered him, for after the rescue he manifested no indications of intoxication." That same uncertainty about Healey's sobriety obtained through the rest of the testimony.

The first witness at the morning session on the day Hutton testified was Chief Engineer A.L. Broadbent of the *Corwin*.[8] He had served in the same capacity on the *Bear* under Captain Healey. Broadbent testified that on the night of the social aboard the *Pheasant* the captain had imbibed quite freely, but he did not think he drank more than the other officers present. The next two nights, however, were different stories.

A prosecutor asked Broadbent whether he was on friendly terms with the captain. The witness acknowledged that there had been a slight misunderstanding between them on the evening of the *Pheasant* social, but he brushed it off as inconsequential. Then Broadbent offered a bit of damaging testimony. He said he had seen the captain apparently intoxicated at a reception given by the officers of the Alaska Commercial Company at Unalaska on the night after the *Pheasant* affair and again on the following night at a social event aboard the *Corwin*. But, Broadbent stressed, he had never seen Healey inebriated when on duty.

The prosecution switched gears again to ask about the captain's efficiency. Broadbent stated that on occasions of danger, when Healey was afraid to entrust the management of the vessel to his subordinates, he had spent from thirty to sixty hours on deck and as much as two days and nights consecutively in the crow's nest. Broadbent characterized the captain as a severe disciplinarian, but said he could not find any fault with him beyond a rather despotic demeanor toward his subordinates.

The next witness, described as "a vision in broadcloth, gold lace and white gloves,"[9] was Lieutenant Dorry, one of the three original complainants against Healey. He said he was an assistant engineer on the *Bear* and had known the captain for about twenty months. Dorry echoed Broadbent when he said the captain was never, to his knowledge, under the influence of liquor while at sea. On the other hand, at the social events Broadbent mentioned, Healey's language had been far from choice—actually insulting, in fact. Dorry concluded his testimony with an admission that he had not heard anyone criticize the captain except during the *Bear*'s most recent cruise.

Buhner followed Dorry. He opined that Captain Healey's behavior on the *Pheasant* was no worse than that of the other participants. Buhner did not recollect having seen Healey intoxicated on any other occasion. He, like Broadbent, said he considered the captain too strict in his method of conducting the vessel, and said there was some ill-feeling among the officers in consequence.

Next in line was William C. Meyers, the *Bear*'s second engineer, who corroborated the testimony of the other witnesses regarding Captain Healey's hilarity on the occasions cited. But, Meyers averred, he did not feel competent to criticize him as an officer. Meyers emphasized that he would trust him in command of any vessel in any sea. Some of his testimony was a bit surprising. Meyers revealed that he had felt rather sore toward the captain for having refused to shake hands with him in front of other people on one or two occasions, but cherished no resentment against him on that account.

Purportedly, the prosecution's final witness was Chief Engineer C.W. Coffin. Events proved that was not the case. The prosecutors had one more witness in the wings, who caught everyone by surprise by his hostility toward Healey. Until he appeared, Coffin took the stand and said pretty much the same as his predecessors.

Coffin made clear that he had completed two cruises with Captain Healey and had experienced some differences with him, but nothing serious. That opened the door for the defense, which recalled Coffin, who testified that the captain had injured his back quite severely when he fell from the wharf at Unalaska. He could not say whether the captain was under the influence of spirits on that occasion or not. Coffin could say, however, that he had never seen him drunk at sea.

George G. Connell, first lieutenant of the cutter *Perry*, said he had known Captain Healey for six years and had made two cruises in his company. He had never seen him drunk, but had heard rumors to that effect. The question was whether the board was interested in rumors as opposed to facts—and in who was expressing them, such as Captain Hooper, the senior officer of the fleet, who followed Connell.

Hooper testified that he had made a brief appearance at the "whisky and tobacco" event aboard the *Pheasant*, but he had not noticed any undue exhilaration on Captain Healey's part during that time. The prosecution asked him whether he thought it was probable that the captain succumbed to the effects of the alcohol. His answer was a bit surprising: "Well, perhaps he did. I would be much surprised if I heard that one of the men present at the social went away sober. I don't see that there's anything so dreadfully scandalous in a man getting a little happy when he's off duty, anyhow."[10]

Captain Healey took the stand for a short while on his own behalf, which many trial attorneys never think is a good idea. He simply said that he had drunk a little on certain occasions named and let it go at that. In retrospect, that might not have helped his cause. On the other hand, it might not have come as a surprise to anyone.[11]

As testimony continued a bombshell dropped. Rumors surfaced that Hamlin was interfering in the proceedings by influencing witnesses to testify against Healey. The rumors were so rampant that some people suggested Congress should impeach Hamlin.

The secrecy around the proceedings had tightened as they progressed, but enough of the details had leaked out to show that some extraordinary things had happened. Among them was the news that Hamlin had taken action that many critics deemed highly unbecoming in an official who had Captain Healey's fate in his hands.

Hamlin had telegraphed Lieutenant Buhner of the cutter *Hartley*, who had been the executive officer of the *Bear* when the bad feelings broke out between Captain Healey and Lieutenant Daniels, the chief instigator in the affair, to "Tell all you know; hold back nothing."[12] Buhner and his friends considered that a direct insult. Ultimately, the lieutenant testified strongly in Healey's behalf, for which he later paid a price.

Soon it was learned that Hamlin had sent messages to other members of the court-martial panel, which critics inferred to mean that he was determined to convict Healey. The captain's friends vowed that Hamlin's attempts to influence the court would not go unnoticed. They swore to introduce a resolution of impeachment against Hamlin in Congress. Hamlin, to no one's surprise, denied the charge.[13]

He issued a public relations statement on February 8 saying that "the story sent out from San Francisco that he had attempted to interfere or influence the proceedings of the court-martial conducting the trial of Capt. Healey of the revenue steamer *Bear* was too silly to be dignified with a denial." He added that it would be singular indeed if an officer could be impeached for merely doing his duty, and that he did not care to make any statement in regard to the matter—even though he just had. Nothing ever came of the threat anyway.

The trial went on as if nothing out of the ordinary had happened. The promised parade of witnesses continued. If nothing else the board was willing to listen to as many officers, enlisted men, and civilians in various capacities as they could. The prosecution brought in even more at the end to make sure Healey was brought down. The last-minute fireworks on the final day of the trial were notable.

As the trial drew to a close the prosecution called Dr. Benjamin Sharp of Philadelphia, a noted scientist and long-time nemesis of Healey, who had been the captain's guest during a scientific expedition. That pleased Healey's supporters.

> "The case against the captain has fallen through," said a warm personal friend of Healy's, whose rank entitles him to be present at the sessions of tile court. "The prosecution, in fact, has no case whatever, and today they begged the captain's side to allow them a little time in order to fetch Dr. Sharp from the East. They expect great things from Sharp, but they are going to be badly fooled. All that Dr. Sharp can do will be to show his deadly personal enmity toward the captain. He has, in fact, sworn repeatedly that he would do Healy up whenever he should get a whack at him."[14]

The captain's friend was correct in his assessment of Sharp's testimony. Unfortunately, it did not help Healey's cause in the final outcome. At least the captain got to take a final shot at his old nemesis. Sharp and Healey had several disagreements while the doctor was on board.[15] As a result, Sharp left the ship. One of his charges was absurd in context of the trial. He accused the captain of mixing potatoes and gravy with his fingers, which Healey flatly denied.

The first witness examined on the last day of testimony was the aforementioned William Boundy, whose evidence tended strongly to weaken the statements of Dr. Sharp. In his testimony Dr. Sharp stated that when crew member Robert Wilson was in irons the captain was heard to say to Boundy, "Hit him and report to me in two days."[16]

Boundy told a different story.[17] He told the court that Wilson had damaged one of the gun-covers and was placed in double irons forthwith in punishment of his carelessness. The captain, happening to pass by when the man was in irons, remarked jokingly to Boundy, "I remember the time when you would hit a man a whack that would lay him up for a couple of days for less than that." No more was said and the man was liberated after having been in irons for about an hour.

Boundy added that on various occasions he had heard Dr. Sharp refer to the captain in terms that were most insulting and contemptuous, calling him in the presence of the officers and crew as "that damned old brute, and similar names." The witness also said that Dr. Sharp had told him he hated the old man and had made up his mind to "do him up."

Boundy finally reported, on other occasions during the voyage the doctor had announced his determination to "make it hot for the captain." Boundy averred that Sharp's allegations against the captain were, as far as he knew, all without any foundation in fact. Sharp might have wished he had not testified.

J. N. Nice of the North American Commercial Company flatly denied Sharp's statement to the effect that Captain Healey had endeavored to pick a quarrel with Agent Gray of the Alaska Commercial Company at Unalaska. Nice testified that the captain's demeanor on that occasion was dignified and becoming. He merely remonstrated with Mr. Gray on account of a supposed slight on the part of the Alaska Commercial Company's employee toward the *Bear*'s officers. The captain did not display any rancor whatever on that occasion of the alleged spat, Nice concluded.

Then Buhner stepped forward to shoot down the doctor. He noted that Sharp had told the board that he had complained to Buhner about the intolerable society of the captain, and had expressed a desire to live and eat with the crew rather than with Healey. Buhner denied that Sharp had ever offered that remark or anything like it to him. In fact, Buhner said, since the inquiry opened, he had received a letter from Dr. Sharp bitterly taking him to task for not having testified more strongly against the captain during the investigation.

One more witness, F. Tilton, captain of the whaler *Andrew Hicks*, stepped up to testify on Healey's behalf.[18] He swore to Captain Healey's sobriety during the month of August 1895, off Icy Cape. He said he had known the captain by reputation since 1881, and personally since 1888 and had never heard anything against him in all that time. Tilton stressed that it would be impossible to find anyone capable of filling Captain Healey's place in the event of his death or removal. Then Healey's turn came to address Sharp's allegations against him when he was asked for his statement. The captain did not hold back.[19]

> "Dr. Sharp made a mean, outrageous and utterly mendacious remark about me during his testimony," Healey roared. "The man had the shameless effrontery to assert that it was my custom to mix potatoes and gravy on my plate with my fingers." I characterize that statement as being false as hell, but not so false as the heart of the man who uttered it. I was kind to Dr. Sharp, and treated him on the ship as though he were a respected and honored guest in my own house. I gave him objects of rare interest for his collection of curios and endeavored to accord him every courtesy.
>
> You have seen, gentlemen, the manner in which he has repaid me. As for the charges contained in the complaint, I meet them with a simple and unqualified denial. The testimony will corroborate my utter repudiation of them.

That marked the end of witness testimony in the trial. The judge advocate and Captain Healey's attorneys announced that it was time to present their final arguments, which would be transmitted along with the testimony and other papers in the case to the federal authorities at Washington. The waiting began.

8

The Fallout Hurts More than Healey

> "Coast Guard officers in the late 19th century had to possess certain traits that were not common in all men. They had to be intrepid, brave, courageous, hardy, flexible, fair, adaptable, innovative ... the list goes on. Captain Healey had all these qualities in abundance. That's what made him a legend in Alaska. And then he fell."[1]

Folks had to wait a long time before a verdict was rendered. The usual rumors swirled regarding the outcome. The most popular seemed to be that Healey had been reprimanded and would be transferred to the command of a vessel on the East Coast.[2] Others said that since Healey had been found guilty on almost all of the specifications preferred against him he would most likely be suspended for a few months at least.

The speculation was that since he had an excellent record, especially when it came to his enforcement of the laws against seal poachers in the Bering Sea, authorities would deal leniently with him.[3] Hamlin and Shoemaker were not tipping their hand, if they even knew what the decision was, and they denied that they did. Meanwhile, influential people in Washington, D.C., were advocating on Healey's behalf for a decision—hopefully in the captain's favor.

U.S. Senators Stephen M. White (D-CA) and George Clement Perkins (R-CA) approached Hamlin to discuss Healey's case and ask how they could help him.[4] Perkins knew Healey personally. White was inquiring on behalf of some of the captain's friends.

They pointed out to Hamlin that Healey had a remarkable 35-year record in the service and that he deserved consideration for that alone. Hamlin thanked them for their concern and promised them he would move fairly and cautiously with the case. He also convinced them that, contrary to public opinion, he was not prejudiced against Healey.

The senators also asked about details of the findings of the court that had tried the captain. Hamlin told them what he told everyone else: he couldn't say anything about the case until judgement was decided. They went away satisfied.

Hamlin and Shoemaker repeated to reporters in late March 1896 what they had said to White and Perkins: there had been no decision. The voluminous records of the court-martial hadn't arrived at the Treasury Department until March 17, 1896, so the public and everyone else would have to wait for a decision. Hamlin said, "The report of the findings embraces 1,500 pages of typewriting. As yet it has not been examined. Not an individual in this department knows its contents and all stories of its approval or disapproval are fake, pure and simple."[5] He was right. It was another three months before the outcome was made public, and it shocked a lot of people.

It wasn't until June 9 that Carlisle announced his controversial decision, which he alleged was based on a recommendation for mercy.[6] He announced that the board had recommended that the captain should be dismissed from the service. Instead, Carlisle claimed that he mitigated the sentence by ordering Captain Healey to be placed at the foot of the list of captains, suspended from rank and duty, and placed on waiting orders and pay for four years. But he couldn't let it go at that.

Carlisle added the usual bit of humiliation afforded Coast Guard and Navy officers convicted of court-martial charges: Healey was to be publicly reprimanded on all revenue cutters by the publication of the Secretary's order. Additionally, he admonished Captain Healey that if he should ever again be found guilty of excessive use of intoxicants he would be summarily dismissed. That was a harsh sentence in light of the claim of mitigation.

Carlisle did not explain what the chances were of Healey ever being charged again with drinking on duty, since in all probability he would not be commanding a ship for four years. In the long run, Captain Healey paid a heavy penalty for his transgressions. Whether the punishment fit the crime was in the eye of the beholder. For some folks, it was a public black eye for the Coast Guard.

Healey received some vindication. Supposedly he was "on the beach" for four years following his conviction for gross irresponsibility and "scandalous conduct." Happily, in 1900, due partly to a need for more cutters in Alaskan waters following the Alaska gold rush, Healey was placed in command of the cutter *McCulloch*. Eventually, he returned north, but he met a sad fate.[7]

It was reported on July 17, 1900, Captain Healey attempted to commit suicide after a period of strange behavior aboard the *McCulloch*. The cutter was diverted from Dutch Harbor to Port Townsend after the crew reported Healey was acting strangely and they had to keep a close watch on him. It was a harrowing voyage, which took eight days to complete.

The officers and crew members noticed the captain's suspected dementia on their first day out on the *McCulloch*.[8] Right after the cutter set sail he came on deck and issued some orders relative to handling the ship. Then, surprisingly he attempted to leap overboard into the sea. Luckily, before he reached the railing several crew members grabbed Healey and escorted him to his cabin, where a guard was placed over him. His erratic behavior continued nonetheless.

During the night, unobserved by the guard, he secured a medicine bottle and broke it. He used a piece of the glass to cut a blood vessel in his left arm. The guard was alert enough to witness what was going on and discovered the wound before Healey lost much blood. He bound the wound with a handkerchief and called for assistance. Once the cutter reached Port Townsend Captain Healey was taken to the United States Marine Hospital and put in a straitjacket.

Shortly thereafter he was examined by the County Board of' Physicians and pronounced insane. The results of the examination revealed that during four years, while on waiting orders, he had been subjected to many attacks of insomnia lasting from a week to ten days. Consequently, Doctor Gardner, who was in charge of the hospital, ordered that Healey be committed to an asylum. Speculation was that he would be sent to Washington to the national asylum. It seemed to be an ignominious ending for a national hero who had served his country faithfully for so many years. Once again, he rebounded quickly.

In December 1901 another crisis in Alaska arose when 115 miners were reportedly stranded on the *Ralph J. Lung* at Unalaska. The United States government prepared to send them relief. Captain Healey was ordered to be ready to proceed at once to the far north in command of the *McCulloch*, which was prepared to sail. The government was awaiting more specific information concerning the situation before dispatching the cutter on the relief mission. It was significant that the service trusted Healey enough to put him in charge, even if that did not turn out to be his time to command.

It was another four months before Healey received an official command assignment. The news was received with unrestrained glee by members of the press, albeit in restrained terms[9]:

> After suffering humiliation for years from being his own worst enemy, Captain Michael Healey is soon again to resume the prominent place in the revenue cutter service from which he was relegated some years ago, and the news will be received with pleasure by the many who know that despite his former failing, Captain Healey is of the material from which brave men and heroes are made, as can be attested by many a poor devil of a whaler who owes his life to Captain Healey's courage and perseverance.
>
> For years Captain Healey was "the" revenue officer in Bering Sea, known and respected by every native and whaleman in the land of the midnight sun. One day at Unalaska congenial and other spirits played havoc with the old sea dog, and a court of inquiry at San Francisco later in the season did the rest.
>
> Now, however, all that is a thing of the past, for under orders recently issued from the Treasury Department, Captain Healey is assigned to command of the converted man-of-war *Thetis*, now in the revenue service, and will, unless some hitch occurs in the arrangements, be the first to enter the frozen north this season.
>
> For some time past Captain Healey has been in command of the customs boarding tugs *Golden Gate* and *Hartley* in San Francisco harbor. It is believed that Captain Buhner, late of the *Manning*, and who recently went south, will be detailed to one of these vessels.[10]

Buhner, who had been promoted to captain in 1901, was relieved of his command and sent to San Francisco to await further orders.[11]

Healey's last two years of sailing in Alaskan waters were aboard the *Thetis*. It was business as usual, e.g., transporting U.S. senators on secret visits, crime witnesses, and shipwreck survivors, losing U.S. Marines.... That was the story on September 12, 1903, when the *Thetis* arrived in Valdez.[12] On board were the usual suspects: U.S. Senator Charles Dietrich (R-NE) and his daughter, passengers and crew of the wrecked schooner *Abbie M. Deering*, and witnesses for murder trials.

> The Senator is traveling on the quiet, but was discovered and prevailed upon to stay over until Sunday morning, a local reporter wrote. Horses were provided by W.S. Amy, who accompanied the Senator and his daughter on a trip over the trail as far as the summit.
>
> They returned early Sunday morning and immediately departed on the cutter. In the hurry

8. The Fallout Hurts More than Healey

The cutter *Manning* (USCG Historian's Office).

of departure a marine was left behind, and will have to remain here until the arrival of the *Rush*. There were also on the *Thetis* two witnesses in murder cases sent down from Unalaska for the coming term of court.... Wm. Hawes, who left overland for Fairbanks this spring, was a passenger on the *Abbie M. Deering* when wrecked. He went to Seattle on the *Thetis*.

Nothing had changed. Captain Healey was back where he belonged. He retired in 1904 at the mandatory retirement age of 64 and died one year later. Neither the story of his court-martial nor his legacy died with him, though.

The fallout from the situation hit more people than Healey. He may have been the only person on trial, but others paid the price, Lieutenant Buhner among them. In April 1896, shortly after he had testified on Healey's behalf, Buhner was transferred from the West Coast to New Orleans. He had come under fire for taking Healey's side of the dispute in the dispute with Daniels. The charges against him were not sustained, so he did not suffer the same punishment that his former commander was facing. Unfortunately for Buhner, his connection with the scandal was so pronounced that Secretary of the Navy Hilary A. Herbert ordered that he be transferred for the benefit of the service.

Herbert promised to make other changes—and soon. He was determined to restore at least a degree of harmony among the officers of the different Coast Guard vessels on the West Coast. As he saw it, the quarrels and scandals that were becoming more common among the officers and men in that region were casting a bad light on the Coast Guard in the public's eye, which he could not tolerate. But, if authorities wanted to bring peace and harmony they did not go about it the right way with one of their first directives after the court-martial ended. The negative fallout from the Healey trial continued.

The Bering Sea fleet comprising five cutters carrying a total of 35 officers and 185 men had been ordered to sail from Port Townsend at noon on April 28, 1896. The *Bear*, as usual, now under the command of Captain Francis Tuttle, since Healey was still awaiting the outcome of his court-martial, had different orders than the other four, which were confined to the Bering Sea patrol.

The *Bear*'s mission was to sail to Point Barrow to break up a smuggling gang which had been operating there for a long time—and the cutter would stay there. The four cutters that patrolled the Bering Sea would return to Port Townsend about October, but Captain Tuttle had orders to remain at Point Barrow until November 15. All five captains were ready to heave off—and then they received a disheartening order that was related to the Healey case.

On the afternoon of April 27 instructions arrived from the Treasury Department ordering the commanders of the Bering revenue cutters not to take aboard any spirituous liquors.[13] They couldn't have arrived at a worse time. The fleet was ready to sail, but the men were compelled to land their private supplies anyway. They and their captains would have to become teetotalers during their tedious six-month cruise, as the new orders prohibited them from carrying on board even the mildest intoxicating beverages.

Needless to say, the order was met with disapproval throughout the fleet. To their credit, none of the officers expressed an intention to resign rather than obey the department's instructions. It is safe to assume, however, that the name of Healey was uttered often in a pejorative manner as the crew members offloaded their alcoholic beverages before they sailed.

It was the consensus that the order emanated from the scandal and general charges of drunkenness unearthed in the Healey case. That may not have been a surprise. What was shocking, however, was the revelation that one-third of the Coast Guard officers on duty in the Bering Sea fleet were accused of intemperance. Yet, they still managed to do their demanding jobs, despite the accusations. The truth? That was a different matter, just as it was with the Healey trial.

The court-martial did not have a major impact on Dorry's career apparently.[14] He was still aboard the *Bear* ten years later. Reportedly, in May 1905 his wife teamed with two other ladies to convert the *Bear* into a tearoom for an afternoon, Refreshments were served on deck and the tea tables were made brightly attractive by garlands of golden coreopsis blossoms. The ship was "gaily decorated" with flags. The afterdeck was converted into a cozy corner composed of pillows and numerous handsome Navajo blankets. Refreshments were served on deck and the tea tables were made brightly attractive by garlands of coreopsis blossoms. Ironically, Captain Tuttle's name did not appear on the guest list.

9

Ellsworth P. Bertholf, the Santa Claus of the Coast Guard

> *"Congress, in combining the revenue cutter service and the life-saving service into the new coast guard service for the first time in the history of the world, has brought about the establishment of a military branch of government primarily for humanitarian purposes."*[1]

One of the first lessons a *Northland* commander had to learn was the position of Santa's headquarters at the North Pole. Well, not really. But there was a close connection between the *Northland* and Christmas. To numerous Alaskans its commander and crew were Santa Claus and the elves and reindeer experts, at least symbolically.

June 5 was Christmas Day for some people in Nome, Alaska, the *Northland*'s summer base and the outfitting center for all Alaska exploring expeditions. That was the day the *Northland* traditionally arrived there to begin its Arctic adventure. Part of its cargo included Christmas presents from the preceding season sent from the States. Delivery of those presents had been a tradition for the *Bear*. It continued with the *Northland*, although to a lesser extent, despite technological advances.

There was no telling what the *Northland* was carrying in its holds as it sailed north. The assorted cargo was a logistics officer's nightmare. It left on its sixth annual northern cruise in 1933 loaded with lollypops, "talkie" films, medicine, soda pop, toothpaste and numerous other articles eagerly sought by the natives.[2] After all, it was the crew's job to do everything from rescuing stranded sailors at sea to pulling natives' teeth and protecting the seal herds around the Pribilofs from poachers to delivering the mail. Those diverse duties did not change as the *Bear* gave way to the *Northland* and the new Coast Guard moved ahead at full sail.

Poachers were less of a concern to the *Northland*'s crew than they were to the *Bear*'s. That was evident in a 1938 report from Captain Zeusler.[3] He said that upon leaving Nome on July 14 on its annual voyage to Point Barrow, the *Northland* cruised south to Unalaska to prepare for the trip. The ship searched the Bering Sea area for vessels but did not locate any.

The *Northland* stopped at St. Lawrence and Nunivak Islands, where doctors rendered medical attention. After leaving Nunivak Island, the *Northland* visited St. Matthew Island to search for poachers. Crew members did not uncover any indications of recent activities. They found a house not more than two years old on the northwest end of the island, but there was no one at home—and there was no mail for it. There was still plenty of mail for the rest of the islands though, although the Coast Guard was slowly cutting back its delivery service.

By the time the *Northland* replaced the *Bear*, postal service from the states to Nome had been upgraded through improved dog sleds and those newfangled airplanes. Nevertheless, the Christmas gift traffic into Nome was still light. As late as 1930 it cost statesiders $1 an ounce for shipping. It was less expensive to ship the gifts on the *Northland*.[4] The cutter was heading for Nome anyway. Just one more service provided by the United States Coast Guard!

The Coast Guard was the orphan of the U.S. military structure. Unlike the Army and Navy it was not created to fight wars, although it did at times. Its original purpose as specified on August 4, 1790, when it was created, was to protect the nation's revenue. A new law authorized ten cutters for the job and gave birth to the name revenue cutter service. Changes came quickly.

In 1797 Congress authorized the president to increase the strength of the service and cause the said revenue cutters to be employed to defend the seacoast and to repel any hostilities to their vessels and commerce. In 1798 the president was authorized additionally to employ any of the revenue cutters for the purpose of defense against hostilities near the seacoast. That was the point at which the service truly became a "coast guard" and a military force whenever the need arose. In every war after 1798 revenue cutters were consolidated with the Navy and employed for defensive and offensive purposes.

The service's responsibilities increased as the years passed, commerce increased, and the country's merchant marine developed. In 1837 Congress enacted a law directing the president to authorize cutters to sail along the nation's coasts during severe weather seasons and aid distressed navigators when needed.

At the same time cutter commanders were suppressing piracy in the Caribbean Sea and on the Gulf of Mexico and breaking up the slave trade, while still preventing smuggling to protect the revenue. That was not the end of it. They acquired responsibility for enforcing navigation, quarantine, and immigration laws and preventing filibustering expeditions (irregular, unauthorized attacks launched from the territory of one country against that of a friendly country without the involvement of the legal government of the friendly state).

In addition to all that, cutters maintained ice patrols in the North Atlantic and destroyed dangerous derelict vessels at sea. Somehow those ice patrols became romanticized and drew people's attention to Coast Guard activities in the "north land." That accounts for why the activities of the *Bear* and the *Northland* became popular across the country, even as the revenue cutter service's responsibilities continued to evolve.

There was a significant change in 1878 when the life-saving service was established to guard the coasts in a different manner. Until then there were very few stations on the Atlantic Ocean coast to assist stranded vessels. Those few were supervised perfunctorily by revenue cutter officers. The revamped structure increased the number of stations and created a supervised force that led to more assistance in saving life and property.

Essentially, then, the revenue cutter service had two branches under the aegis of the Treasury Department, one to guard the coast, to enforce the laws along it, and to assist navigation, and the other to guard mariners from dangers threatened by the sea. Their duties overlapped at times, and they cooperated closely in peace and war. For example, during the Spanish-American War of 1898 the life-saving service performed a valuable role by converting its stations into signal stations upon which the Navy relied. It was inevitable that at some point they would be united as a single service.

One officer in particular, the legendary Ellsworth P. Bertholf, pushed for the merger, which Congress authorized in 1915, and named him as the "captain commandant."

"Realizing that much better results could be obtained by combining the two services under one head, Congress has amalgamated them and has adopted the logical name, coast guard, since neither of the old names is properly descriptive," Bertholf explained.

"While the military idea has prevailed to an extent in both old services, it becomes more pronounced in the new, for it is realized that promptness of action and efficiency in emergencies can best be secured under military discipline. The fact is to be emphasized that the coast guard is essentially military in its organization and discipline. It is the only military organization ever formed by any government purely for humanitarian purposes."[5]

The revenue cutter service had grown up and was continuing to grow. Bertholf had grown with it.

"The new service is the beginning of a potent naval reserve to be used in the national defense should the occasion ever arise," he said. "The old revenue cutter service, always organized on a military basis, contains thirty-six cruising vessels and nineteen smaller vessels, patrolling all the coasts of the United States, from Maine to Florida, the gulf, the entire west coast including Alaska, and Porto Rico and Hawaii.

The personnel is made up of 1,900 officers and men. Officers for the service are trained at the revenue cutter academy at New London, Connecticut," from which he graduated with the Class of 1887.[6]

It was customary at the time for graduates to serve two years at sea before they received their commissions as third lieutenants in the Revenue Cutter Service. Bertholf received his on June 12, 1899. Later, he became the first Revenue Cutter Service officer to attend the course of instruction at the Naval War College in Newport, Rhode Island. Bertholf served through all grades of the service on ships stationed along various parts of the coast of the United States and Alaska. That's where he began to build a reputation for himself as a member of the *Bear*'s crew, and later as its captain.

In August 1897 Bertholf, then a second lieutenant, had completed several years at sea. He was assigned to shore duty at headquarters in Washington, D.C., which was his first assignment on land. In typical Bertholf fashion he seized the opportunity to expand his professional portfolio and started taking law courses in his evening hours. He was thinking of leaving the revenue cutter service and becoming a lawyer. That didn't happen.

In November that year word reached headquarters that hundreds of sailors of the Arctic Ocean whaling fleet were trapped at or near the tiny settlement of Point Barrow, Alaska, the northernmost point of the United States' possessions. Three ships were trapped at Point Barrow and there were another three or four stranded about fifty miles to the east. The number of sailors involved ranged between 200 and 400, depending on the source. Their captains had waited too long in the ice of the Bering Strait, which separates Alaska and Siberia by about fifty miles, before sailing to warmer waters. Two of the ships had been crushed already.

That wasn't the first time whalers had made that mistake. Unfortunately for some of them they paid for their poor decision making with the loss of their lives or their ships—and sometimes both. The *Bear* and its companion cutters were in the region to prevent, or at least cut down on, the number of such dire outcomes. This was one of those times when captains' poor decision making was backfiring on them and jeopardizing their crew members' lives.

An estimated 250 men had run out of provisions but had made their way to Point Barrow. The arrival of 250 men put a strain on the villagers' resources. As a result, the new arrivals and the few native and white inhabitants were in imminent danger of starving to death. A call went out for the Coast Guard to send an expedition to their relief. Captain Tuttle, commanding the *Bear*, theorized that he would receive orders to sail to the Arctic and try rescuing the stranded whalers, but privately he was not sure the effort was worthwhile.[7]

The Treasury Department sent him a brief telegram to get the attempt underway. "Can beef, rice, beans, canned goods and cardbreak [sic] be obtained in large quantities in Seattle? Hurry repairs on *Bear*."

Tuttle assured the department that supplies could be bought there in any quantities, that the *Bear* would be ready to start at the end of the week, and it would carry

Members of the Coast Guard Overland Expedition approach the stranded whaling fleet at Point Barrow in 1898 (USCG Historian's Office).

100 tons of provisions. He was not particularly sanguine about the voyage, as he told reporters: "I do not see of what avail my going will be, as there is hardly a remote chance of the planned expedition reaching the whalers until next August. As I have said, I think the whalers will be able to punch through on short rations. I shall take a year's provisions for the *Bear*, as we might ourselves be caught in the ice. In fact, I look for that very thing to happen."

The dubious Tuttle did not think it was possible to send relief parties by reindeer, which could be used for food and transportation, and dogs, as some people were proposing. The idea was nothing new. Captain Healey had discussed the introduction of animals into Alaska in his detailed account of a cruise in 1891, dated September 15, in which he discussed the places visited and the services performed during his two-and-a-half months' cruise.[8]

> Cape Prince of Wales was reached on July 7, and it was found impossible on account of the ice to proceed further north, and it was determined, instead, to gather information regarding the introduction into Alaska of tame reindeer procured from the Siberian coast. The *Bear* entered the Arctic and arrived at Point Hope on July 29. Point Belcher was reached on August 11, and it was found that the ice pack was solid to the north and east along the shore with no signs of moving, and it was found impossible to reach Point Barrow relief station to deliver the coal and provisions brought from San Francisco. Word was received from the superintendent saying they had coal and other supplies sufficient to carry them comfortably through another year.
>
> During the cruise much information was gained concerning the reindeer, and the matter of the introduction of the animals in Alaska has taken such a hold upon both the natives and whites that it is an important question before the country. Deer seem to be the solution of three vital questions of existence in the country, viz: food, clothing, and transportation, and I believe that under the care and attention of white men the usefulness of the animals may be immeasurably improved over what it is now in Siberia.

Despite Healey's optimism and Tuttle's misgivings, Tuttle was bound to follow orders, so he prepared to leave Seattle, sail directly to Unalaska, and continue up the straits between Nunivak and St. Matthew Island until ice stopped the *Bear*. Public pressure made the voyage a certainty.

The cry for help was picked up by a San Francisco newspaper, *The Call*, which sponsored part of the expedition. The cooperation between *The Call*, a few other newspapers, and the Coast Guard was unprecedented. Without those newspapers, the *Bear* might never have sailed because the government could not afford to finance the mission and countless whalers might have died. (The story of the unique alliance is recounted in Chapter 10.)

The personnel were selected and orders issued. At the last moment 29-year-old Lieutenant Frederick C. Dodge, the officer nominally assigned to command the land expedition segment of the mission, notified the authorities that he could not go. The story was that Dodge had volunteered for the mission, as a result of which he was named to replace a Lieutenant Hooker. A *Call* reporter wrote that Dodge had not been named the land commander and charged that a rival newspaper, the William Hearst–owned *New York Journal*, was making up news about the expedition rather than reporting the facts.

According to *The Call* correspondent *The Journal* concocted a transcript of the succinct conversation between Shoemaker and Dodge and printed in boldfaced letters that the commandant had assigned Dodge to head the land operation. That should not have been surprising. Hearst and his newspapers were known for the yellow journalism hallmarked by little or no legitimate, well-researched news and emphasizing sensationalism and human interest stories while using eye-catching headlines for the sake of increased sales.

Hearst began his publishing career in 1887 after his wealthy father, U.S. Senator George Hearst, gave him control of *The San Francisco Examiner*. Naturally, then, Hearst tried to get in on the *Call*'s deal. *The Journal*'s version of the subsequent telephone call went like this[9]:

"Hello! Is that Lieutenant Dodge?"
"Yes."
"Well, lieutenant. I want you to report to the commander of the *Bear* immediately and head the overland expedition for the relief of the Arctic whalers."
"Aye, aye, sir," responded the lieutenant.
"Good-by [sic]."
"'Good-by."

The Call reporter denied that the conversation took place. He said he was in Shoemaker's office when the commandant was talking via telephone with Dodge. The two men had spoken by phone, but not one word was said about Dodge heading the overland expedition, the reporter avowed. The man from *The Call* also said that when Shoemaker read *The Journal*'s version displayed in big type, he could hardly express his disgust. And, he used some language that would not look good in print—at least not in *The Call*.

In hindsight, *The Journal* was more than likely trying to divert attention from *The Call*'s up-close-and-personal involvement in the planning and impress its own readers with its access to the central figures. As the planning and implementation evolved, *Call* leadership grew somewhat defensive about their rival newspapers' involvement and made their feelings known in print. At any rate, Dodge's withdrawal opened the door for Bertholf to "volunteer," which is one of the first lessons members of the military are advised never to do.

"Bertholf, we are up against it," Coast Guard Captain Commandant Charles F. Shoemaker said to Bertholf when he showed up for work one fine November morning. "Dodge can't go," he continued. "We need a volunteer."

That was bad luck for Lieutenant F.C. Dodge, but good luck for Bertholf and the officer appointed to replace Dodge, Lieutenant David Jarvis. Like Bertholf, Jarvis, an eight-year veteran of the Arctic service, had a long way to go to reach Point Barrow, and getting there was a particular hardship for him. He was on the 1897 version of paternity leave when the call came and he had to report immediately back to Seattle.[10]

Jarvis had been granted a leave of absence in early September 1897 when the *Bear* was at St. Michael. He had learned that he had become the father of a daughter, so he was excited about visiting his family, which lived in New Bedford, Massachusetts. (Some newspaper reports stated he lived in the small community of New Bedford, Pennsylvania, which was unlikely, since it was just east of the Ohio border, nowhere near a Coast Guard facility. Either way he had a long distance to travel to return to the West Coast.)

Jarvis left St. Michael on the steamer *North Fork* and reached Dutch Harbor on September 22, where he was delayed for more than a week. Finally, he continued his journey home on board the cutter *Corwin*, which arrived in San Francisco on October 13. He finished his journey home. It was a quick turnaround for him, but duty and humanitarianism called. Jarvis returned to Seattle as quickly as he could.

The fact that headquarters assigned three officers on the East Coast to the Arctic expedition was an indication of how highly valued Arctic officers' experience was to the Coast Guard when it came to operations in that region—especially for rescue missions of this magnitude. It was unfortunate for Lieutenant Dodge that his wife wouldn't let him go. At least that's what reporters made it sound like. She may have pulled a few strings. After all, she was the daughter of the wealthy inventor Cyrus McCormick, the head of the company that manufactured reaping machines.

Captain F.C. Dodge when he was captain of the cutter *Unalga* (USCG Historian's Office).

Dodge, who was assigned to the cutter *Dexter*, was reportedly the first choice to command the land expedition. But, allegedly his wife intervened. She feared that he was physically unable to make the trip, so she appealed to their family physician, Dr. J.C. Shaw, who agreed with her. He wrote a note to Shoemaker to that effect: "Lieutenant Dodge has been under my care all this summer, and he is not in physical condition to go with the *Bear*. He has never recovered from the effects of a similar trip, and I doubt whether he ever will. John O. Shaw, Physician."[11]

She had planned to travel to San Francisco with him and their child and stay there with relatives until his return from the Arctic. As far as Dodge was concerned there was a bit of mystery involved in the assignment process, which he vowed to solve.[12]

The lieutenant was eager to go. It would not be his first rescue mission of the sort. In 1891 he led a mission to save the crew of the American schooner *Dove* off the coast of the rugged Vancouver Island. He was itching to participate in another mission of that type. Once he recovered from his surprise and disappointment at the unexpected change in his plans and orders, Dodge began efforts to reverse the decision to replace him. He telegraphed the Secretary of the Treasury and told him that he had nothing to do with the request for a change in the original plan.

Dodge stressed that it was done without his knowledge and that he wanted to go on the expedition. He even asked for a review of his physical condition by a government medical board and pleaded for permission to proceed with his original orders. The Secretary was in no hurry to respond.

Dodge had been in New York when he received his initial orders. He prepared for his departure to Seattle should the Secretary change his mind. Instead, he received orders revoking his assignment and telling him to return to the *Dexter*. He was greatly disappointed, but he accepted the fact that orders were orders. The lieutenant knew that the expedition would have been taxing and recognized the perils he was likely to encounter, but he stepped aside as ordered. He predicted that the expedition would succeed. Bertholf, meanwhile, did not hesitate to take advantage of the opportunity afforded him.

"All right," he said, nonchalantly to Shoemaker when asked to join the expedition. He flicked away his cigarette and said simply, "I'll go."

His quick decision ended any thoughts he had ever considered about a law career and benefited the Coast Guard for years to come. A few hours later he was on his way to Seattle. He left so quickly that all he carried was a supply of cigarettes and a change of linen. Here he was headed for one of the coldest regions in the world and he didn't even have an overcoat! The one he had was old and tattered and Bertholf had left it with a tailor for repair. It was not serviceable and, in truth, he couldn't afford a new one.

Bertholf was earning a mere $150 a month as a second lieutenant, so purchasing an overcoat was far down on his list of priorities. He had the foresight to telegraph people in the Seattle office and ask them to arrange for an Arctic outfit. Thus equipped, he joined the crew of the *Bear* upon arrival. The cutter got underway quickly. So began one of the most famous rescue missions in Coast Guard history.

10

A Unique Partnership

"Many lives may soon be in jeopardy as the result of a want of sufficient food to nourish and stimulate the body to a winter endurance in the frozen Arctic."[1]

As soon as word got out about the whalers' plight at Point Barrow, executives at the San Francisco *Call*, one of the city's leading newspapers, made a bold move: they offered to help underwrite an expedition to rescue the trapped whalers. At first government officials were reluctant to take them up on it. They changed their minds after a rigorous debate, however, and news of their acceptance, project development, and mission execution gripped the nation.

Government officials had legitimate reasons for turning down the initial offer to fund the expedition themselves. The chief reason was money. There was a risk the Congress might not appropriate the funds for the expedition, at least not for the supplies, as Secretary of the Navy John Davis Long explained to a reporter: "But are not your San Francisco friends aware of the fact that even if we had a vessel available for the purpose we have no money to provision the vessel. You know that Congress always has to appropriate money for such relief, as they did in the case of the Mississippi flood sufferers and in many other instances."[2]

That explained why *The Call* offered to pick up the tab for the provisions. There was a more practical reason. The federal government could not afford to finance a rescue mission of the magnitude required to save the stranded whalers because it was getting dangerously close to engaging in a war with Spain. Officials did not want to have to choose between fighting a war or rescuing stranded whalers, especially since, as Leon Blum, of Roth, Blum & Co., a San Francisco meat packing company, alleged, the government was partly to blame for the situation. Therefore, it had a duty to save them.

"The Chamber of Commerce has asked the President to do something for the relief of the whalers," he explained. "It is the duty of the Government to send a revenue cutter there to bring needed relief. All the whalers are nearly out of provisions, and there is nothing to be had at Point Barrow, for two years ago the Government sold out its stores there to the Pacific Whaling Company ... it is no more than right that Congress should do something to relieve them."[3]

Captain Shoemaker acknowledged that the government had sold the stores, but it wasn't entirely at fault for doing so. He explained that the relief station had been abandoned because it had never been of any use, and that at the time they did not think it would ever be, so they sold the provisions to private parties with the understanding that they would keep the provisions there and establish a kind of trading post. But, the purchasers did not hold up their end of the deal and removed the supplies from Point Barrow. The longer the debate over the approval of the rescue mission went on the more issues there were wrapped into it, and not just on the government side.

There were more public opinions and suggestions on how and whether to conduct the mission than there were drops of water in an iceberg. Not surprisingly, California's politicians were not giving the government much choice as they turned the situation into a political football by trying to placate their constituents. They were all for saving the whalers' lives, especially since most of the sailors were based in San Francisco. That local connection was also behind *The Call*'s interest in the expedition. One after another the politicians wrote to *The Call* in support of the mission.[4]

> Hon. John D. Long, Secretary of the Navy, Washington: Information from the north seems to make it imperative that something be done at once to save the crews of several American whaling vessels now near Point Barrow. Provisions need cause no uneasiness, as they are already promised. A Government vessel is a necessity. Would respectfully urge that you use your endeavors to secure favorable action in this matter at Tuesday's Cabinet meeting. George C. Perkins, Senator from California.
>
> Hon. John D. Long, Secretary of the Navy, Washington: Latest advices are to the effect that the crews of many American whaleships are in danger of starving to death in the Arctic, owing to being caught in the ice pack near Point Barrow. Plenty of provisions are available, but it would seem to be the duty of the Government to provide a vessel to carry them north. At Tuesday's Cabinet meeting would respectfully ask that you present the matter and urge immediate relief, as it is a case of urgent necessity. S.G. Hilborn, Congressman Third District, California.
>
> Hon. John D. Long, Secretary of the Navy, Washington, D.C: In view of the imminent danger of starvation to 300 American sailors who are icebound at Point Barrow, Alaska, and the offer of the proprietor of the San Francisco *CALL* to provision any ship that may be sent to their relief, I urge that you take such immediate action as possible to provide transportation for the provisions offered. James G. Maguire, M. C.
>
> To the President, Washington, D.C.: It would seem that humanity demands that the Government take prompt action toward sending succor to the crews of the whaling vessels now fast in the ice of the Arctic Ocean. I join the other members of the delegation in urging that immediate steps be taken in this matter. H.F. Loud, M. C.

"When Senator White saw The Call of Saturday, which arrived today, he became much interested in the account of the icebound whalers. He said some such plan of relief as suggested by U.S. Navy Lieutenant George M. Stoney should be carried out by the Government. The Senator will send a strong telegram to Secretary of the Navy tomorrow urging action," a reporter for *The Call* said.[5]

Lieutenant Stoney had developed a plan for the rescue and volunteered for the mission. His plan, which seemed simple on paper, suggested that a ship suitably equipped and provisioned could reach Norton Sound before the ice grew too thick for navigation. From that point supplies would be transported on dog sleds to Port Clarence, only a short distance overland from Norton Sound, where the government maintained a large herd of reindeer.

Provisions would be hauled from Port Clarence to Point Barrow along the coast on sleds pulled by the reindeer or packed on their backs. When the reindeer and drivers reached Point Barrow they could easily transport the needed supplies to the stranded vessels there and to the east. At Point Barrow, at least, the captains had kept their ships as close together as possible for mutual protection. They could be provisioned through the use of smaller boats.

Could the plan work? Planners turned to Captain Healey to get his opinion. He allowed that it could and some folks believed he and the *Bear* should be the ones to carry it out. A reporter interviewing Secretary Long told him: "I have also received word that Captain Healey of the revenue cutter marine, whose experience and knowledge of Arctic travel is not surpassed by any other man, says that the expedition is entirely practical, and that the journey from Cape Prince of Wales to Point Barrow can be accomplished with reindeer in from thirty to fifty days. Captain Healey says that what is needed above all is promptness, and that there should be no delay."

R. M. Lindsay, manager for James McKenna, agreed that a relief expedition such as that outlined by Stoney would be successful if undertaken at once, especially if Healey approved it. He was not alone in that regard. There was a campaign launched in San Francisco to get him reinstated and assigned to the mission, and if the Coast Guard did not want to do that, then perhaps a privately owned whaler, the *Thrasher*, should be substituted for a government vessel. Even Lieutenant Stoney could support that idea, although he preferred to do the job himself on a government ship.

Lieutenant Stoney believed that there was no man so thoroughly learned in Arctic navigation as Captain Healey, who had on numerous occasions picked his way safely through the floating ice where others would consider it certain destruction to venture. Members of several whaling ships agreed. Twenty-one of them signed a petition for *The Call* to request that Healey be assigned the task of rescuing their fellow whalers[6]:

> The *Call*, San Francisco, Cal.: To your kindness and forethought the imprisoned whalers are indebted for the prompt action taken by the Government in preparing to send the cutter *Bear* to their relief.
> To insure the success of the undertaking we, the undersigned members of the whaling fleet lately returned from the north, respectfully request you to use your influence with the Government to have Captain Healy placed in charge of the expedition, not only on account of his ability as an officer and seaman, but also for the great influence he has over the natives.
> He knows the language of every tribe, and is so well acquainted as to be able to call every native between Point Hope and Point Barrow by his name, and they entertain for him both fear and respect, and they will go to any extreme to render him assistance.

Then, the San Francisco Chamber of Commerce sent a telegram to President McKinley requesting that Captain Healey be appointed in charge of the whalers' relief expedition.[7] The president forwarded the request to Secretary of the Treasury Lyman Gage with his endorsement. Gage consulted with some Treasury Department officers, who informed him that assigning Healey was impossible, since he was on "waiting orders" while serving a sentence imposed by court-martial.

Gage informed the president accordingly, so the idea was abandoned. Tuttle was the man, but backers of the mission thanked *The Call* for trying. They just wanted to get the mission started, although there were still diehards who advocated for Healey's assignment. As Lindsay said:

> The *Call* deserves a great deal of credit for the course it has taken in regard to the whalers who are frozen up in the North. The Government should fit out a vessel at once, for it is a duty which it owes to its citizens.
>
> I think that Captain Healey would be the best man that could be found to command a relief expedition. He is thoroughly acquainted with the northern waters and the conditions prevailing there, and if there is a chance to reach those men he is the man to take that chance. The *Bear* is the best boat for the trip.[8]

Captain Thomas Scullion agreed:

> I have not been in that country since 1872, and I was a young man then, but it seems to me it will be a most perilous trip, though it ought to be undertaken if such a man as Captain Healey says it can be done.
>
> He certainly knows that region like a book, and what he says ought to be heeded. It is a thing that no one has ever undertaken before, and I think The *Call* deserves the thanks of all seafaring men for the interest it has taken in their cause.... It might be that the trip would be made all right, and it is certainly worth an honest trial.[9]

The bottom line was that Healey was not available, but at least the *Bear* was, which the people mulling the feasibility of the rescue mission knew as they continued debating the pros and cons. Before they could assign a ship they had to decide if they were going to okay the mission. They were under enough pressure from within and outside the government to do that, let alone pick a vessel.

And, what if they accepted *The Call*'s offer, launched the mission, and then learned that the private funds had dried up? That would leave the government on the hook for completing it. Certainly, if the mission had to be aborted midstream for financial reasons the adverse publicity would redound badly on the government at a time when it was trying to curry the public's support for a war that a lot of Americans did not think was justified.

Then there was the issue of assigning a ship and a crew. The Bering Sea fleet had ended its summer patrols and was back in port preparing for 1898. The cutters needed repairs and the crews needed down time. Was it fair to order them back into the frozen Arctic at the worst time of the year, or even ask them to volunteer? More important, was it worth risking the loss of a cutter and crew for a single mission, even if 300 or so civilian lives were at stake?

Timing was also a consideration. The service could not put together overnight everything needed for the mission. It would take time to gather supplies, outfit the officers and crew with clothing sufficient for the time of year, make whatever vessel selected seaworthy... The logistics were daunting, to say the least. But, again, there were hundreds of lives at stake.

Government officials at the highest levels discussed all the pros and cons. Secretary Long spoke with President William McKinley about the stranded whalers on November 9, 1897. Immediately thereafter, Long met with Secretaries Gage and Russell A. Alger (War), Commandant Shoemaker, Commodore Melville, chief of engineers of the Navy Department, and Commander Dickinson of the Navy. They had some reservations about working with private financial backers to fund their effort and about their own ability to carry out such a mission.

10. A Unique Partnership

Ironically, one of the strongest arguments against the expedition came from the man who would eventually lead it, Captain Tuttle. He outlined his objection in a telegram to Secretary Gage as discussions about mission feasibility progressed[10]:

> Repairs to boiler, air pump, bridge walls, new sails and docking vessel, cost 15 hundred dollars. Before *Bear* can reach St. Michael, the bay will be frozen over. Vessel cannot winter at St. Michael, as the ice would carry it away.
> There is no harbor north of Unalaska that does not remain frozen until late in June. Bering Strait is closed by ice in November and remains so until June.
> The whalers at Point Barrow are within six miles of the point and 18 miles of the former refugee station. I understand from Captain McGregor of steamer whaler *Karluk* that Liebe's (a Hawaiian-owned whaling company) agent at the refuge station has about 300 barrels of flour. With this and the provisions of the vessels, there should be no starvation. Those frozen in at demarcation point have the supply station at Herschel Island to fall back upon.
> While it will probably be necessary to abandon the vessels, I do not apprehend the crews will meet with anything worse than privations and hardships. The *Bear* can be ready to start in two weeks. There is plenty of coal at Unalaska. I can see no way of rendering assistance until the ice opens in July. No vessel can do anything on the Arctic Ocean until July.

The council took Tuttle's advice under consideration. But it may not have sunk into Long's head. He in particular considered the situation extremely urgent.

Long decided not to wait for the report of the commandant of the Mare Island shipyard, whom he had telephoned the night before regarding the viability of the mission, or input from McKinley's cabinet, which was meeting the following Tuesday. Finally, exigency won over indecision. The officials opted to approve the mission.

Gage summed up the goal of the mission succinctly in a letter to Captain Tuttle in which he included general observations about what was expected from the rescuers, even though he was a bit confused about who they were rescuing[11]:

> The routes and methods outlined in the foregoing are suggestions for your consideration. You doubtless have formed plans of your own, and believe such can be executed with better success.
> You will understand that your movements are not, by anything herein contained, in the least hampered. The whole situation may be summed up under two heads—to wit:
> First—Food must be got to the starving miners [*sic*: no doubt he meant whalers].
> Second—The best and most feasible method of doing this is to be adopted.

On November 13, 1897, Commandant Shoemaker sent this message to the proprietor of *The Call*[12]:

> To John D. Spreckels, Proprietor of "The *Call*," San Francisco, Cal.
> Washington, D. C.,
> Will gladly accept your offer to provide fur clothing, etc., for the officers and crew of the *Bear*. I think it would be well, if you feel disposed to do so, to forward a lot of warm clothing for the persons to be rescued from the whaling fleet, for when found they will doubtless be destitute.
> Captain Tuttle was instructed today to accept all donations on the above lines.
> We propose to rescue these people if human effort can accomplish it.
> The *Corwin* will follow the *Bear* very early in the spring to supplement her work.
> C. F. Shoemaker,
> Captain and Chief of Revenue Cutter Service.

The terse message was noteworthy for two things: Shoemaker's attitude of confidence that the mission would be successful and that the cutter assigned was the

Scan of original postcard image of cutter *Algonquin* breaking ice along the Columbia River, dated 5 December 1919, one of the *Bear's* specialties. Postcard kindly donated to the U.S. Coast Guard Historian's Office by Linda Pachkowski (June 2022). Original now in *Algonquin* Cutter File (USCG Historian's Office).

Bear, Captain Tuttle commanding. No surprise there. Representatives of the Coast Guard and *The Call* started planning with alacrity. Their individual responsibilities were 180 degrees apart, which made the planning a bit difficult. Civilians and military personnel were not used to working together to put together a mission like this, but that did not deter them from establishing communications with one another and getting the job done.

The Call offered to supply clothing and assorted supplies for the officers and crew of the *Bear*. Its staff lined up correspondents for the expedition, invited other newspapers, some of which they disdained, to help financially or otherwise, coordinated logistics with their military liaisons, and addressed myriad minor details that had to be completed. *The Call* captured the excitement about the situation in a front-page article[13]:

> The *Call*'s Appeal is Answered: Government to Send the Cutter *Bear* to Save the Whalers
> President McKinley and His Advisers Act Promptly on the Appeal of "The *Call*" to the Heart of the Nation.
> The urgent appeal of the *Call* for the relief of the 403 American whalers at this moment imprisoned and facing possible starvation in the icepack near Point Barrow has found immediate and noble response from the Central Government at Washington. Thanks to the timely and thus far successful efforts of the *Call* in their behalf, the brave men in the ice-locked ships in the polar waste will not, if human aid can now avail, be left to glut the gorge of the beast of death that prowls by the glacial sea.
> The *Call* offered to furnish all the provisions if the Government would dispatch a ship to the aid of our fellow-countrymen in the white desert of the Arctic. Within twenty-four hours the answer flashed across the continent and the people of the republic will applaud the promptness and the humane spirit that characterize the action of the administration in

ordering the revenue cutter *Bear* to be prepared with haste for an expedition to the coast of Northern Alaska.

The whole American nation is deeply concerned in the race of the life ship, and the universal prayer will be that the *Bear* will reach the 400 whalers before cold and famine have reduced their ranks. The thousands in their comfortable homes in this mild clime will pray "God speed the *Bear!*"

The officious Captain Tuttle sent Spreckels a message the same day as did Shoemaker to initiate the logistical effort, which the paper printed boldly on page 1. *The Call* had every intention of letting its readers know what was going on step by step, with the expectation, of course, that they would follow the expedition's progress through its pages. Tuttle's message read[14]:

"Your offer to supply furs and clothing for the crew on the *Bear* and for the whalers when they are rescued is accepted. I will, as soon as possible, notify you just what is required.

F. TUTTLE, Commanding *Bear.*"

Whether Spreckels had any realistic idea of what he was getting into was questionable.

11

Providing Provisions

> "When the revenue cutter Bear sails on Thursday next the full complement of officers will include men who have already done meritorious service. They will put forth every energy to insure the success of the expedition which has been ordered by the Government as a result of The Call's efforts to that end. They are brave and persistent men, who are determined to surmount all obstacles in order that the end desired may be attained."[1]

Captain Tuttle took a personal interest in ordering the provisions for the mission. "Hurry repairs on *Bear*," the Treasury Department ordered.[2] Game on!

Tuttle planned to carry 100 tons of provisions. Even that amount would put a strain on Seattle's resources. Any concerns about availability were alleviated somewhat by goodhearted citizens who chipped in. Supplying the expedition became a community effort, even to the point of turning the *Bear* into a virtual ark.

Communications in the far north were notoriously poor at the turn of the 20th century. Indeed, they weren't exactly top-of-the-line on the mainland. Coast Guard officials were just beginning to get the hang of the telephone to complement the telegraph. So, one San Francisco carrier pigeon fancier stepped in to help the miners, whalers, and other people living in the Arctic regions communicate. His donation was a bit late to help the Point Barrow expedition party though.[3]

The individual gave the United States government eight pairs of his very best birds to form the nucleus of a carrier pigeon service among the more remote portions of Alaska. The plan was to take them north on the *Bear* and distribute them to various points such as St. Michael, Point Barrow, and Herschel Island. Someone would take care of them at those places until they became thoroughly acclimatized. The offspring of the original eight pairs of birds would become the messengers of the future between isolated miners and whalers and the outside world. That was a good plan, but it was not going to help anyone on this trip.

E. Hayden, manager of the Hayden Packing Company, donated 200 pounds of granulated potatoes, which was equal to one ton of fresh potatoes.[4] *The Call*'s rival newspaper, *The Examiner*, contributed $1,585.85 worth of provisions and its baseball team contributed an equal amount for goods.[5] Even *The New York Journal* got in on the action, much to *The Call*'s amusement and dismay. The writers made it known on their front page that *The Journal*'s intentions may have been good, but the *Bear*'s crew members may have suffered as a result[6]:

The officers of the *Bear* know how well The *Call* has fulfilled its agreement. It has not supplied quite all the clothing, for the vermiform (resembling or having the form of a worm) appendix of the *New York Journal*, envious of The *Call's* efforts undertaken to care for the crew, after first making a futile effort to pass around the hat. It did succeed, however, in pilfering from a charity fund it held in trust a few hundred dollars, on which, it attempted to build a reputation for philanthropy.

Then the writers explained how *The Journal*'s contribution was really detrimental to the crew's welfare:

> With these diverted proceeds in hand the yellow sheet clapped poor Jack on the back and told him he would be sent to the Arctic as well prepared to withstand the rigors of the winter as his superiors of the wardroom, and Jack, believing in the fair promise of the Hearstlings and true to his improvident nature, spent his pay for the sweets of life, with the result that today, when handed his outfit, he found himself on the eve of departure for the far north with but little better provision against the icy blasts than the sheepherder on the upper slope of the sunny Sierra.

The Call charged that the clothing provided by *The Journal* wouldn't keep the crew members comfortable in the middle of a blazing furnace: "When the distribution was made each seaman found himself the possessor of a sheepskin coat—the poorest of all skins to protect one from the cold—a pair of blanket trousers, boots, a few socks, mitts, and a cap. Not a sign of underwear, and no blankets to cover himself with when he stretches himself out in his narrow bunk!"

If *The Call*'s assessment was true the timing was bad. While officers throughout the Coast Guard—and the Navy—were volunteering in large numbers to go along on the expedition, crew members were not. They had just returned from a lengthy voyage to the Arctic, and were not eager to return so soon, especially not at a time when conditions up there were at their worst.

According to *The Call*, when the *Bear* was towed out of its berth at Seattle on November 16 by the tug *Defiance* for its three-hour trip to Quartermasters Harbor to be placed on the dry dock for maintenance work preparatory to its voyage north, it went without a full crew. The previous night four crew members "took unceremonious leave of the cutter." They included a fireman, master of arms, and two sailors. That should not have been surprising to people. The timing of the new cruise was just not right for many of the *Bear*'s crew members.[7]

When the *Bear* had reached port nearly two weeks earlier each sailor had six months' pay due. That amounted to $150 to $200 per man. Few of them had not spent it all by the time the *Bear*'s new mission was announced. Sailors reputedly did not like the idea of giving up a few weeks of contemplated fun just to go out again on a long voyage during which there was little opportunity to let off steam. So, rather than give up their celebrating, many of the sailors asked for their discharges. Others simply took their leave of the cutter without going through any formalities.

The men who worked in the fireroom were particularly averse to spending another eight months or more in the northern seas. Consequently, on the morning of November 20 they all deserted the ship. That did not cause any great alarm in Tuttle's mind. There was no lack of competent seamen available. For every man who wished to leave there were two to take his place, especially on such a publicized and patriotic mission as this.

"It is an open secret that but few of the sailors relish the special trip north at this season of the year," *The Call*'s reporter warned. "Several have already asked for their discharges and been refused. Other desertions will undoubtedly follow unless a close watch is kept on the men and shore leave refused them."[8] That was a potential problem for Captain Tuttle, and if news spread to crew members that they would be sailing with second-rate clothing it would get worse. It was somewhat mitigated by the fact that he had authority to hand-pick his crew, which meant he would more than likely pick the best sailors at his disposal.[9]

Sure enough, the same day the firemen vanished, Tuttle was deluged with offers to enlist.[10] He referred the men he selected to Dr. Eagleson, the local Marine Hospital physician, who put them through a physical and color blind examination.[11] Those who safely passed were given the places of the men who were not inclined to go north. Captain Tuttle chose the new enlistees wisely. He did not believe that a dissatisfied and disgruntled sailor would contribute to the success of the expedition.

The Call's reporters tried to ease everyone's concerns about the quality of the crew. They acknowledged that there were many mutterings of discontent among crew members, but they did little good. But, they declared, "if Jack is cold he will at least shiver on a full stomach, for *The Call* provisioned the ship, and has filled every locker and every inch of space below decks with the best quality of provisions and enough of them to last a full year."[12]

That was certainly true, and the officers went out of their way to compliment the newspaper for its largesse. That didn't do much to assuage some of the crew members who looked at themselves as poorly dressed second-class citizens who would have to do most of the hard work while the officers stayed comfortable in their chamois underwear and top-of-the line fur parkas. The one thing that the captain did not need was friction between the crew and the officers that could spill over and make a perilous voyage more difficult.

Sadly, neither Tuttle nor his officers seemed to recognize the lifestyle differences between them and the crew members as they wrote effusive letters of thanks to *The Call*. They would be living a privileged life with wine, cigars, haute cuisine, music, and other niceties of life while the crew would be less well provisioned. Tuttle's letter summarized the other officers' appreciation and occasional references to the crew's welfare[13]:

> The generosity of The *Call* is simply without limit. I have signed requisitions for clothing for the officers, stores for officers and crew, and other things, until I have felt as though it were an imposition to draw on The *Call* for another dollar's worth of supplies. I accepted The *Call's* offer in the spirit in which it was made, and intended to outfit my officers comfortably, but not lavishly, but every requisition I have made has been more than filled.
> Instead of the ordinary furs I had expected, I find my Arctic clothing to be of the very best Eskimo dog skin, and, besides, there is everything else a man could think of to take on such a trip, including chamois and silk underclothing, boots, socks and mitts, and even silk handkerchiefs for the face. Every officer on the *Bear* is provided for exactly as well as I am, and I am sure everyone extends his thanks to The *Call*.
> Then there is the mess for both officers and men. It is safe to say that no United States ship

ever left port as well provisioned for both officers and crew as does the *Bear*. When finally I thought the last of The *Call's* supplies had been placed on board I was notified today that another car load of provisions had arrived. Where I am to store them I don't know, but we'll have to find room somewhere.

The *Call* has not overlooked a single thing. Even the officers' wine mess has been packed to its fullest capacity, while a fine library of several hundred cloth-bound volumes has been sent aboard for us. I can only say to the *Call* that I thank it and its proprietor for what it has done for the officers and men of the *Bear*.

Perhaps the captain should have trod softly on his reference to the fine wine, since the Treasury Department had banned alcoholic beverages after Healey's court-martial. But, this was a once-in-a-lifetime rescue mission and a few perks for the officers and crew would not hurt. Besides, there was so much cargo to be stored aboard the *Bear* that no one would notice a few bottles of wine.

Imagine: whereas the planners had once worried about where they were going to get the supplies they needed for the expedition they now had a surfeit, almost enough to require a second vessel to carry some of it.[14] Then, they realized they needed even more supplies and personnel. The Treasury Department instructed Captain Tuttle to secure as many sleds as he considered necessary to transport provisions overland, with all appurtenances such as sleeping bags, while planners sought to fill out the crew and take care of minor assignments like contracting correspondents and photographers for various newspapers and soliciting letters for the stranded whalers.

Spreckels realized that it would not be a wise business decision to monopolize coverage of the news and photos on the trek. He also recognized that there would not be a lot of room aboard the *Bear* for a bevy of reporters and photographers. So, he arranged with officers assigned to the cutter to act in their stead. Second Lieutenant John G. Berry took on the roles of exclusive reporter to *The Call* and *The New York Herald*. First Assistant Engineer H.M. Wood agreed to be the photographer for the same papers. Shoemaker assigned Lieutenant E.P. Bertholf to act as exclusive reporter and photographer for both publications, which was significant because he was part of the land party.

Then it dawned on folks that another physician might be needed, since the ship's surgeon, Doctor Samuel Call, a highly experienced seaman who had made three previous trips to Point Barrow with the *Bear*, was going with the land party. Lieutenant Cochrane could provide some medical help in an emergency. He had originally planned to enter the Navy as a medical officer and had taken medical courses in Cincinnati and New York, but he wasn't a doctor.[15] *The Call* offered to furnish one and invited 38-year-old Dr. E.H. Woodruff of Marysville, California, a graduate of Harvard University and McGill Medical College, to join the team. He accepted the invitation and one more critical part of the puzzle was in place.

The Call also offered to take charge of sending letters to the stranded whalers. Staff members realized that their friends and relatives wanted to correspond with them and the whalers would welcome their letters for morale purposes. So, the paper invited people to submit their letters to the newspaper, which it would forward to the *Bear*, and set a deadline of November 20, since it took three days to send the mail from San Francisco to Seattle.[16] The number of letters was voluminous. The deadline was a stark reminder that the start of the voyage was imminent—and that mail service was slow even in those days. Slowly but surely everything was coming together.

At five o'clock on November 26 the final pieces fell into place when a large truckload of boxes and barrels of provisions arrived on the Arlington dock in Seattle. The cargo was added to a huge pile of other boxes and barrels heaped up in front of the berth where the *Bear* was waiting. It was the last load of supplies furnished by *The Call* for the expedition that was scheduled to start the next day to provide relief to the hundreds of ice-bound whalers at Point Barrow.

The supplies had to wait on the dock until the following morning, when they would be stowed into the hold of the *Bear*. Everything else was on board. The last of the soft coal was stowed in the bunkers and a carload of hard coal for use in the cutter's stoves was sacked and piled between decks.

Tuttle dreaded the loading process of the last shipment of supplies from *The Call*. It would take several hours to get them all from the dock to the hold, and the captain wasn't sure he could find room. Then again, he wasn't sure the mission was going to be a success, but there he was.

He was not a man who would give up trying to complete a job. Everyone knew he would find the room. After that, the crew would turn to, clean up the thickly strewn litter on the docks, and the *Bear* would set sail for Point Barrow—or at least motor that way. People had faith in Captain Frank Tuttle. He did not disappoint them. By this time he was convinced that the mission would be a success and the wives and children of the whalers would be forever grateful. His "setting sail" letter reflected that.[17]

SEATTLE, Nov. 26. John D. Spreckels, Proprietor, *The Call*, San Francisco, Cal:

In the annals of newspaper generosity there may be instances where greater liberality has been extended, but in my experience I know of no case that equals the unselfish patriotism and boundless generosity with which The *Call* has furthered the humane project to send a relief-ship to the rescue of the unfortunate men cut off by the ice floes of the Arctic from the comforts of civilization.

The first to agitate the sending of a relief expedition to the far north, and having succeeded in inducing the Government to order the *Bear* on this special cruise, The *Call* has most generously extended every possible aid that might tend to expedite the arrangements so as to insure an early sailing and to further enhance the success of an expedition that at best is fraught with many dangers by so liberally caring for the material wants of the volunteers who are about to set out on this project.

The many acts of kindness, courtesy and liberality that have been extended by The *Call* have been frequently and favorably commented upon by the men on the cutter who have been the recipients of these favors. They are most appreciative, and marvel at The *Call's* forethought in equipping the officers and crew with outfits complete to the minutest detail and supplying the officers with a high grade of provisions and luxuries such as will tend to strengthen and fortify them for the hardships to be endured.

Upon the eve of the departure of the United States revenue cutter *Bear* to the frozen fields of the north I cannot refrain from extending upon behalf of myself and men our most grateful appreciation and public acknowledgement of the unparalleled favors extended by The *Call*. That our mission will ultimately be successful we have but little doubt, and when the 265 unfortunate whaling men are rescued from the ravages of starvation and mental suffering and returned to their homes in a land of sunshine and plenty truly then will wives, mothers, daughters and sons bless The *Call* for having instigated an expedition that means so much to them.

Sure enough, on November 27, 1897, the *Bear*'s lines were cast off and the navigator turned the cutter's prow to the icy north on its errand of mercy. One of the greatest rescue missions in U.S. maritime history was underway, and people around the world held their breath awaiting news of its outcome. They had a long time to wait, but the outcome was worth the effort and expense for some people. Skeptics wondered if the mission was worth the costs, since many of the stranded ships didn't need the help after all.

By the time the *Bear* arrived at Point Barrow, two of the ships trapped, *Orca* and *Freeman*, had been lost. The schooner *Rosario* was the only other vessel that was crushed in the ice. The other vessels—the *Newport, Jeannette, Fearless* and *Belvedere*—were all out of the ice and either on their way to unknown destinations or had continued on their whaling cruises. The *Wanderer*, which had gone into Herschel Island in the fall of 1897 when its captain ascertained that it could not get out of the ice, was known to be safe. But it had not put in an appearance when the *Bear* left Cape Smythe on August 16. To make matters worse, the *Bear* got trapped in the ice after it had rescued sailors from some of the ships.[18]

Correspondent Lieutenant John Berry wrote about the cutter's embarrassing plight:

> With all the shipwrecked sailors on board the *Bear* is lying jammed in the ice off Point Barrow as solidly as any of the vessels here have been jammed during the winter. We arrived here on the 26th of July [1898], got nipped between the shore ice and the drift, backed up by the pack, on August 2, and are now waiting as patiently as may be, ready to steam out should occasion offer: ready to go ashore and wait for the customary Arctic relief expedition for the relief of the first Arctic relief expedition if it should turn out that way.

Berry was not worried though, as he continued: "We have a large supply of provisions on deck, ready to dump them on the ice if we are crushed. Our propeller is jammed so that it cannot be moved and the ship herself is immovably fixed in the ice. We cannot budge her an inch with all the lines we have."

Fortunately, the rescuers did not need rescuing. The *Bear* finally broke free of the ice on August 17 with the help of some ships that were already sailing in open water. The short imprisonment in the ice did not diminish the romance of the mission in the public's eye however.

12

Relief at Point Barrow

"Of course it will take some time to bring the Alaskan Indians around to the new mode of life; but Capt. Healy is convinced that they will see the advantages to be derived, and soon become interested in the breeding of reindeer."[1]

Early in December 1897, the *Bear* landed the relief on the ice three miles off Nunivak Island on the Bering seacoast of Alaska, 1,700 miles south of Point Barrow. That was as close as any vessel could get to the settlement at that time of year. It was remarkable that any ship could have reached such a northerly point by December. But this wasn't just any ship. This was the *Bear*. It was built for ice work, with 18 feet of solid teak in its bows. That certainly helped—as it did so many times.

Bertholf, Jarvis, and Call set out to gather a few hundred reindeer and herd them to Point Barrow. The fact that they had to walk 900 miles to the government reindeer stations at Prince of Wales before they could travel another 800 miles to Point Barrow was a mere inconvenience. Moreover, it was taking a bit of a chance to deprive the *Bear* of Dr. Call, its physician, so he could participate in the round-up, even though Dr. Woodruff was aboard.

Reindeer station? In 1891 Sheldon Jackson, the United States Commissioner of Education for Alaska, conceived the idea of importing reindeer from Siberia into Alaska. Although he is generally credited for his role, he had a champion: Captain Healey. Not much of note happened in the Arctic region at that time without his involvement or input.

As the search for the North Pole accelerated explorers sought his ideas on how best to reach it. On that matter he kept his views to himself. He was more interested in the welfare of the natives in his area of responsibility. He was a man with a keen sense of observation. One of the first things he noted while cruising in the Bering Sea was that the Siberian Eskimos were much more prosperous than those on the American peninsula. He wanted to know why.

Healey ascertained that the climatic conditions were almost alike for both groups. He investigated the puzzle and determined that the Siberians' advantages were due in great part to their reliance on reindeer. The Siberians used them for food, shelter, and clothing. The American Eskimos did not use reindeer for anything, which led to great misery for them.

They relied more on fishing and hunting seals and walruses for their sustenance. When fish became scarce the Americans suffered greatly. To compound their problems, white hunters were driving away the seals and walruses. Healey acted on his observations to stop the cycle.

He petitioned Congress to appropriate $15,000 to introduce reindeer to the natives on the American peninsula. That effort failed. The bill passed the Senate twice but failed in the House both times. That did not deter the determined Healey. He started a public fundraising campaign that brought in several thousand dollars. He had the seed money for his project, but he realized quickly that was the least of his worries. He had to convince the Siberians to sell some of their reindeer.[2] That was like asking Superman to give up his powers to become a cockroach farmer.

The 1898 Point Barrow Overland Expedition Leaders: Lt. Ellsworth Bertholf, Dr. Samuel J. Call, and Lt. David H. Jarvis (left to right) (USCG Historian's Office).

The Siberians were very superstitious and their folklore had taught them to believe that an awful fate would overtake the man who parted with his reindeer. There were very few non-natives in the region who could dissuade them of that belief. Captain Healey could—and did. He capitalized on his years of service to the Siberians to persuade them to sell a few reindeer. They agreed after some delicate negotiations with Healey and Dr. Jackson, whom they favored because of his efforts to educate them. Jackson got the credit; Healey got the reindeer. They still had obstacles to overcome.

Both men and their supporters theorized that the animals could be used as pack animals and sources of food and provide employment for ranchers. Skeptics scoffed at the plan. They claimed that reindeer could not be rounded up—at least not alive—and transported on boats. Moreover, they said, the reindeer would not thrive in Alaska if by some chance they did survive being rounded up and transported, because the Alaskan natives had no interest in living among them. Jackson and Healey brushed aside the arguments and declared that their plan to purchase and transport reindeer was feasible.

Coast Guard officials were on their side as long as the pair could purchase the animals. They offered Captain Healey's *Bear* as a seagoing cattle car to test their theory. Jackson recognized that Captain Healey had for a long time been interested in such a project and gave it his earnest support. His intimate knowledge of the natives and their confidence in him was of great value, so his assistance was critical. The venture began a long Coast Guard and reindeer relationship.

Jackson boarded the *Bear* and they headed for Siberia.³ He and the captain visited several communities before Jackson found someone who was willing to sell them a few reindeer. He purchased 16 domesticated animals at $10 apiece: two geldings for pack work and 14 bucks and does for breeding. Jackson paid for them with a mix of guns, ammunition, tobacco, cloth, flour, etc. Just for good measure he contracted for 100 more to be shipped the following year. It was money well spent.

The next question was how to transport the 16 reindeer safely back to Alaska. The crew of the *Bear* may have been versatile, but they were not reindeer experts. The solution was to tie the animals' feet together and place them in pens. The process worked. Despite naysayers' claims to the contrary, reindeer could withstand sea voyages. They reached Alaska safely. Over the years the numbers of reindeer grew significantly and they became assets to the territory.

The reindeers' trip from Siberia to Alaska was their first major Alaskan survival test. Bertholf's 1897 rescue attempt was their second. The experiment was more than just an attempt to save the lives of a few hundred people. It was also a practical test of the endurance and traveling qualities of the reindeer that had been—and still were—considered by some people to be a folly in Alaska.

One dark Arctic night shortly after their arrival at Nunivak, Bertholf, Jarvis, and Call set off on their journey equipped only with the supplies they could carry on their backs. They completed the dangerous trek, collected the 500 reindeer, hired some Eskimos to help herd the reindeer, and headed for Point Barrow, 800 miles away. They endured some hardships en route, and did not arrive at their destination until April 25, 1898—with 300 reindeer in tow! (Some sources say there were 500. Either way the arrival of fresh meat on the hoof was a welcome relief for the folks waiting in Point Barrow.)⁴

In retrospect, what Bertholf, Jarvis, and Call accomplished was nothing less than a miracle. They drove a herd of reindeer hundreds of miles through rough, barren country in the worst season of the year. The reindeer proved capable of finding their own food. They dug out moss from under the snow.

Critics marveled that the deer could be driven that distance, through a bare, unpeopled country during an Arctic midwinter, with the temperature from 25 to 50 degrees below zero, find their own food, arrive safely at their destination and still drop a large number of healthy fawns there. That was all the evidence supporters of the project needed to prove the value of reindeer to people who lived in the Arctic. Bertholf gave all the credit to the reindeer. The Coast Guard officers serving aboard the *Bear* certainly deserved a large share of it as well.

The expedition did not get any easier once the officers reached Point Barrow. The people there were starving, scurvy-ridden, and surly. Whalers were, at their best, not model citizens or the easiest people to deal with for authorities. They needed a lot of governing, an assignment that fell on the *Bear's* officers by default. They handled it well.

The officers put the whalers to work for their own physical, mental, and moral well-being. They figured that if the men were working they would be a bit distracted from causing trouble. That didn't pay off at first. Many of the whalers mutinied, but Bertholf, Jarvis, and Call stood fast. None of the mutinies got very far. That was in large part because Bertholf was not only adept at organizing expeditions and events, but he was a fair executive who handled people well.

The sailors who served under his command recognized him as a strict, but efficient, disciplinarian. They also knew that he had their interests at heart and would fight for them. The whalers recognized that too and behaved as well as whalers could be expected to behave. Whether they considered him as the "idol of the enlisted man," as some people did, was up for debate.

At any rate, they all survived the trials and tribulations at Point Barrow. In July 1898, the *Bear* arrived at the settlement and took on board some of the crew members of the vessels that had been wrecked. The other refugees returned on their own vessels. Bertholf had learned a lot between November 1897 and July 1898 about organization and leadership. Likewise, the Coast Guard had learned a lot about him and his bright future as a leader. Bertholf had one regret, though, which said a lot about him and his devotion to the Coast Guard and his country.

After they returned to the states Bertholf, Jarvis, and Call learned to their chagrin that the United States had been in a war and that it had ended before any of them had been able to participate. The *Bear* had to sit out the war. Congress assuaged them by awarding each one with a gold medal. The Coast Guard recognized Bertholf as a great prospect for arduous missions—and a reindeer expert.

Somewhere along the line Bertholf had learned to speak Russian and Eskimo. So, in 1901, when the Department of the Interior launched a program to improve the breed of reindeer in Alaska by introducing bigger stock from Siberia, the home of the Tunguse reindeer, his name came up.[5] Bertholf was assigned to lead the mission. He went into Siberia via Moscow and the Trans-Siberian railroad to Lake Baikal. From there he traveled 2,000 miles by horse to Lena. He completed the final 1,000 miles partly by reindeer post and partly by dog sled.

Finally, he arrived in the interior, far removed from the Sea of Okhotsk, where the big reindeer were living. Notably, all of this traveling had to be done in wintertime, when sled travel was at its best. At least he did not have to walk, as he had done during the Point Barrow rescue mission. He could ride reindeer.

The lieutenant was somewhat of a mystery to the people he encountered along his route. He completed the entire journey while mingling with aboriginal and sometimes savage people, many of whom had never seen a native Russian, let alone an American. His only companion was an interpreter. This trip was not quite as uneventful or successful as his 1897 expedition; neither was it entirely wasted. He delivered 254 reindeer to their intended destination.

The purpose of his assignment was to acquire via barter and purchase and transport about 400 "Tunguse" reindeer, which were much larger than most breeds, to the Teller Reindeer Station in Alaska. Their large size was attributable to the abundant food supply in the area of Siberia in which they lived. The Tunguse were much larger than their "cousins" in Lapland. They stood as tall as five feet and could carry 200 pounds on their backs. They were often used for riding. Authorities in Alaska felt that these animals would be well suited for use there.

"Send for Bertholf," they said. His assignment was unusual and risky for a Coast Guard officer, since the people with whom he was negotiating were not easy

The revenue cutter *Hudson* outfitted for the Spanish-American War at Norfolk, VA, Navy Yard, April 21, 1898. The crew of the *Bear* missed their chance to participate because of their Port Barrow rescue (USCG Historian's Office).

to deal with on any level. That did not faze him. Truth be told, the animals fascinated him.[6] "The Tunguse deer are certainly magnificent animals, for they can carry a full-grown man several miles through deep snow," he said. "In fact, when we were sighted from their camp, two Tunguse came out to meet us riding deer that at times sank in the snow nearly to their shoulders. In winter, when sleds can be used two of these deer easily draw a load of 600 or 700 pounds, and when used as pack animals 150 pounds is considered the proper pack."

After some difficult negotiations Bertholf purchased 428 large reindeer and drove them down to Baronesskorf Bay in the spring, where he expected to arrive in late May and meet the *Bear* in July for the voyage to Alaska. He did not know that the *Bear* was unavailable and that due to communications breakdowns no one knew where he was. It was as if Bertholf had dropped off the face of the planet and fate was conspiring to abort the entire mission.

Captain Francis Tuttle, the *Bear*'s commander, discovered in Washington State that the vessel had a broken shaft.[7] There was no hope of immediate repairs because there was a machinists' strike in progress. Union workers refused to make the necessary repairs, so the ship was taken to the Bremerton naval yard. Unfortunately, the work could not be completed in time for the *Bear* to reach its rendezvous point with Bertholf. The venture had to be put on hold for a year. Bertholf was on his own.

Setbacks like that were minor obstacles for the lieutenant. He arrived with his

12. Relief at Point Barrow

depleted herd at Vladivostok, Russia, the key to eastern Siberia. There, he chartered a steamer to transport the herd to Port Clarence, Alaska. Sadly, he experienced a great deal of difficulty on the way to the animals' new home. Only 254 of them survived the journey. Even that was remarkable in some people's opinion.

Russian officials who knew of his expedition marveled at his success and the absence of serious trouble he encountered, as if losing 174 of the original herd wasn't devastating. That he delivered any animals alive should not have surprised anyone. Bertholf simply relied on his ability to deal with people and animals, whether they were sailors, aborigines, government officials—or reindeer. Once again Bertholf had demonstrated his prowess as a leader. It's a wonder the Coast Guard didn't name him Santa Claus.

13

1900—A Year of Death, Disease, and Devotion

"Alaska Famine Kills Hundreds—Government Will Send Rations to Starving Indians. Unburied Dead in Houses: At Teller Station Half the Natives Have Died. Salmon are running but not enough well Indians to catch many"[1]

That heartbreaking headline depicted the seriousness of the dire straits in which people in and around the Bering Straits were living in 1900. If ever there was a year that was atypical for the *Bear*—and the Coast Guard in general—1900 was it. It was a year that taxed the Coast Guard's resources and its icon, Captain Healey, attempted suicide. It was also a time when the service's personnel demonstrated beyond a shadow of a doubt how valuable their services were to the residents of the north land—and how they extended Semper Paratus to folks outside their circle.

The year began for Tuttle and his crew as normally as he could hope—his second crew at least. The first one walked out on him along with crews from several other cutters.[2] It took a while to sort out that most unusual labor dispute.

There was labor unrest throughout the Coast Guard in early 1900, and unless the government was willing to pay the regulation wage in force on the coast there would not be a fleet of cutters in the Bering Sea and the Arctic Ocean that year. Sailors on the revenue cutters were earning $5 a month less than their counterparts on the ships stationed on the coast. The men of the north land fleet were not going to let that situation obtain.

When payday came around the crews of the *Manning*, *McCulloch*, *McArthur*, and *Rush* demanded a pay increase. Their demand was refused. The crews quit en masse. They knew replacements were scarce and they could find suitable employment on other ships. Almost every vessel on the coast was involved in the gold rush fever and the subsequent Nome trade. Therefore, good sailors were at a premium.

The captains of the revenue cutters and coastal survey steamers realized they would have considerable trouble in recruiting new crews, even if the Secretary of the Treasury approved an advance in wages, which he seemed in no hurry to grant. In the meantime a large fleet of poachers was heading for the Bering Sea, where they could operate with impunity if the cutters were to be delayed two or three weeks. The poachers could haul in quite a catch of seals without fear of interruption in that case.

Also, there was some unusual interest attached to the voyage, because the *Bear* was assigned to prevent the British steamer *Alpha*, which sailed from Vancouver

April 5 carrying 250 passengers and a considerable load of freight, from landing its passengers and cargo at Nome.[3] The Treasury Department had issued orders that no Canadian vessels would be allowed to trade at Cape Nome, and had asked the American Consul in Vancouver to notify authorities in Washington to alert it as soon as *Alpha* sailed. It was the *Bear*'s job to stop *Alpha*. Tuttle promised that *Alpha* would not be allowed to get closer than twelve miles off the Nome shore.[4] But he had to assemble a crew before he could worry about intercepting the Canadian vessel.

Although Tuttle suspected the *Alpha* probably had a head start and was well up into the Bering already, he believed it could not get through the ice to Nome before he arrived. He was wrong. *Alpha* arrived in Nome on May 25 with 154 passengers and their supplies and cleared customs with no problems. It started its return trip to Vancouver on May 30.[5]

Meanwhile, not to be outdone, the *Bear*'s crew joined the strike. They refused to go to sea at the old wage, so when their demands for an advance were inevitably refused they walked out in a body. The *Bear* was left without its cubs, but Tuttle vowed to go to Alaska alone if he had to.

Progress was slow—almost nonexistent—when Tuttle tried to replace the crew that had deserted. There were formerly 20 men on the deck. By April 11 only three had signed up to sail with the *Bear*. Tuttle said he would go to sea with four men, two to a watch, if he could not do any better. As observers noted, it was very difficult to obtain sailors at the government rate of $28 per month, as masters of coasting vessels were paying as high as $40.[6] That was a significant difference.

Tuttle appealed to the Secretary of the Treasury at Washington for permission to raise the crew's wages. It was ironic that he had to fight for sailors' pay. The cutter commanders weren't exactly enjoying financial security themselves.[7] It wasn't until April 1902 that Congress addressed the issue. That was when the House overwhelmingly passed the Senate bill to promote the efficiency of the service by a 135 to 49 margin, but it wasn't easy. The opponents of the measure fought it to the last ditch.[8]

The bill gave the Coast Guard's commanding officers these relative ranks: captains with majors in the Army and lieutenant commanders in the Navy; first lieutenants with captains in the Army and lieutenants in the Navy; second lieutenants with the first lieutenants in the Army and lieutenants (Junior grade) in the Navy, and third lieutenants with second lieutenants in the Army and ensigns in the Navy. It also awarded the officers service longevity, pay equivalent to the corresponding rank in the Army, and provided for their retirement with three-fourths pay for disability or upon reaching the age limit of 64 years.

Charles Edgar Littlefield (R-ME) championed the bill. In a significant speech in favor of the measure he declared that the Coast Guard was legitimately a part of the war arm of the government. Since it was the settled policy of the government to retire officers of the Army and Navy, the Coast Guard's officers who stood on the same footing in time of war should be entitled to the same privileges in regard to longevity pay and retirement. Tuttle did not have a crystal ball in 1900 though. His immediate concern was filling out his crew.

It took two weeks for the secretary to approve Tuttle's request. But, even if he could pay the new ruling rate of wages he still didn't have anyone to pay them to.

After a great deal of trouble he recruited a new crew and the *Bear* started for the Arctic after a delay of nearly three weeks.

The *Bear* left Seattle on its northern voyage on May 6 with little fanfare.⁹ So, little, in fact, that the news of its departure was buried on p. 12 of a local newspaper. Everything was routine:

> She goes first to Port Townsend, where the officers and men will receive their monthly pay from the government, and thence to Comox for coal. Sitka will be her next port of call. At the capital Special Treasury Agent Evans and Col Wright, collector of customs for the St. Michael district, will be taken aboard: also four Yukon Indians who were witnesses in the celebrated Bird murder trial.
>
> These natives gave important testimony against Bird, who was convicted of murdering his two Yukon mining partners, and in view of their disposition to uphold the enforcement of the law, the government will return them to their tribes.
>
> Dr. Sheldon Jackson, head of the government educational affairs in Alaska, will go north on the *Bear*. Miss Tuttle, daughter of Commander Tuttle, will accompany her father north as far as Sitka, thence returning to Seattle via the steamer Cottage City.
>
> The *Bear* will go out loaded down like a merchantman. She is taking a large quantity of stores and supplies to give the Point Barrow natives as a reward for their services in aiding the *Bear* expedition during their efforts to rescue the whalers imprisoned in the Arctic ice.
>
> Supplies and stores will also be taken north for the river revenue cutter *Nunivak*, which wintered on the Yukon.

There was nothing out of the ordinary there. But there would be soon. If anything could go wrong in Alaska in 1900, the height of the gold rush, it did. Ships filled with people ill-equipped to cope with the harsh environment of the region descended en masse into the Cape Nome area. The passengers were primarily would-be miners who aspired to get rich quick and return quickly to their homes in the states and elsewhere. The number of vessels in the Bering put additional strain on the Coast Guard to provide assistance where and when needed. The *Bear* had no sooner arrived in the Cape Nome area than it received its 1900 baptism in a notable rescue.

A strong gale hit the area June 5–6, leading to the first big disaster in the rush to Nome. The bark *Alaska* went ashore during the gale and became a total wreck.¹⁰ Several other whalers, revenue cutters, and passenger vessels were in the open roadstead, but they managed to weather the gale. During the storm, the *Alaska's* anchors started dragging. As soon as Captain Tuttle saw that the whaler's crew was in danger he weighed anchor and went to the rescue. It was a most dangerous venture, as the slightest mishap would have sent the *Bear* ashore also. Even though his own crew was new, they responded as bravely and efficiently as any of their predecessors.

They extracted the *Alaska's* crew before anyone was lost. The *Bear* rode out the gale without any damage. The *Alaska* was not so fortunate. A few minutes after the crew was removed, the old ship was pounding on the beach. Its masts were destroyed quickly, and thirty minutes later the *Alaska* broke clean in two. Its 600-ton cargo of general merchandise was strewn along the beach.

The surf was so heavy that not a single case of goods was left intact. The only things that escaped total destruction were cans of salmon, meats, and fruits. At least that was salmon that even this *Bear*, rolling in the waves after yet another successful rescue operation, could not eat. The irony of the situation was that only a few days earlier the *Alaska* had been involved in a significant rescue itself, which ultimately led to another unhappy mission for the *Bear*.

On June 1, only a few days before the fateful gale struck, the *Alaska* rescued a stranded, starving, near-death sailor named James Murphy of New York on St. Lawrence Island.[11] Murphy had endured four months of fearful suffering during which he helplessly watched one after another of his five companions die from cold and/or starvation.

They left San Francisco on November 3, 1899, bound for Nome on the schooner *Eacrett*, captained by J.H. Johnson. After an unusually rough voyage, the *Eacrett* was driven ashore on the island. It landed high and dry and the men made an easy landing. They managed to get most of their scanty supply provisions and baggage ashore. The weather was severely cold and the men had very little shelter. Strangely enough, they were not too far from relief.

The island was inhabited by natives and there was a Catholic mission somewhere nearby the landing site, which Captain Johnson set out to find in January 1900. He froze to death on the way. Perhaps he had misjudged the distance to the mission, which was seventy miles away. One by one the other members of the party succumbed as well.

A party of natives found Murphy and Mate Charles Elliott on March 20. They were escorting the two survivors to their village, carrying Elliott in a litter. Sadly, Elliott died the next day. Murphy, however, reached the village, where he was well cared for by the natives and quickly recovered his strength. The bodies of his companions lay scattered about the camp of the shipwrecked party.

Once Murphy reached Nome and Tuttle heard about the five unburied corpses on St. Lawrence Island, he assumed responsibility for their interments. He promised to go to the island and give decent burials to the five victims. Murphy accompanied him to locate the bodies, after which he expected to return to New York. That was just one more indication that Tuttle was a man with a heart, which he and his crew members, new and old, showed time after time no matter the circumstances. As it turned out, the unburied bodies were the least of the cutter commander's problems.

The flood of people to Cape Nome brought with them diseases that led to a health epidemic and martial law, with two companies of U.S. soldiers (about 300 men) to enforce it. But even they weren't enough to stop the rampant crime or disease.[12] Things got so bad the Treasury Department assigned Lieutenant Jarvis as a special agent in Nome to cope with the problems and granted him wide emergency powers to enforce the law there. That left Tuttle one officer short. Meanwhile, he had his hands full trying to deal with the famine that was killing so many Eskimos in the islands he patrolled. It was a hectic time for everyone, as Tuttle summed up in his July 6 report to the Treasury Department[13]:

> It is estimated that there are within a radius (taking the United States post office at Nome as a center) of ten miles 25,000 people. Most of them are living in tents either on the beach or tundra. The sanitary condition of the portion of the city where houses have been erected is simply frightful. Typhoid fever is raging and smallpox is steadily gaining. All possible efforts are being made to stamp out the smallpox, but with so many thousands of tents scattered over

miles of territory it is impossible for the health authorities to keep track of all cases. Gen. [George M.] Randall is commanding with a firm hand, and, having troops at his disposal, will maintain order until such time as civil government is organized.

I understand the natives all along the Siberian coast are suffering from influenza and pneumonia, and are not disposed to trade for reindeer at present.

The "firm hand" Tuttle referred to was a euphemism for martial law. General Randall, U.S. Army, had explained to authorities in Washington, D.C., in a July 11 telegram from Nome via San Francisco why he had imposed it[14]: "At request of Chamber of Commerce have assumed control of affairs in town of Nome until the arrival of the judge and the establishment of municipal government under recent act of Congress. Estimated this date 16,000 people in the town and no effective civil organization for protection of life and property."

Randall was not exaggerating. Few people, if any, could have predicted a month earlier the state of confusion which existed on the Nome beach at that time or that so many marine accidents would have occurred in the Bering Sea or the Nome beach area in June and July. The 16,000 people already in Nome were a drop in the bucket according to prognosticators. Thousands more were en route.

According to estimates, not more than two-thirds of the number of vessels engaged in the northern Alaska trade had already reached Cape Nome on their first trips. All the steam vessels that served the area expected to make three more round trips from San Francisco or Seattle to Nome before the end of the season—and all of them were looking for large passenger lists on every trip except perhaps for the last ones.

Some of them, such as the steamship *Tacoma*, carried as many as 650 passengers.[15] The steamer *St. Paul* sailed into Seattle in early November with 132 passengers and $100,000 in treasure aboard.[16] At least the steamship companies and their employees were making money, which was no doubt part of the reason the Coast Guard had so much trouble recruiting sailors.

On the bright side, two large steamships, the *Ohio* and the *Santa Anna*, had been quarantined in Nome because of an outbreak of smallpox on board. Wisely, authorities would not allow a single passenger or a pound of freight to land from them. The beach was glutted with freight until the waves threatened to wash it away. At least nine-tenths of the inhabitants were existing in tents or had no shelter at all. The smallpox alone was disconcerting to Jarvis. He needed help from Randall and Tuttle. But, the captain had his own problems with the natives outside Nome.

While Randall was trying to impose order, Jarvis was confronting the smallpox and typhoid epidemics at great risk to himself.[17] Reports about the epidemics started coming to authorities from multiple sources. Many of them mistakenly believed that the problems had been abated though. Officers aboard the *St. Paul*, 13 days from St. Michael en route to San Francisco, with 54 passengers and $1,500,000 in gold dust, brought reports of a great many cases of smallpox and typhoid fever at Nome.[18] When the *St. Paul* left Nome the officers believed that the further spread of the diseases had been checked and so informed authorities in San Francisco. That was not the case.

In fairness, even Lieutenant Jarvis believed the epidemic was tapering off. The

13. 1900—A Year of Death, Disease, and Devotion

Treasury Department in Washington received a telegram from him on July 11 saying that there had been only 20 cases of smallpox up until to July 2 at Cape Nome, the day it was dated. But, he was not taking any chances on letting it spread. In that same telegram Jarvis asked for medical officers and supplies and stated that measures had been taken to isolate the cases and combat the disease. He did not say whether the cases he mentioned had appeared in the crowded camp of Cape Nome or on shipboard.

Part of the reason no one could get a handle on how much of a problem health authorities were facing was due to the vagaries of communications. Shortly after the Treasury Department received the first telegram on July 11 a second showed up. This one was dated June 29—three days earlier. It read[19]:

> Ten cases smallpox at this port in last three days. One death today. All were passengers from steamship *Oregon*. *Oregon* sailed for Seattle. Have established camp and removed cases there. Urge proper officers and sufficient vaccine matter be sent. Fifteen thousand people in immediate vicinity. Absolutely no civil authority here and I have had to take measures to isolate and prevent spread of disease. Steamers *Ohio* and *Santa Anna* released from quarantine. Passengers all vaccinated and vessels cleaned as well as possible. Patients on Egg Island improving. No new cases arrived by vessel.

To make matters worse, authorities on two other vessels en route to Cape Nome from Dutch Harbor reported that they had found smallpox aboard shortly after leaving port. It was possible, they said, that the cases broke out on board the ships, but the chances were good that they had started ashore. Neither Jarvis nor his health services counterparts could pinpoint where the diseases originated or how widespread they were at the point, which made treatment and stoppage more difficult. The Treasury Department didn't take any chances. It dispatched several physicians to Nome, along with 1,000 doses of vaccine. Everyone hoped that was a sufficient quantity.

Jarvis couldn't catch a break. A case of varioloid, a mild form of smallpox affecting people who have already had the disease or have been vaccinated against it, was discovered in the great mining camp. That suggested the disease could spread more rapidly. The authorities set up a place of detention for the smallpox patients on the deserted Egg Island, 12 miles west of St. Michael. The *Ohio* and the *Santa Anna* anchored nearby. All was not well with the passengers on the *Ohio*, which added to Jarvis's problems.

There was almost a complete absence of civil or military government in the Cape Nome district. In fact, the absence extended to the entire territory of northwestern Alaska. That was a factor when the *Ohio* arrived around the first of July with its two smallpox patients. They and the other passengers strenuously insisted on coming ashore. The no-nonsense Jarvis would not hear of it. He immediately took radical measures to maintain everyone's health and to avert the imminent danger of an epidemic.[20] He did so at great risk to himself.

Jarvis took full advantage of the emergency powers he had been granted and ordered the *Ohio* to proceed to Egg Island and remain in quarantine there for at least ten days. He then had a cargo of lumber shipped to the island for the construction of a "pest hospital." Jarvis visited the island to oversee personally the quarantine arrangements.

Not surprisingly, the passengers on the *Ohio* were less than pleased. They had come to the area to dig gold or engage in associated business enterprises, not sit in a crude hospital on some deserted island overseen by a Coast Guard officer. They protested vigorously that the loss of time was detrimental to their interests. Jarvis did not care.

The lieutenant had to think of the thousands of other people in Nome who were at risk of contracting smallpox or some other dread disease and possibly losing their lives, not just other people's time. He appealed to the authorities of the company that owned the *Ohio*. They submitted to his orders with a slight protest. Then, Jarvis learned he had other eggs to fry.

Only two or three hours after he returned to Nome following the Egg Island showdown the steamship *Santa Anna* appeared a mile offshore flying a yellow flag, denoting disease aboard. Jarvis and the health officer appointed by the municipal government of Nome went out to the ship to investigate. They discovered one passenger on board with smallpox. Jarvis sent the *Santa Anna* directly to Egg Island before night fell. He was not a man to trifle with.

Gradually the disease epidemic ended, for the non-natives at least.[21] General Randall reported on August 11 that the natives all along the coast were dying of measles and pneumonia. Smallpox had been checked in Nome though. No new cases had been reported in 12 days. That may have been good news for the general and the thousands of people who had flocked to the area, but it was not for Captain Tuttle, who was still dealing with the natives' sad plight. He summed up their deprivations in a September report about his operations since July, which related principally to the condition of the natives along the Alaskan coast and adjacent islands.[22]

He said that everywhere the vessel stopped, officers went ashore to investigate the residents' condition and reported that they had never been in worse condition. At Teller Station in particular affairs were desperate. One-half of the natives there had died. In some cases entire families had disappeared and in others parents had died leaving helpless children. There weren't enough people to catch salmon or hunt and thus provide food for the present or for the coming winter. The ravages of disease had been so great that a panic had seized the natives and the dead natives were left unburied in their houses.

Captain Tuttle concluded his report with a dire message:

> At a conference with Governor Brady of Alaska and J.F. Evans, special agent of the treasury, Dr. Sheldon Jackson and myself. In reference to the deplorable condition of the natives, it was declared that rations must be afforded them or they would perish during the coming winter. Special Agent Evans at once ordered a load of supplies, which was put on board. I steamed to Unalaska to get some stores to be out on board.

For some odd reason the newspapers back home were loath to report the full story. Getting all the facts was like pulling teeth for some readers.

The Astoria, Oregon, *Morning Astorian* printed, "Captain Tuttle says he is going to make another trip north." The Maysville, Kentucky, *Daily Public Ledger* added a few words: "Captain Tuttle says he is going to make another trip north *to distribute the few things that were received and to attend to the government business.*"[23] The Waterbury, Connecticut, *Evening Democrat* closed out the sentence with even more:

13. 1900—A Year of Death, Disease, and Devotion   99

"[Captain Tuttle] reports that the natives are thoroughly demoralized through their condition and fright and superstition."[24]

One more addition, from the Condon, Oregon, *Globe*, was even scarier: "This is the first time they have not secured their winter supply of food. Captain Tuttle says he believes that if it were not for the little relief he is taking to them on his present trip, there would not be 10 percent of them alive next June."[25] It was a good thing Tuttle had an accurate picture of the natives' real exigency. Not everyone back in the states did, unless they read a significant number of newspapers.

Tuttle did the best he could to continue helping the natives until the *Bear* returned to Seattle on November 21. He knew it was not enough. So did General Randall. In his 1900 Annual Report, in which he stated that order had been restored in Nome, Randall noted that "the Eskimo has been unnoticed by those he befriended and has been allowed to die for the lack of proper care and food. The revenue cutter *Bear* had been distributing supplies to the destitute natives ... the work of Lieutenant Jarvis, who is in charge of this relief, is highly recommended."[26]

In the long run, if it hadn't been for the work of devoted people like Randall, Jarvis, and Tuttle, a lot more natives and non-natives would most likely have died around Cape Nome in 1900. Randall convinced the U.S. government to bring from Nome to the states—at its expense—several thousand sick and destitute persons before winter set in in 1900. He deserved as much credit as the men he praised.[27]

Those were tributes well earned by Tuttle and Jarvis, but they were of little consolation to the natives they were trying to help. All they could do was hope 1901 would be better. They and the *Bear* couldn't save the world—but they would be back again to try; 1905 in particular was a trying year.

14

The *Bear* Takes a Hawaiian Vacation

"Ten wild steers from Hawaii broke loose from the cattle pen and began to swim down channel. Captain Hamlet of revenue cutter Bear *tried to check them. Had to call for aid from the boat boys."*[1]

If ever there was an omen that 1905 was going to be unique in the annals of the *Bear*'s history it appeared in the first few months, when the cutter was in Hawaii. Ostensibly, the *Bear* had sailed in December 1904 from San Francisco to Honolulu primarily to deal with bird poachers in the western Hawaiian Islands. The assignment turned out to be much more than that.

Many people wondered why the *Bear* was sent to Hawaii. There was a surplus of U.S. naval vessels in the Hawaiian Islands that year. Normally there was only one stationed at Honolulu, the USS *Iroquois*, which speculators thought could handle everything required of the naval service. One writer commented, "There is absolutely no work for the naval vessels to perform that the *Iroquois* in the course of ordinary events could not do or transact. The fact that makes more certain the government has material reasons for maintaining vessels at Honolulu is the presence of the revenue cutter *Bear*. She has been on duty at this port for months. It is her regular duty to attend to work that the naval vessels might otherwise have to perform. There seems less reason for the warships to be maintained at Honolulu."[2]

Perhaps the reason was the possibility that the neutrality of Honolulu might be infringed upon by Russian or Japanese warships. The two countries engaged in an eight-month war starting in February. "In view however of the fact that the Russian Baltic fleets are now in the waters of the Far East, the necessity of maintaining a naval vessel here, other than the *Iroquois*, would seem to have passed," the writer concluded.

But, the *Bear* stayed as crew members rounded up swimming cattle, got involved in firefighting, hosted parties ... in short, life was anything but usual for them in the islands. Perhaps crew members glimpsed a harbinger of things to come that year when they saw a Hawaiian volcano erupt, which was a change of pace for them.[3] They considered themselves in luck to be near Hawaii while Kilauea was erupting. The spectacle may have been a surprise for them in a voyage filled with surprises.

Whatever the reason, the *Bear* was there and the officers and crew were going to do whatever they were assigned—even if the ship's name might change.⁴ A piece of news that caught a lot of people off-guard was that the *Bear* might disappear. At least its name would. There were rumors that year that the Coast Guard was thinking of changing the names of its cutters to celebrate Indian heritage. The *Bear* was in Honolulu harbor in January when the information was revealed that a year or two earlier the Treasury Department had adopted a plan to name its cutters after Indian tribes. The changes were to take place gradually.

The service had already started with the cutter *Galveston*, which was being rebuilt at a shipyard at Wilmington, Delaware. It would be renamed the *Apache* when it returned to service. That killed two birds with one stone, since the Navy had a ship named *Galveston*. Changing the cutter's name would eliminate confusion among people who worried about such things (which did not include the crew of the *Bear*).

The possibility of a name change was not something the crew had to worry about at that point—and it never happened. Maybe it wouldn't have mattered anyway, since some people couldn't identify the *Bear* under any name. On one cruise it returned from Kauai late at night, and it was reported as a foreign steamer. Its name didn't matter if no one knew what it was. What mattered was that the vessel's engines were in need of repairing.⁵ That accounted for why it arrived off the harbor so late at night.

The *Bear* had made slow progress en route from Kauai to Honolulu in the face of the strong trade winds that had been blowing for two days. That was not the time for such problems. The *Bear* was getting close to its departure date for Alaska. For the nonce, however, the crew was more concerned about carrying out its normal duties in Hawaii, which turned out to be anything but normal. But the abnormal was normal for them, which was one of the beauties of their lives.

Some of the antics in which the crew participated in 1905 were way out of the ordinary, even for the *Bear*. But neither they nor Captain Oscar G. Hamlet, whose son Harry later became a Coast Guard officer, were going to be cowed by their responsibilities, even though they got their chance to be. One of the crew's memorable experiences was an open-water round-up of frightened cattle in the Honolulu harbor.⁶ It was no doubt a first in the *Bear*'s history—and possibly the entire Coast Guard's. As usual, the crew members were up to the task of saving the cattle from— and for—certain death.

The steamer *Helene* arrived in Honolulu on the morning of February 2 carrying a herd of cattle consigned to the Metropolitan Meat Company. The cattle were pretty wild following their voyage. After they were off-loaded and the steamer moved away, the excitement began. Someone forgot to close the gate to the pen completely. One of the animals discovered the opening and made a break for the wharf. Several of its companions followed. Chaos ensued.

Ten of the steers jumped into the water and swam about 200 yards down the channel toward a lighthouse. The *Bear* lay at anchor in the stream between them and the structure. Captain Hamlet was in a small boat near the cutter—and directly in the path of the swimming cattle, who apparently had no respect for a Coast Guard officer. He acted quickly.

The captain realized immediately that they must have escaped from the cattle

A typical cutter engine of the early 1900s. This was taken aboard the cutter *Mackinac*, which was put into service in 1903 (USCG Historian's Office).

pen. He steered the boat toward the swimming cattle. His goal was to turn the cattle out of the deep water and drive them back toward the cattle pen. The cattle weren't afraid of the *Bear* or anyone from it. They were beyond control. The animals ignored Hamlet and the yells and gestures of the crew members aboard the *Bear*. Instead of being frightened, they headed for Hamlet's boat and practically surrounded it.

Hamlet guessed their intention. He believed they would try to get their front hooves over the gunwales of the small craft in order to rest. The captain was ready for that maneuver. He steered his boat toward the landing to seek help. It was like he was the pied piper of Honolulu. The cattle swam after him.

Hamlet called to some workers on the wharf to help get the cattle. Six of them responded, each in their own boat. The posse determined that the cattle were going to try a new tactic when they started swimming toward the Oceanic and Allen & Robinson wharves to get underneath them. If they reached them it would have been a very difficult and dangerous task to get them out.

Each "boat boy" singled out a steer and pursued it. It was as if they had been to this rodeo before. They had to lasso the cattle to hold their heads out of the water before they drowned. The animals were not known for their long-distance swimming abilities. And, they were badly winded and tired out. They had swum fully a quarter of a mile in the harbor since jumping from the cattle pen.

The rescue was a dangerous undertaking. The shore boats were lightly constructed and subject to serious damage if a mad cow hit them. Hamlet and his crew watched the operation with amazement. Eventually the boat boys, aided by crew members of the *Helene*, saved all ten animals. That was an amazing experience for Hamlet and his crew. There were more to come before the *Bear* left Hawaii.

Three days later Hamlet and his executive officer, Lieutenant E.E. Meade, became enmeshed in the "Great Mystery Cruise" incident.[7] A steamer named *Iwalani*, moored in Honolulu harbor, was about to embark under secret orders on a voyage that was so secretive even the ship's captain, George Piltz, didn't know where he was going or what he was going to do when he got there. The ship was chartered by W.H. Underwood of New York City, a prominent merchant, and Le Grand Brown of Rochester, New York, a noted civil engineer. They seemed to be the only people who knew what their mission was. Or, many people suspected, Hamlet did and he wasn't telling.

Underwood and Brown had arrived in Honolulu aboard the steamer *S.S. Sonoma* on February 8 and registered at the Young Hotel. They did not tell anyone why they were there, but they presented letters of introduction from well-known references in the states. Then they loaded a strange cargo aboard the ship: four good-sized cases and one small can, several pick axes, an adz, a crowbar, and half a dozen shovels. That only heightened the mystery.

There was speculation among locals that they might be searching for buried treasure, looking for a lost island, or engaging in some other nefarious venture. It had been reported to the local Collector of Customs, E.R. Stackable, who seemed to think the *Bear* was his personal cutter, that the men were heading a foreign expedition in which they were contemplating indulging in some violations of the shipping regulations. Stackable approached Hamlet and asked him to unravel the mystery.

Hamlet and Meade conducted an interview with the two mysterious characters in an effort to find out what they were up to. The men did not go into too much detail, but they convinced the officers they were engaged in a legitimate private enterprise. What little they told Hamlet and Meade was sufficient to fill them in on the general character of their destination and expedition. Then, Underwood dropped a name that sealed the deal.

He told the officers that if they needed additional references regarding their mission they could contact their commander-in-chief, President Theodore Roosevelt, for details. Underwood said he was a personal friend of the president. That was all Hamlet and Meade had to hear. The *Iwalani* sailed on February 14 with the Coast Guard's blessing, carrying provisions for about a month. Hamlet dropped a hint about the ship's destination after the interview, which only added to the speculation about the mission.[8] There were some folks who theorized that not only did Hamlet know more about it than he was letting on, but he was in charge of it.

Their proof was that Hamlet and one of his lieutenants were aboard the *Iwalani* a few minutes before it left port.[9] They were carrying charts and nautical books with them and were seen in the captain's room pointing out something on the charts to Piltz and two unknown passengers. "Was Hamlet giving them their route?" the onlookers wanted to know. If that was the case then he definitely knew their destination—and they were no doubt sailing under his orders. Hamlet would not give anyone the satisfaction of revealing the details, but he did drop a hint or two.

He supposedly told somebody that he understood the *Iwalani's* destination was Johnston Island, about 600 miles west by south of Honolulu. There were other reports to the effect that the expedition was bound for the lost De Greaves Island or the site where the U.S. Navy's sloop-of-war *Levant* had disappeared without a trace in 1860. Why anyone would be investigating a lost ship 45 years after it disappeared was a mystery in itself. Reporters noted that even though the *Iwalani* started west, as if it were going to Kauai, it might have sailed right past and kept moving to its unknown destination.

Eventually the details about the mystery emerged. Hamlet was correct, and he had more than dropped a hint. One reporter got the full story from him. Underwood and Brown were going to Johnston Island to investigate the value of the guano (fertilizer) beds there.[10] They simply wanted to ascertain the extent of the guano deposits before investing the necessary capital to exploit the fields. As far as Hamlet was concerned the entire mystery was much ado about nothing—and perhaps the wrong play for Underwood and Brown to make in surrounding the venture in mystery.

The next great adventure of the season was another unusual assignment for a ship: a response to a forest fire on land.[11] E.R. Stackable kindly placed the *Bear* at the disposal of the territorial authorities to transport the territory's chief forester, Ralph S. Hosmer, and Frank S. Dodge, Superintendent of the Bernice Pauahi Bishop Estate at South Kona, Hawaii, where a major forest fire was raging, to help control it. The *Bear* got underway on February 25.

The *Bear*'s crew was not expected to fight the fire. Its job was to get Hosmer there as quickly as possible to save what he could. There were about 100 acres burning, and more valuable timber in the tract was under threat of destruction. Hamlet understood the gravity of the situation.

His assignment was to take Hosmer to a spot on the coast where he would meet a launch to take him the rest of the way to the fire. Hamlet did one better: he volunteered to sail to Kawaihae, which would cut a day off the chief's trip. That took the *Bear* out of its way, but that did not bother Hamlet. His haste paid dividends. Dodge returned to Honolulu a few days later to announce that the fires were mostly under control.[12] The crew could relax, read its mail, and collect its pay. Whether or not they could spend it was another story. It was paid in gold.

After transporting Hosmer and Dodge to South Kona the *Bear* returned to Honolulu. It appeared off the harbor on March 1 to await its mail from the vessel *Ventura*, which was lying to seaward, and its pay.[13] Getting both was a complicated procedure. Stackable delivered the pay by traveling out to the *Bear* in the customs launch *Waterwitch* with two bags of gold. He continued to the *Ventura* to pick up the cutter's mail. At least the crew got their morale-boosting pay and mail and remained ready to continue its mission.

Saving cattle from drowning, playing "Smokey the *Bear*," solving maritime mysteries... such jobs were all in a day's work for Hamlet and his crew, whether they were in Hawaii or Alaska. The cutter's service in Hawaii was scheduled to end June 1, when it would set sail for the mainland.[14] But scheduled dates and actual sailing dates didn't always coincide. First, the *Bear* had to undergo repairs to its boilers, which were predicted to take three weeks. After that, it was back to Alaska, where its "Year of Strange Events" continued.

At 10:45 a.m. on June 6 the *Bear* steamed out of Honolulu harbor with many caps and handkerchiefs fluttering from its decks.[15] The cutter sparkled from a shiny new coat of white paint and every spar was polished. The locals were not sure they would ever see the *Bear* again.

"It will be months before the cutter comes back from the frozen seas, perhaps years before she is in this port again," a reporter noted.[16] That was a long-term outlook. Its Hawaii vacation was over. In the short term the *Bear* had a tough few months ahead of it in Alaska.

15

The *Bear* Rides the Waves to Bust a Crime Wave

> *"The revenue cutter* Bear, *under command of Captain Hamlet, has returned from a cruise into the Arctic, where for several weeks during the summer she was engaged in breaking up the illicit traffic in liquor between the white men and the Indians, and in meting out punishment to Americans who had betrayed the natives in other ways. In many instances trials were held aboard the* Bear, *with Captain Hamlet sitting as Judge."*[1]

Anyone who looked at the account of the *Bear*'s late 1905 northern cruise under the command of O.C. Hamlet would think that it was nothing out of the ordinary.[2] It read in part:

Frank G. Churchill of the Interior Department and W.T. Hamilton of the Educational Department were taken on inspecting tours of the reindeer stations and the school facilities in Alaska.

Axel Johjnsen, a coxswain, died October 2 from apoplexy and was buried with full honors at Unalaska.

"The Society of Nanooks, or True Polar *Bear*s," was organized on the *Bear*, membership being limited to any person "abaft the mast" who has been within the "Arctic" circle. The grand officers of the Grand Den are: Grandkeeper, Captain O.C. Hamlet; grand oracle, Frank G. Churchill; grand surgeon, James T. White; grand secretary, J.E. Dorry; grand keeper of seals and *Bear* claws, W.L. Hamilton; grand marshal, C.C. McMillan.

All of the officers on the *Bear* and the revenue cutter *Manning* were initiated. The emblem is a polar *Bear* carved from a walrus tooth. The President of the United States and the Secretary of the Treasury and other notable officials will be elected honorary members.

The *Bear* was under sail for 70 hours on the passage home owing to a crack in the high pressure crank pin.

Passengers brought home were Dr. Hultberg, a dentist, and Captain Hultberg of the schooner *Mary Sachs*; Captain Applegate, an otter hunter, and Emil Eltner, an employee of the North American Commercial Company, returning after three years of service in the Arctic.

Officers on the cruise were: Captain O.C. Hamlet; lieutenants, E.E. Meade, H.H. Wolf, P.R. Shoemaker, and L.C. Covell; chief engineer, J.E. Dorry; assistant engineers, C.C. McMillan and J.W. Glover, and surgeon, J.T. White.

There was no indication in those entries that late 1905 was unique for the *Bear*, but it was. It was more of a crime crusade than a standard voyage. The results proved that beyond a doubt.

Reports had been circulating in the Arctic region and Washington, D.C., for some time about mistreatment of the Eskimos by some of the American ship captains and traders plying their trades in the native communities. Even some of the natives were guilty of crimes against their neighbors. The Department of Justice acted in 1905 to investigate and curb the alleged abuses. It assigned a special commission to Captain O.C. Hamlet of the *Bear* to carry out the mission. Hamlet started on his duties at once.

The *Bear* traveled from Hawaii to the north land in 1905 with a different mission than normal. Captain Hamlet held a commission as a judicial officer from the Department of Justice to facilitate the crusade upon which the vessel was bent. He picked up Assistant United States District Attorney W.N. Landers, United States Marshal Hugh Lee, and an interpreter at Nome for the northern cruise. The search for evidence and offenders against the federal laws, which was conducted from July to September, covered the entire Alaskan coast as far as Point Barrow. The combined voyage took almost a year, which was a highly unusual time period for a cutter to be away from home. But, the results were worth the time spent.

The complaints made against the captains, traders, and natives were numerous. They involved the illegal use of whiskey, kidnapping, human trafficking, rape, debauchery, and overall pillaging. The majority of the crimes were perpetrated by a handful of people, all of whom were headed for federal court if indicted. Hamlet vowed to make sure they were, although not everyone was convinced that he would be even-handed in the process. That was another unique factor in the 1905 cruise. Newspaper editors started widely criticizing the service that had maintained peace in the region for so long, which started a battle among them. The Coast Guard wasn't used to coming under such fire.

One editor accused another one of biases: "The Nome Gold Digger gives out the impression that the Revenue Cutter *Bear* only captures those 'hooch peddlers' who have no pull."[3] Other editors took sides. Regardless, Hamlet did what he was supposed to do.

An editorial in the Nome *Nugget*, written by E.J. Knapp, who a rival newspaper, the *Daily Alaskan*, dismissed only as someone who had been in charge of a mission school last year, castigated Hamlet and the *Bear* as well.[4] Knapp characterized the entire revenue cutter service in Arctic waters as a farce:

> The revenue cutter service, so far as those waters is concerned, is little better than no service at all. Indeed, it is a fact that the revenue cutter officers do not wish to be bothered or hampered by having to devote a little time to seeing that the laws are enforced and the lawbreakers brought to punishment. They have shown by their actions that they do not care what havoc the whalers work among the natives.
>
> Their trips to Bering Sea and the Arctic are merely junketing excursions, during which they may enjoy themselves, and trade and traffic with the natives as much as they please.
>
> The trip of the *Bear* to the Arctic during the present season was little more than a farce. It is alleged, and we believe the statement to be true, that Capt. Hamlet showed little disposition to overtake the whaling vessels, which it was charged carried hootch, and were disposing of it to the natives. The whalers had ample opportunity to get out of the revenue cutter's way.
>
> There are even worse stories than this told of some of the *Bear*'s officers, with truth enough in the stories to demand that the service in Bering Sea be given a thorough shaking up.

Despite Knapp's opinion, the investigations conducted by Captain O.C. Hamlet and his staff uncovered a considerable amount of evidence that they handed over to law officers at Nome. The *Bear*'s staff gave the authorities a plethora of material the legal authorities could use against the illegal traders in liquors among the natives and the Americans who had kidnapped young girls from their parents and committed what complainants considered unspeakable offenses against morality.

Hamlet paid particular attention to the trafficking in native girls, many of whom willingly testified against their suspected assailants. The captain saw to it that they were transported to Nome as witnesses in trials. One of them was a young child who had allegedly been kidnaped by Captain E.W. Newth of the whaler *Jeannette*.[5] Newth was considered to be one of—if not the—most despicable violators of the law, and one of the ringleaders of a group of whalers who participated in the crimes against Eskimos.

The captain considered himself to be a law above all others in the region. Newth treated his crew with contempt, which came back to haunt him in 1907, and he pandered to the natives for favors, often of a lascivious type. There was a bit of irony in the crew's complaints, since they were not generally considered by most people to be citizens of high moral character.

Newth and his crew, who were generally recruited from the lowest class of criminals in the region, had been carrying out serious crimes against the natives for many years. Their modus operandi was to stop at a native camp and swap a few bottles of alcohol for valuable furs. While the Eskimos reveled in a wild, drunken orgy, the crew members grabbed the best looking young girls in the village and carried them aboard *Jeannette*. They did not release their victims until after the girls had been shamelessly debauched. (Newspapers of the time shied away from using the words rape or sexually assaulted, which was what "debauchery" really was. They preferred to use words like debauchery or outrage.)

Jeannette's crew had been getting away with their crimes for years. Newth had become so brazen that he visited Nome in July 1905, seized two young native girls aboard his ship, and tried to debauch them. It was no wonder federal authorities wanted to have a word with him. One particular story epitomized his venality.

Eskimo parents told Nome authorities that Newth had attempted to abduct their two daughters, aged 9 and 12. The family went aboard the *Jeannette* to conduct some business. Newth plied the adults with liquor. Then, he lured the two girls into his cabin, locked it, and assaulted them. Their cries for help alerted the mother, who rescued them after a hard physical fight with the captain.

The parents told their story to Nome District Attorney Hoyt a few days later, but someone warned Newth. He and the *Jeannette* left Nome hastily, and they were well out at sea before the local police could catch him. His escape was only temporary. Hamlet saw to that.

Hamlet had in hand a warrant for Newth's arrest when his crusade began. The *Jeannette's* captain, however, was as elusive as a furred seal when poachers were around. He was charged with having lured young native girls aboard his whaler and carrying them off, a fancy term for kidnapping. Hamlet was unable to apprehend Newth because of the adverse open sea weather conditions in the region in 1905. There was a lack of ice that year that helped him sail away unscathed. But the miscreant couldn't hide forever, even in the vastness of the Bering Sea. The weather would see to that.

While Newth hid, the *Bear* continued its voyage. At Diomedes Islands the officers found evidence of two murders among the natives, carried out under the influence of liquors sold to them illegally. Sadly, the officers could not make any arrests because too much time had elapsed between the murders and the investigation and any evidence that existed had disappeared. They did not sail away empty-handed however. They apprehended one whaler's cook and sent him to Nome for selling whisky to the Indians. And, they captured the notorious "Pig Iron" Jones, who allegedly had been making money north of Point Hope in his illicit whisky traffic. Both arrests were detailed in Hamlet's 1905 annual report.[6]

There were other successes as well. One of the men the officers apprehended was a man known as Jerome, a shore whaler at Wainwright Inlet.[7] He was so notorious that Hamlet decided to give him a hearing aboard the cutter before binding him over to the Grand Jury at Nome. Jerome was accused of buying native girls from their parents in exchange for guns and ammunition. Hamlet transported him and girl witnesses to Nome on the *Bear*.

The staff also apprehended several other shore whalers and a man named Olson, who had been charged with selling liquors illicitly. They were turned over to the federal officials. Newth remained Hamlet's focus though. At St. Lawrence Island several native girls were found who gave testimony that would be used against Captain Newth when he was arrested and brought to trial. Hamlet had an inkling of where he would find his nemesis. He was patient. He knew that Newth was safe until 1906 and that he wasn't going anywhere because of the weather. Hamlet could bide his time until then.

The *Bear*'s crew was a bit disappointed that Newth had escaped, but they felt that overall the crusade had been worth the effort and the time away. They had not ended the criminal activities in the region, but they had put a dent in their spread. As widespread as the crime spree had grown, and despite the efforts of the authorities to check it, the *Bear*'s cruise had such a moral and morale impact on the crew that the officers believed a strong check had been put on the evil practices they had encountered. By any measure that was success enough in their view.

Sure enough, when the *Bear* left for a cruise to the states on August 1 the weather conditions were ideal—for the *Bear*. At the time the Arctic was remarkably free from ice. The whalers had all sailed off to the east while an offshore wind drove the ice to the north. Before the *Bear* left Dutch Harbor rumors of the whaling fleet's fate began circulating along the coast. It was iced in, à la 1897–98. The *Bear*'s officers determined that the whalers were widely separated, and hundreds of miles apart, for the ice pack closed in upon them too quickly for the vessels to reach a rendezvous, which was their usual practice to weather out the winter.

They opined that the whaling crews were not in any danger of starving. The herds of government reindeer at Point Barrow and Herschel Island were large and the *Bear*'s officers felt confident that they could be used for food supplies. Newth would no doubt prevail upon them at some point. So, when Hamlet returned he could easily pick up Newth's trail. That's what happened, although the outcome wasn't quite the way Hamlet had imagined it would be.

The crew of the *Jeannette* did not fare well during the time they were ice bound. In typical Newth fashion, he treated them poorly. According to crew members, the food they were compelled to eat consisted mostly of four thin slices of bread, a little deer meat, and some warm, dirty water that was labeled tea. That was their daily ration for months.[8]

Meanwhile, the captain was supplying the natives with the food the crew members should have been getting. When they complained, he told them simply that when they were in the Arctic aboard his ship only one law applied: his. Under the circumstances, people might have thought that none of the crew members would shed a tear when Newth was ultimately captured. At least one did, but that was a year later.

Hamlet returned to the Arctic region in 1906 in command of the *Thetis*. Just as he had predicted, someone reported the *Jeannette's* whereabouts. Newth and his crew had gone into winter quarters at Herschel Island, where they had been iced in from August 29, 1905, to July 10, 1906. When the famous explorer Roald Amundsen arrived there he sent out word of the *Jeannette's* position.[9]

The *Thetis* arrived in the area in early September and apprehended Newth after he left Herschel Island. The *Thetis* overhauled the *Jeannette* near Point Barrow and made Newth a federal prisoner.[10] The *Jeannette* was sent to Nome under the control of Mate Ary. Newth was transported there separately, thence to Seattle. Nobody was taking any chances on his escaping this time. He was transported in irons. Eventually he was indicted by a federal jury in Seattle on November 18 for abducting native children for immoral purposes, and released on a hefty bond.[11]

The local folks were happy. They predicted that Newth and his band of desperate criminals would be spending a long time in the penitentiary. The wheels of justice turned slowly however. In fact, Newth escaped any punishment for his misdeeds—at least from a legal standpoint.

On September 3, 1907, Newth was arrested again. He was apprehended on Fillmore Street in San Francisco on a complaint issued in 1905 by United States Commissioner Heacock.[12] He was accused of securing a sailor named Stephen P. Talbot to Jeannette's rigging for an hour while the vessel was on the high seas. Newth was released on $2,000 bail. Talbot proved to be a more compassionate man than his former captain.[13]

The trial stemmed from an incident in which Newth subjected Talbot to beatings, exposure, and starvation. The crewman would not confess to stealing a pair of trousers, so Newth had him tied by the wrists to the ship's ratlines (a series of small ropes fastened across a sailing ship's shrouds like the rungs of a ladder, used for climbing the rigging) and exposed, half dressed, to the piercing Arctic cold for about an hour. Apparently, when Talbot saw Newth in court the former captain looked worse than Talbot had after an hour tied to the ropes.

Talbot ascertained quickly that Newth was dying. The captain was tottering and feeble, supported by the arm of his wife. "Nothing but pity and forgiveness shown in the face of Stephen P. Talbot, a common seaman, when he asked the court in San Francisco to be lenient with Capt. E.W. Newth, formerly of the whaler *Jeannette*, who is in a dying condition," a reporter said.[14] "Affected by the magnanimity of the man who forgave all because he pitied the captain, United States Commissioner Heacock dismissed the case."

Ironically, Talbot was also a physical wreck and it was not expected that he would live any longer than Newth. The scene was highly emotional as Newth motioned his thanks to Talbot, who looked at him with eyes of compassion. Good had triumphed over evil in this case, but it did nothing to help the young Eskimo girls that Newth and his crew members had attacked.

Despite the fact that Hamlet and the Coast Guard had been severely chastised as a farce in 1905 and Newth had avoided serious punishment for his crimes, Hamlet was pleased with his success that year. Some of the results from his aforementioned log bore that out:

> Three prisoners were brought to Nome on August 11 and lodged in the federal jail on unspecified charges. At St. Lawrence Island, the first stopping place on the crusade, a native was taken into custody on complaint of Dr. K.O. Campbell, the missionary there, but as there was not sufficient evidence to convict, he was discharged by Commissioner Hamlet.
>
> At Little Diomede Island two natives were tried for peddling hootch, and each sentenced to two months in jail. These natives were left at the jail in Teller. In Port Clarence two steam whalers were boarded, and although no arrests were made one native girl belonging to Teller was taken from the *Belvidere* and set on shore.
>
> The *Bear* then went north as far as Cape Smythe, a few miles from Barrow. Near Point Belvidere Capt. McKenna's schooner, the *Charles Hansen*, was boarded, and Jos. Jones, the steward, was arrested and taken before Commissioner Hamlet, charged with furnishing liquor to natives. He was found guilty and fined $200. In default of the payment of the fine, he was brought to Nome to serve the time in the federal jail.
>
> On the mainland near the Sea Horse Islands, just north of Pt. Belcher, about 60 miles this from Pt. Barrow, two Portuguese whalers were conducting a whaling station. Jos. King, one of these whalers, was tried for peddling hootch, and fined $200. He was brought to the Nome jail. His partner, Jerome Lopez, was charged with rape, and bound over to the grand jury.

A newspaper reporter asked Marshal Lee if he considered the trip a successful one. He said that although some good had been accomplished, the evil had continued for so many years that it was impossible to stamp it out in a single month.[15] Lee acknowledged that the whalers were all pretty well scared knowing that the government was cracking down on their activities, and the chances were that they would be much more careful in the future.

He concluded that many of the captains made themselves scarce as a result of the *Bear*'s vigilance. Only three of them remained in the area. Since they had all been warned of the Coast Guard's intentions by one of the Nome newspapers, they had skedaddled north, and some of them did not stop until they reached British waters, far to the east of Point Barrow. Lee was certain that they would be more careful in the future, and a continuation of the crackdown in future seasons would quickly put a stop to the depredations that had prevailed for so long on the Alaskan shore of the Arctic Ocean. Hamlet shared Lee's sentiments.

In his 1905 report he advised Treasury Department administrators that the liquor trade among the natives of northwestern Alaska was abating. The commander recommended that the cutters get an early jump on enforcing the laws each year. He urged the department to start their voyages into the Bering Sea from Dutch Harbor in June, rather than later. Hamlet believed the Coast Guard was doing something right, even if some of the people it served did not. After all, it was his opinion that counted.

16

The Only Ship the Bering Patrol Lost

"Officials of the revenue cutter service have strong hopes that Congress will this session authorize the building of four new revenue cutters to take the place of antiquated vessels now in service. Should the new vessels become a reality they will displace the cutter Woodbury *on the Portland, Me., station; the* Manhattan, *at New York and the* Winona *at Mobile. The fourth vessel will be designed to take the place of the cutter* Perry, *which was lost in Bering Sea."*[1]

One of the Coast Guard's most important missions was to protect the seal rookeries in the Bering Sea, primarily the rookeries at the Pribilof Islands. The islands were the only home of the fur seal, which explained why they attracted large numbers of poachers from several countries and Coast Guard cutters to interdict them. Sealskins meant big money for poachers, and they went to extremes to slaughter them. Conversely, the cutters and their crews did the same to catch the poachers, often to their detriment.

There was perhaps no more an inhospitable sailing territory in the world than the seas around the Pribilofs. Even the most accomplished cutter captains could not always navigate the waters around the islands with any degree of confidence. They simply took their turns guarding the islands and hoped for the best. Always two, and generally three, of the revenue cutters were kept at the Pribilof islands, while the fourth went to Unalaska for sufficient coal and water to allow it to remain at sea another two weeks. Each vessel remained at sea until its fuel and water were exhausted.

While on patrol around the islands the crews had to exercise the utmost vigilance under unfavorable and exasperating conditions. The climate was raw, humid, and disagreeable. There was almost always a high wind or heavy fog present, sometimes both. They were complemented by plenty of mist and rain. To make matters worse—as if anything could—the region was poorly charted and at night in particular there were currents of unknown strength and direction to befuddle the navigators.

The atmosphere was foggy practically all of the time during July and August, and there were no lighthouses, fog signals, buoys or other aids to navigation on the islands. It was remarkable that in all the time the revenue cutters patrolled the islands only one was lost due to the harsh conditions. Many, including the *Bear*,

16. The Only Ship the Bering Patrol Lost

went ashore and sustained damage at times, but the *Perry*, one of the oldest and smallest of the cutters in the Bering patrol, was the only one that was wrecked and abandoned.

The *Adams* struck Tonki Point in 1898, but was refloated. The *Corwin*, *Bear*, *McCulloch*, and *Manning* had also run aground there at various times, but those vessels had wooden bottoms and escaped serious damage. The *Perry*, unfortunately, had a metal hull, which the rocks pierced, so there was no hope of escape for the tiny cutter, even if there had been equipment available to save it.

Ironically, despite the number of cutter groundings around the Pribilofs, the service did not maintain any rescue or salvage equipment there to aid its stricken vessels. The captains were pretty much left to their own devices if they ran into trouble. That was Captain F.J. Haake's predicament on July 28, 1910, the day the *Perry* ran aground at Tonki Point, on the east side of St. Paul Island.[2]

The 161-foot long *Perry* was built in 1884 at Buffalo, New York, the same year the *Bear* entered service. The *Perry* was assigned originally to duty on the Great Lakes, then transferred in 1893 to the Pacific Coast, where it performed admirably in Alaskan waters for 17 years. It carried a crew of 50 officers and men the day it ran aground.

Captain Foley, the senior officer of the Bering fleet, responded to the scene of the wreck, which was in an extremely dangerous locality. There was a reef there that projected about one-and-a-half miles offshore. The ship was filled with water and beyond saving, since there were no wrecking appliances in the neighborhood. Foley ordered that the cutter be stripped and abandoned and its complement be distributed to other vessels. Fortunately, there had been no lives lost.

Captain Foley included the details of the incident in his report to the Treasury Department[3]:

The *Perry*, the only cutter the Bering Sea Patrol lost (USCG Historian's Office).

The *Perry* was hard and fast ashore, forward and amidship, and all her compartments below the decks were filled with water. I decided to abandon her after consultation with the officers of the *Perry* and *Manning*, being convinced that it was absolutely impossible for us to save her without wrecking appliances that were not on hand or available. Even if we should succeed in pulling her off the rock it would be only to have her sink and I have had to admit that we should be risking another and much more valuable vessel in the foul ground around her.

The *Perry* is lying in a very exposed condition, the tide ebbs and flows in her, and in my opinion she will break in two in the next blow from any quarter, except directly from land, which may occur at any time now. I therefore ordered her stripped. A large part of her stores and outfits had already been put ashore.

The accident happened while the *Perry* was on her way from Northeast Point to East Anchorage, St. Paul Island, for mail. The *Tahoma* (Captain Foley's cutter) heard the distress signals of the *Perry* at St. George's Island and proceeded at full speed to her assistance, but was unable to give aid, because on her arrival the hold and fireroom of the *Perry* were full of water and she was pounding on the reef.

Navigation about the Pribilof Islands, and in particular about St. Paul's Island, which is fringed with dangerous reefs, is very difficult because of the fogs, dense at times, which prevail during the sealing season, and the treacherous currents varying in force and direction according to no known law.

The vessels must cruise in fogs to make the patrol efficient, because it is in foggy weather that the sealers approach the rookeries and the cutters must keep in touch with the land in order not to lose the islands. In the past season the *Bear* lost them for three days and other vessels have cruised about them for days without finding them!

As a final measure, Foley reassigned Captain Haake from the *Perry* to the *Tahoma* to be his aide. Captain Worth G. Ross, chief of the revenue cutter service, commented on the report: "It is as Captain Foley says, the waters around the seal islands are the worst in the world. You strike a current sweeping along, and when you get into it again it is running in the opposite direction." That was a lesson many of the cutter captains assigned to the Bering patrol learned the hard way. It didn't make losing a cutter any easier for any of them, even if it wasn't their own. The Pribilofs had claimed one more victim, but that did not deter the Coast Guard. The remainder of the Bering fleet picked up the slack until a new cutter was assigned to it and life went on.

The islands, which were discovered by the captain of a Russian ship in 1786, were located 2,000 miles as the crow flies from Seattle, and 214 miles from the nearest frozen coast of Alaska. They were only about six by 12 miles in extent, with a population of 253 people in 1906. Their value as a sealing center was established in 1799 when the czar of Russia granted the right to the Russian-American Fur Company to take seals in the surrounding waters. The rights reverted to the United States after they purchased Alaska from Russia in 1867, although the Russians did not give them up easily.

Legally, by the treaty of cession, the right to protect the seals was transferred to the United States at that time. It included the right to protect seal life on the islands and in that part of Bering Sea included within the boundary of the territory conveyed. Russia continued to claim that it had the right to control the waters of Alaska and only pretended to transfer this right with the title to the territory when it ceded Alaska to the United States. It based its claim on discovery, on first occupation, and on peaceable possession for a period of half a century.[4] The U.S. ignored those claims.

The government may have been overly protective when it assumed ownership of the Pribilofs. It issued a contract to only one American firm, the Alaska Commercial Company, to conduct sealing operations in the islands, and no independent sealers were allowed to hunt within three miles of them.[5] That restriction was displeasing to sealers from outside the United States, particularly the Japanese, British, and Canadians. Arguably, the limit was only a minor inconvenience for them, since most of the killing of seals did not take place on or immediately around the islands. That was a source of contention among sealing nations for years.

Independent sealers simply positioned their vessels just outside the boundary and killed the seals when they swam out to sea, sometimes right under the noses of the cutter crews. The practice, known as pelagic sealing, devastated the seal population. One of the most serious results of the practice was that the hunters killed the animals indiscriminately without regard to their gender. They killed them first and let them float until they could harvest and skin them.

Sadly, not all the seals died at the hunters' hands. Inevitably pups died from starvation after their nursing mothers were killed. Statisticians averred that despite the Coast Guard's protective efforts hundreds of seals were killed at sea by poachers. They estimated that many thousands of fur seal pups died of starvation each year after their mothers were killed.[6]

Cutter commanders were helpless to stop the off-island deaths, since they were restricted to the interior of the limit, and there was a whole lot more water outside it than inside. That was frustrating to the commanders, but they did everything in their power to enforce anti-sealing laws where they could. But, they couldn't just save the starving pups, and there was no way for them to get food, unless…

17

Judge Not, Lest Ye Be "Thurbered"

> *"Atagh dove, came to the surface and turned, what schoolboys call a 'flip flop'; Ennatha perched high on the smooth rock in the center of the tank, flapped first her right flipper down and then left, making a sound not unlike that of a whack of a barrel stave on a stone pavement, and then dove off the rock into the water, going through the same performance her young mate had just completed."*[1]

Scientists sought a way to feed orphaned seal pups in order to save the species. They knew that the fur seals were headed for extinction if hunting them continued unabated. Therefore, saving every seal they could was a necessity. Unfortunately, the pups were not amenable to forced feeding by humans. The scientists were at a loss about how to do that until Boatswain Judson Thurber, a *Bear* crew member, "a quaint, quiet Yankee, with a reputation for observing much and saying little,"[2] gave them hope.

Thurber made it his mission to find a way to feed the orphaned pups. Late in 1909 he began a series of experiments to discover the proper technique. He demonstrated that fur seal pups in captivity could be domesticated enough to accept food from the hands of humans. His discovery excited scientists, statisticians, and experts in other fields. More important, he established a precedent in the field where only failures had been the norm previously and he proved that members of the Coast Guard could do more than just carry out the routine tasks associated with their ranks.

Not all government officials looked at Thurber's discovery from the prism of a scientific breakthrough. The "bean counters" evaluated it in terms of monetary value to the government. That was especially true with the officials of the Department of Commerce and Labor, the agency that regulated the sealing privilege in the Pribilof Islands and other Alaskan waters. Dollars flashed in their eyes when they heard about Thurber's success.

The government received from $12 to $15 for each seal lawfully killed. Each seal killed illegally or outside the department's jurisdiction represented a monetary loss to the government. The permanence of this source of revenue resided in the conservation of the natural resources and the protection of the mother seals and the healthful upbringing of the seal pups.

Pelagic sealing was the bane of the sealing grounds, and it cost money to maintain the fleet of cutters assigned to curb it. The way the "bean counters" looked at it, saving pups meant saving dollars that could be used to underwrite the fleet's operations. The bean counters' attitudes also raised a salient question: what was the purpose of saving the pups? Was it just so they could be returned to their natural environment ultimately to be killed by hunters? It was a vicious cycle, which did not amount to a hill of beans in Thurber's eyes. All he wanted to do was save the seals.

Until the fall of 1909 there had been no verified case of Alaska fur seals being fed in captivity and living for any length of time in other than their natural environment. In fact, there had not been a recorded instance of anyone even trying to accomplish the feat since the early 1880s, when the Alaska Commercial Company placed two live fur seals between two and three years of age in Woodward's Gardens in San Francisco as part of an experiment to see if they could be fed in captivity. Both animals died of starvation after over a month's incarceration. Neither one ate a morsel during that time.

The outcome of the experiment convinced people that fur seals would not feed in captivity. Judson Thurber debunked that theory when he induced two fur seal pups to take food voluntarily. They thrived in captivity for at least two months. It was a start, and success did not come easy. It came as a surprise to Thurber, who never expected it to come at all.[3]

James Judge, an assistant agent of the seal fisheries, a division of the Bureau of Fisheries, was on St. Paul in late 1909 taking a census of the seals as the *Bear* patrolled the nearby waters.[4] He and other bureau agents were also seeking a way to save the lives of the thousands of starving seal pups. Judge captured a couple pups and settled on the old method of feeding the pups milk from a bottle. He asked Doctor Fox of the Public Health and Marine Hospital Service, who was also the surgeon on the *Bear*, to feed the pups.

Doctor Fox was unsuccessful. Not only did his attempts to feed the pups fail, but in his efforts to make the pups suck the nipples on the bottle he broke their frenums, the piece of skin lodged at the base of the tongue that keeps the tongue of an infant seal fast to its mouth at the gum. Thurber had been watching the experiment closely. After Doctor Fox gave up in despair, Thurber adopted the pups for pets. He had no intention of solving the problem of feeding orphaned seal pups.

One afternoon while he was playing with the pups he noticed that their tongues would occasionally hang from their mouths like a dog's, unlike any other seal pups he had ever seen. The phenomenon aroused his curiosity and he began to watch the pups more closely. Then he recalled that the frenums of both seals had been broken or cut. That was when he started pondering the question of how he could train the animals to feed themselves.

Thurber began his experiments by forcing condensed milk down the throat of a starving pup. He found that the animal experienced difficulty in swallowing. Thurber attributed this to the fact that the movement of the tongue was restricted by the frenum. He rectified the problem by forcibly severing it with his finger. Soon after, the pup began to eat fish. Unfortunately, it died.

Thurber acquired two other pups, both born in July 1909, in which he noted the same frenum impediment. One, a female named Ennatha, succeeded in breaking her frenum through her own efforts. She began to eat a few days later. The male, Atagh, did not break his frenum, so Thurber anesthetized him and cut his membrane. Immediately Atagh stuck out his tongue and nosed a fish in its enclosure.

That was an encouraging step forward for Thurber, who was a skilled and patient researcher. He moved on to another step. Thurber began feeding the seals by holding their mouths open and pouring evaporated cream mixed with bits of fish down their throats. The pups did not take to the mixture, but small quantities reached their stomachs. That gave Thurber another idea.

The boatswain started with the most basic piece of knowledge. Seals ate fish, which they caught while swimming. He procured a large fish which he cut into strips that he tied on the end of a long piece of twine. Then he carried the pups back to St. Paul and put them in a tank of water to see if they were helpless. When they began swimming he knew they were not, so he inferred they could feed themselves.

While the seals were swimming in the tank Thurber dragged the pieces of fish through the water in front of them. At first the pups paid no attention to the movement. But he was patient and stuck to his task. It wasn't until three days later that Atagh finally grabbed a fish. Thurber cut the twine holding the piece of fish and the pup swallowed the food.

Apparently Atagh developed a taste for fish. Thurber turned his attention to Ennatha, who was loath to fall for his trick. As soon as he began trailing a fish through the water in front of her, Atagh grabbed and swallowed it—along with the twine to which it was attached. Thurber realized he was on the verge of a significant discovery, but he still had to teach Ennatha how to eat.

He placed the pups in separate tanks and concentrated on her. It took two days, but she began to eat. After that he fed them both by hand and within a few days both pups began to look for his appearance and the strips of fish he supplied. Buoyed by his success, Thurber took the thriving animals, the only captives of their kind in the world, back to the *Bear*. But, had he really saved them?

The upside was that Thurber had found the only feasible method of saving the lives of thousands of pup seals, if rescuers could supply enough people to feed the orphans. The downside was that he was also consigning the saved seals to fates as pelts for the market. That paradox might not have interested Judge who, elated by Thurber's success, immediately notified his boss, George M. Bowers, the Commissioner of Fisheries, about what the boatswain had accomplished. Bowers asked Judge to bring the seal pups to Washington, along with the suddenly famous Thurber, who was reluctant to go.[5]

The boatswain did not like the limelight or the city. He was born a whaler, and social Washington did not appeal to him. In fact, once he got there he wanted to leave early, but he was ordered to stay for a few days longer. The administrators in the capital eagerly awaited his arrival. Some people did not. Bowers' request set off an uproar in the city.

When several fur-seal experts heard about the project they aired immediate concerns. Their chief argument was that the pups would not survive in Washington. First, they claimed, seals could not live in fresh water. Second, the climate was too mild for them. The experts wanted the seals sent to New York instead, as if 200 miles farther north was going to make a difference. Bowers ignored them and procured a furlough for Thurber. The boatswain arrived in Washington in November, accompanied by Ennatha and Atagh.

The experts had been partly correct. The pups had a problem adjusting to their new surroundings, but it had nothing to do with the water or the climate. Thurber had overlooked one important fact about seals' eating habits, which he quickly corrected.

The pups were ensconced in a tank about 60 feet in circumference and about three feet deep on the first floor of the fisheries building on the "Mall" in D.C. The tank was filled with Potomac River water, the same water the residents of the city drank. Each day for two months Thurber fed them strips of fish and they seemed to thrive. In fact, they gained weight. Suddenly, and inexplicably, they began to decline.

Ennatha and Atagh refused to eat and their weight losses continued. Thurber began to worry that his pets were going to die. He wracked his brain for an answer as to what was causing their decline. Then it hit him! Seals did not eat every day, as other animals do. He realized that he had fed them too much. Thurber determined not to feed them for at least three days, during which time he stayed away from their tank.

On the morning of the fourth day, well before any of the bureau's employees appeared, Thurber visited the tank. He expected to see his seals dead, if he saw them at all. His heart skipped a beat when he looked in the tanks and saw it empty. Then he heard a shout of alarm from above—and laughed.[6]

He looked up and back toward the rear of the room. There was a guard sitting on top of a pile of boxes, looking down at two healthy seals on the floor below. They were squatting on their hind flippers, their mouths wide open, and their eyes blinking. The guard held a club in each hand, ready to whack the animals as they rose on their flippers. He told Thurber that he had been there for three hours, and that the pups were the "livest" dead seals he had ever seen. Thurber happily agreed with him. The guard explained to Thurber that the seals had climbed out of their tank and started to meander around the room. He had tried to chase them back to the tank. Instead, they attacked and cornered him on his tenuous perch. All that Thurber cared about was that his theory about overfeeding was correct.

From that point on he cut their rations. They began immediately to thrive again. By the time Thurber returned to the *Bear* in January 1910 the pups were adding weight at the rate of five pounds a month. Moreover, throughout the long, hot summer months in Washington, when the water in the tank was rarely below 80 degrees Fahrenheit, Ennatha and Atagh thrived and grew fat. That he had saved them was no surprise to the Coast Guard administrators who knew him—including the commandant, Captain Worth G. Ross.[7]

"Sailors are the kindest hearted mortals in the world," Ross said. "Thurber probably fussed around with the cubs during every minute that he could call his own, gave them remedies when they were ailing, brushed and washed them, and mothered them generally. This kindness without doubt had much to do with keeping them well and contented."

That they were well and contented was evident. A year after Thurber returned to the *Bear* each of them weighed about 50 pounds. They had defied the experts' beliefs about their inability to adjust to a different environment. More important, they were still in Washington, D.C., far away from the rookeries in Alaska. They, at least, would not become pelts thanks to the unique services of a Coast Guard boatswain, who proved it doesn't always take a so-called expert to solve a problem. All it took was common sense, which was a common trait among "Coasties," as Ross explained:

> Thurber merely used common sense and kindness in his care of his cubs. In the first place, he discovered why no one was ever able before his time to raise baby seals. They are tongue-tied and cannot lap milk. He performed the simple surgical operation of cutting what is known as the "freedom" [sic] of the tongues of his charges, and after feeding them for a time with a common nursing bottle, until their tongues ceased being sore, he taught them to lap milk like a dog or cat.
>
> Then he was careful that they had their daily bath of salt water and as they grew older and stronger he changed their diet. Now they will leap two or three feet from the deck to reach a fish suspended over their heads.[8]

Solving the problem certainly wasn't above Thurber's head. There was no limit to the skills of the *Bear*'s crew members.

18

A Lieutenant Makes a Major Discovery

> *"In 1776, Catherine the Great, Empress of Russia, granted trading rights to the Russian American Trading Company and began exchanging goods and services for furs, gold and other items at trading posts throughout Alaska. When the United States bought Alaska from Russia in 1867, the company was sold to San Francisco merchants Lewis Gerstle and Louis Sloss and was renamed the Alaska Commercial Company. From 1868 to the Gold Rush Days of the early 1900s, Alaska Commercial Company was a provider of groceries and general merchandise for trappers, explorers and gold seekers."*[1]

The story behind the formation of the still-existing Alaska Commercial Company, to which the U.S. government offered the first exclusive sealing contract, was long on fantasy and short on facts. According to one fanciful reporter, who was about 80 years off on his facts, the seal rookeries the cutters were guarding were discovered by an unnamed Russian Army lieutenant just about the time the U.S. purchased Alaska.[2] He was aboard a Russian gunboat when it visited the rookeries. The young lieutenant was an entrepreneur. He envisioned a lucrative financial haul in the seal trade.

The officer traveled to San Francisco and proposed a joint commercial venture to several prominent business operators. One of them accompanied him to the rookeries and saw what the lieutenant saw. They formed the Alaska Commercial Company and secured a 30-year lease of the islands from the American government for the privilege of seal hunting. During the lease the Russian officer was treated fairly by the organizers of the company, who gave him a liberal amount of stock. He moved to San Francisco, where he became a wealthy and respected citizen. Whether that was true or not, some facts remained. Their business was legitimate—and a monopoly—but they skinned the government as well as the seals.

Their deal was the company would pay the government a $3 per skin royalty. Government officials tried to monitor the company's activities, but not always successfully or in a timely fashion. In August 1891 the Treasury Department dispatched the *Bear* to visit the seal islands on its trip from Unalaska to Point Barrow and leave instructions with the treasury agents to limit the Alaska Commercial Company's catch of the season to 7,500 sealskins.[3] It was a wasted trip in an age of slow communications. Other sources said that the company had already secured at least that number of skins, and open sealing had been entirely suspended for the season. The government did not learn its lesson.

Federal negotiators signed another long-term lease for the rookeries, this time with the North American Company. The lease was scheduled to end in 1909. The deal gave the company the sole right to kill fur seal on the islands. It did not, however, mean anything to the pestiferous poachers operating three miles offshore, whose activities were monitored by the Bering Sea patrol cutters.

The three-mile limit did not daunt the poachers. They simply waited for the seals to reach the ocean outside it and slaughtered them there while the crew of the *Bear*, very often without orders or authority, was powerless to do anything to prevent the destruction of the seals.[4] The poachers, in sheer defiance of their presence, continued the destructive work until there were very few live seals remaining. The ongoing slaughter offended some critics in the United States who demanded that the U.S. Navy be dispatched to the region to confront the poachers.[5] That was an affront to the Coast Guard, whose ability to interdict poachers was restricted by artificial boundaries and political edicts, not a lack of willingness to carry out the mission they were assigned to perform.

According to the terms of the lease the North American Company paid the U.S. government about $12 per skin. That was about half of the value of each skin, which earned the company from $22 to $25 apiece. That was a lucrative deal for the company, since it did not sustain any significant expenses in the harvesting process. The sealers simply drove the animals ashore by the thousands and slaughtered them there, all under the protection of the Coast Guard, which assigned as many as four cutters at a time to patrol and protect these islands.

The cost of operating those patrols far exceeded what the company paid the government. That was, in the eyes of many detractors, a bad bargain on the government's part—and a losing proposition for the Coast Guard.[6] The cutter crews were fighting a battle against poachers they could not win, nor could the seals they were supposed to protect. The statistics for the years between 1874 and 1909 were tragic[7]:

There existed an estimated 4,700,000 seals in Alaska in 1874
    By 1891 the number was down to 1,000,000
    For every sealskin gathered, two other seals were slaughtered and not recovered
    Another 18 years and there were fewer than 50,000 seals in Alaska, and they were threatened with extinction unless the government provided immediate aid
    The annual revenue to the government was about $317,000 per year during the decade between 1879 and 1889, with about $12,000 per year as the cost of collection and protection
    By 1909 the government's gross revenue amounted to only $149,000 per year, and it cost $340,000 per year to collect it and subsidize the Coast Guard cutters assigned to protect the herds from absolute extinction in one season, which the poachers would have happily completed if they could
    During the 20 years ending in 1890 the United States government made in net cash profit out of the fur seals exactly $5,981,036—when the royalty was only $3.17 per skin
    During the 20 years ending in 1909 the gross revenue to the government on the fur seal business of that period was $3,235,063, and it cost $5,472,607 to protect the seal herd while it was being collected
    The net loss to the government during the 20 years ending in 1909 was $2,247,544

The dollar figures during the period between 1874 and 1909 did not tell the whole story. Along with the money loss, the seal herd was almost annihilated by the poachers. Nor did the dollar figures and seal annihilation take into account the physical threat to the cutter crews who sometimes went ashore to protect the seals at risk to their own safety. In truth, the only way to end the poaching problem would have been to train the seals to remain within the three-mile limit. Circus entertainers may have been able to train seals, but neither the Coast Guard nor the Alaskan natives could, so many of the animals swam out to sea into international waters. There, the poachers became legitimate sealers and the Coast Guard's jurisdiction grew smaller as their coverage area expanded.

The patrol fleet was strong enough and quick enough to make the poachers' operations difficult on the islands. The cutter captains' responsibility was to make sure nobody other than the one authorized company could take seals within the American portion of the Bering Sea or in the Pacific Ocean within three miles of U.S. possessions. The issue of which countries had access to the seals in the Arctic region, how many seals they could harvest in a given time, and where, was changing as several countries' representatives sought an agreement on it at Paris, France. That complicated the captains' enforcement operations.

The patrol fleet was assigned an area almost half as large as the Gulf of Mexico to oversee. If the delegates at Paris decided against the U.S.'s claim about its self-proclaimed territorial boundaries, the cutters' enforcement area would be confined to the Pribilof Islands, St. George and St. Paul in the Bering Sea, and to guarding the coast within a three-mile limit. Until, or if, that happened, the captains followed their orders, and they had very little say in the killing operations on the ground, where the Alaska Commercial Company faced tight restrictions in its take.

The company's agents could not kill more than 7,500 seals in any one year, and they were only allowed to kill them in the presence of a U.S. agent. They could not kill either the females or the old bulls, only the "bachelors," as the young males are called. The process was not difficult. It was described as "the tamest kind of sport," as the bachelors were simply driven apart from the rest of the herd and killed with sticks.[8]

The agent of the company counted the skins in the presence of the government's agent, who sent a tally of the number shipped in each cargo to a U.S. agent at San Francisco. The San Francisco agent, in turn, ensured that there were no more skins than the government agent in the northwest had certified to. Most of the Coast Guard officers in Alaska believed this bureaucratic process was more of an overkill than the slaughter of the animals. They implied that seals would become extinct despite the precautions taken to preserve the species.

Worse, they believed, if the region were opened to all nations and seals were taken with nets, as they had been in the past, the final destruction would be accelerated. Despite their concerns the commanders obeyed their orders every year when the season began anew about the 1st of June or 1st of July. That was when the seals had become well established in the Bering and breeding had begun. At that time the rocky Pribilofs and a few islands belonging to Russia near the coast of Siberia were crowded with thousands of seals, and the animals swam the sea in search of food.[9]

The poachers didn't wait for the seals to reach the protected islands. They simply intercepted them on their way from the ocean into the sea. The cutter commanders were powerless to stop them. They could not interfere with sealing in the Pacific three miles from American shores, so they kept watch on the passes of the Aleutian through which seals and sealers entered the Bering.

The sealers were most busy in midsummer, but it was not unheard of for them to raid the seal islands as late as December, when most of the cutter fleet had left. The patrol fleet stayed on the lookout for poachers generally from May through October, with some slack periods. Sealing in May and through most of June was a rough profession. The weather in the Bering was wintry well into June, and the hills ashore were still snow covered sometimes as late as the 1st of July. That's when the heat of the northern summer began.

The air was mild and the sea was calm most of the time, flowers were blooming, and grass was growing on shore. That was the signal for the cutters to step up their patrols for a couple months. It was a short season. By the end of September, the weather turned nasty again. Squalls became more common and by the 1st of November snowstorms came with increased frequency. That took any fun out of sealing that may have existed.

Healey didn't seem to care what the weather was like. Since he knew the Bering from the Aleutians to the Arctic better than anyone else, and was known to everybody in that region as the embodiment of Uncle Sam's power, he and the *Bear* usually stayed around the seal islands late into the year, after everyone else had gone. Poachers who fell into Healey's hands were likely to repent of their temerity, as folks were fond of saying.

The question was whether the results were worth the efforts he and his counterparts put into their zealous enforcement. The records suggest they were not, but that did not deter their efforts, and explains why Healey was usually the last commander to leave the region.

He occasionally made a foray to the east of the islands, as did some of the other cutters. Sometimes in midsummer the commanders stationed landing parties on one of the islands commanding an important pass. Mostly, they confined themselves to the region around the Pribilofs. Wherever they were poachers didn't pay them a great deal of respect at times.

On occasion a sealer disguised as a different type of vessel would enter the sealing region as a cutter commander watched. If the commander suspected the vessel was there to kill seals illegally he stopped it and demanded an explanation from its captain as to why it was there. Healey and his counterparts knew what they were looking for. A ship equipped for poaching often carried a great many small boats, an unusually large complement of men, and an abundance of firearms.

The poachers' method of killing seals was just as barbaric as the authorized hunters' tactics, except that they used guns. When the sealer captain encountered a herd of seals swimming he lowered many boats carrying armed men into the water. They shot the seals as rapidly as possible and picked up as many carcasses as they could. They did not care about the seals' gender statuses and vital statistics. Old, young, male, female, bachelor … they shot them all. The sad part was that they wasted large numbers of them, which again raised the question of the efficacy of the cutter patrols.

18. A Lieutenant Makes a Major Discovery

Some old sailors estimated that 75 percent of seals shot by the poachers were not recovered. Others maintained that the loss did not exceed ten percent. The sealers who wasted a large number were simply greedy and did not care about extermination as long as they could fill their holds. A small vessel could take $100,000 worth of seals in a single season. The temptation for a poacher to kill as many as he could to reach his limit was strong. And, it was all the stronger because the crew members on poaching vessels worked under a "no catch, no pay" system.[10] Healey and his fellow commanders could not stop them from filling their quotas if they were outside the protected limits, but they tried.

For the most part they did not have a problem chasing down poachers at sea. The ships of the patrol fleet could overtake the swiftest of the poachers, but with a fair, strong wind a trim poaching schooner might have easily escaped. Any vessel a cutter caught captured with seals on board was usually taken to Unalaska, where a prize crew boarded it. The vessel was then sailed to Sitka or Victoria, depending on whether it was American or English.

The poachers were somewhat concerned about what happened if they were apprehended no matter where they were based. They were for the most part sure that the negotiators at Paris were not going to arrive at a decision adverse to the United States. But, they knew that if that were to happen "Uncle Sam" would be the subject of numerous damage suits filed by poachers excluded from the Bering.

Again, that did not faze the Coast Guard administrators who told their cutter commanders to enforce the laws as they were, not as anyone predicted them to be. That was good enough for Healey and his cutter commander counterparts, for whom the war against poachers was a long, lonely, and often futile, venture.

19

Healey and His Counterparts Share a Conundrum

> "*U. S. Government Made a Bad Bargain: The islands are exceedingly difficult to guard from the constant attacks of the poachers. The elements seem to favor them. Heavy fogs hang from the heavens, affording protection to the marauders and obscuring the vision of the watchers. Only by the merest chance can they be apprehended.*"[1]

One of the bizarre twists in the *Bear*'s crew members' lives was their relationship with seals, walruses, and other wildlife in the Arctic region. There were times when they had to shoot them for one purpose or another. Sometimes they shot them for fun or for food. At other times they had to protect them from being shot illegally. They were proficient either way.

Historically the government sent U.S. Navy warships to the Arctic to protect the region from what were referred to as pirates, another name for poachers. The government realized that was a waste of the Navy's money and manpower. The responsibility for the anti-poaching patrols was transferred to the Coast Guard in 1894. That was a prudent move, but it was still a waste of money in many people's opinions, even after Great Britain, Canada, and the U.S. reached a badly needed agreement on August 15, 1893, over the issue of poaching in the Bering region—and they needed to do it fast in some people's opinion.[2] But, as always, government wheels moved slowly.

"As far as the United States are concerned, it would appear that the fur-bearing seal is going the way of the buffalo. While the diplomats are exchanging notes and protocols, the poachers are massacring the seals, mother and cub alike; and by the time the last state paper is drawn up the last seal will have vanished from American waters, and its congeners will have to be sought out in the Arctic Circle," an editor warned.[3] There was a certain amount of truth to that as the years ahead proved.

It became obvious to representatives of the United States, Canada, and Great Britain in 1890 that a treaty of some sort had to be negotiated to control sealing in the Bering, particularly to stop poaching. Failure to do so was likely to lead to a war that none of the countries wanted over a problem that seemed so trifling. Unilateral U.S. government actions had brought matters to a head. The only people ready to go to war, apparently, were bellicose newspaper editors.

"There is a feeling among military people here that the presence of the United

States cruisers in Behring Sea will eventually lead to trouble between the United States and England," an editor at the Halifax, Nova Scotia, *Recorder* declared.[4]

The London, England, *Standard* echoed the statement. "It would seem that a small spark might kindle a conflagration. An officer in one of her Majesty's regiments said it might be confidently expected that Canadian sealers would catch seals in what is disputed territory. It might also be put down as a certainty that some of them would sooner or later fall in with a United States cruiser, and in such case there is bound to be a seizure. What will follow such an event the signs of the times teach."[5]

The Recorder's editor got downright belligerent. "British fleets are not in the habit of losing much time when they set out on a pulverizing mission. Probably a fleet sailing from Halifax could bottle up New York commerce in even less time than Senator Hawley stated. Moral for our American cousins: Get out your guns, polish up your armor, for an experience of 2,000 years has taught the world that there is a heap of truth in the saying that we know not what a day, nor an hour, may bring forth," he warned.

The New York Herald's editors felt compelled to respond and stated unequivocally in a "bring it on" manner that the U.S. government had a right to protect its seal fisheries, noting that two revenue cutters had set sail from Seattle with instructions to capture and dismantle every vessel found sealing in the Bering Sea, whether British or American.[6] The editors also made clear that there were between 30 and 40 Canadian sealing vessels in that sea at the time, so people could expect fireworks.

"Such of them as are caught by our cutters will undoubtedly suffer the penalty prescribed," the writer stated. "It is reported a modus vivendi was proposed by the British Government pending the completion of the negotiations, but this was refused by [James G. Blaine, U.S. Secretary of State] and as Congress has not chosen to change the law, it is the duty of the President to enforce it."

The Herald's editor averred that all the Canadians had to do to end the crisis was stop sealing. "Practically the modus vivendi would have been a command from Salisbury to his semi-independent but irresponsible agent, Sir John Macdonald, to prevent depredations by his people on the fur-bearing animals pending negotiations…. The best modus vivendi with a poacher is an agreement that he shall stop poaching pending negotiations." They did not take the editorial advice.

On July 11, 1889, the *Rush* seized the Canadian sealer *Black Diamond*. The cutter was reportedly pursuing six other vessels at the time. The *Black Diamond*'s captain refused to stop at *Rush*'s command, but complied when the cutter ran out its guns. Two officers from the *Rush*, Captain L.G. Shepherd and Lieutenant Frank Tuttle, the future commander of the *Bear*, boarded the sealer and found 103 sealskins. Shepherd seized the *Black Diamond* and sent it to Sitka.

The Canadian government was not happy with Shepherd's action, but deferred to the British government for guidance. Some irate Canadians called for war. The British government was growing weary of the sealing controversy:

The London Times reported in late March 1892 that it really didn't matter to the people in England where they got their furs and the government was upset with the Canadians for complaining to it. The article put that in perspective[7]: "The controversy only concerns a semi-independent colony who treats us as a commercial enemy. These colonies are always embroiling us in foreign disputes. We are obliged to fight their battles, whilst they treat us as a foreign power. How long is this to last? A few more troubles like the Bering Sea controversy will compel us to face the problem and seriously ask ourselves whether the relations between the mother country and the colonies are quite fair to the British taxpayer."

The U.S. government didn't do much to alleviate the tension. Instead, politicians placed more pressure on Shepherd and Healey due to secret diplomacy. President Benjamin Harrison was bent on establishing a treaty to protect the seals in the Bering. His administration was less than open about the process though. That led observers to label the effort as an amazing chapter of diplomatic history. Exactly what Harrison's negotiators were doing was a mystery.

The president inadvertently disclosed one of the mysteries when he alluded in a speech to an agreement among the maritime powers for the protection of the fur-seal fisheries. Senator George Frisbie Hoar (R-MA) revealed another when he introduced a resolution calling for the correspondence on this question. He also alleged that there existed unjust discrimination against American sealers in the Bering. Then, Captain Shepard admitted in reply to a question from Representative Nelson Dingley, Jr., (R-ME) that he and the officers of the other cutters had received confidential orders before sailing for Alaska in 1888.

Observers began to piece the hints together. They suspected correctly that the U.S. was conducting some sort of diplomatic discussions they did not want made public, and they were willing to throw some outsiders under the bus in the process. Shepherd and Healey were among them, as a look back determined.

In July and August 1886, in accordance with the policy pursued by previous administrations, cutters seized three British sealers operating in the Bering Sea. The government initiated legal proceedings against the sealers in the United States court at Sitka. The case was based on the right of exclusive jurisdiction conferred by the 1867 Treaty of Purchase and the revised statutes. The court condemned the vessels in October and ordered that they be sold. Inexplicably, the government released them in late January 1887.

Canadians applauded this sudden reversal of policy. They viewed the move as a timely surrender of treaty rights to Great Britain. Americans, especially the members of the press, were not so jubilant. They described the release as the American government's renunciation of title to the Bering. Whatever it was, Canadian poachers swarmed in these waters when the 1887 season opened in the belief that they would not be bothered by U.S. enforcement officials, and confidently expected to enjoy immunity from molestation. They were a bit premature in their judgement.

Government officials in Washington were negotiating among themselves to renew previous enforcement policies in the Bering. After a protracted deadlock between the State and Treasury departments the orders signed by Secretary of the Treasury John Sherman during his term of office were renewed. That gave Shepherd and Healey the green light to enforce the law. Between them they captured seven British and nine American vessels during July and August. U.S. courts prosecuted the owners in the United States courts. Their vessels were condemned and the cargoes confiscated. If nothing else, sealers from all nations were confused. Harrison's administration had started on one enforcement track, considered the right one by many Americans, deviated from it, and then returned to the original plan. Confusion reigned—and grew worse as the 1888 season began and Shepherd and Healey prepared to depart from San Francisco en route to Alaska.

They received the same orders that year as they had in 1887—at least publicly. The night before they sailed a special messenger visited the two captains and handed them sealed instructions marked confidential and not to be opened until they were fifty miles at sea. When the captains opened their envelopes they were surprised: the new orders were in direct conflict with the orders given in 1887. This time they were instructed to exempt British vessels found outside the three-mile limit from the consequences of illegal sealing.

That same day officials in Washington privately telegraphed the same orders to their counterparts in Victoria, British Columbia. The Canadians in turn dispatched them aboard a steamer that started immediately for a port at which 13 British vessels lay at anchor. Their captains no sooner received the dispatch than they set sail for the sealing grounds, where they began hunting. All Shepherd and Healey could do was watch. Wise observers might have speculated that the sealers had received advance notice that they would not be harassed.

The Canadian poachers were not only secured against seizure by the *Rush* and the *Bear*, but they did not have to compete against American sealers. They had not been informed in advance of the change of government policy. The turn of events sustained Senator Hoar's complaint of discrimination against American vessels. Critics sought an explanation of the change in policy, which they attributed to duplicitous actions by Secretary of State Thomas Bayard.[8]

Bayard was between the proverbial rock and a hard place, in this case the rocks composing the Pribilofs. A San Francisco opinion writer put it best[9]:

> It is a matter of regret that the abstract question of international law has not been settled before the opening of the fishing season. Sooner or later the two powers must arrive at a conclusion either that Bering Sea is an open sea or that it is a closed sea. They may reach that conclusion by a comparison of the facts and the law between themselves; or they may leave the controversy to an arbitrator.
>
> However the problem is solved, it must be, and without much delay; and, under the circumstances, it is a pity that it has not been solved before the naked question of law is embarrassed by accidents which may be irritating. It may not be as easy to reach the conclusion after British sealers have been captured or after the United States flag has been shot away by some reckless mariner from Victoria.
>
> The lease of the islands is in the nature of a warranty, not a quit claim. If Bering Sea is territorial water the United States is bound to keep sealers out of it in order to secure to the new company the monopoly they have granted.

Bayard agreed that it was time—indeed, past time—for a treaty to be negotiated, openly or secretly. He opted for the latter. Bayard's manipulations began in January 1887 when he had ordered the release of the three British sealers on the ground that the U.S.'s claim of exclusive jurisdiction in the Bering was embarrassing him in the North Atlantic fisheries negotiations. He had already started proceedings to propose to concerned maritime powers an international closed season time agreement for the protection of the fur-seal fisheries and he wanted a clear field for his diplomacy.

Seizures of Canadian vessels would be inconvenient when he was seeking acceptance of his proposal from the governments of Great Britain, Russia, and Germany. That explained why the cutter captains were ordered to avoid interdicting any vessels. As a result, laws passed by Congress were not enforced while Bayard was negotiating his maritime agreement.

The U.S. waived the right of exclusive jurisdiction over the waters ceded by Russia for the season. That prompted an editor to suggest that the country would be highly favored by fortune if that treaty privilege had not been compromised or renounced in the convention which was negotiated. He suggested that Secretary Bayard had a ruling passion for surrendering American rights.[10]

Shepherd and Healey learned that lesson the hard way as they watched the Canadian and British sealers slaughter seals. To say that the situation was confusing was a gross understatement. From the American standpoint it seemed like the government was going out of its way to protect the poachers from the cutters. And there was no guarantee that the cutter captains' hands would be untied soon—yet they were still expected to carry out their duties.

Harrison appointed William Windom as Secretary of the Treasury in 1889. There was some uncertainty as to whether he was going to follow the example of his predecessors in that position and rule that the Bering was territorial water and, as such, under the control and jurisdiction of the United States government. The decision was particularly important to the new lessees of the Pribilofs, who believed—or at least hoped—that he would take that view. They, at least, felt confident that the *Bear* and the *Rush* would make prizes of any vessels found sealing in the Bering, whatever flag they flew.

They did not conceal their belief that without such a measure of protection their lease would not be worth what they had undertaken to give for it. Editors agreed. "The lessees are entitled to demand of the Government that it shall protect them in the occupation of the property leased, and if they can show that, owing to the inefficiency of the revenue service, poaching went on to their detriment, they will have a prima-facie case for refusing to pay rent," an editor for the San Francisco *Morning Call* opined.[11]

Whether Shepherd and Healey felt the same way was a matter of conjecture. They had been badly served but people still expected them to protect their interests. What a dichotomy for the captains! And, when a treaty was finally signed in 1893, it didn't do much to clear it up.[12] To listen to the negotiators, everybody won—except Russia. A tribunal determined that the body of water now known as the Bering Sea was included in the phrase "Pacific Ocean" in the treaty of 1826 between Great Britain and Russia. Consequently, all the rights of Russia to jurisdiction and seal fisheries passed to the United States, limited to the aforementioned cession.

The Americans were happy for the most part, even though it was probable that all the vessels composing the U.S. fleet in the Bering would be withdrawn, except for one revenue cutter, which would be used in maintaining the protective zone in accord with the decision of the arbitrators. The decision would compel the United

States to make compensation to British subjects for abstaining from the capture of seals in the Bering during the pendency of the arbitration.

That determination did not address the question of damages prior to that time, and further information was awaited as to the nature of the finding, with reference to seizures in 1887 and 1889. Nevertheless, U.S senators were generally pleased with the outcome. Senator Matthew Butler (D-SC) said the award gave more than he expected. He added that he never believed the contention that the Bering was a closed sea could be maintained.

Senator William P. Frye (R-ME) predicted the court would hold that the U.S. had a property right in seals, and said the decision raised a very serious question as to liability for past action. Senator John Sherman (R-OH) thought the adjustment of the close season and the extension of measures for the prevention of pelagic sealing was very acceptable. For all their optimism the British press expressed glee over the fact that the U.S. had emerged the biggest loser in the agreement.[13] *The London Daily News* said the decision was substantially in favor of the case advanced by England: "Sir Charles Russel's powerful arguments convinced the arbitrators. Sir John Thompson refused to assent to the regulations. We have not the slightest doubt, however, that these regulations are [in our favor]; even were they not, it is our duty to obey them, and we trust no difficulty will be raised by the Canadian government."

The *Daily Telegraph* said: "Our advocates have traversed the absurdly wide American pretensions very eloquently and learnedly, and the arbitrators brushed aside those finely woven pleas and have given a verdict for common sense and Great Britain. Yet, pleased as we naturally are to see England and Canada win their suit, it is a greater and nobler pleasure still to believe America will loyally accept the decision, and that we thus have witnessed another victory of lofty Christian substitution of rational arbitration for force of arms."

Perhaps the most overlooked inclusion in the analysis of the treaty was the idea that only one Coast Guard cutter would henceforth be needed in the Bering. Just the opposite was true. Two years later officials were clamoring for more Coast Guard resources to patrol the Bering, which should have been renamed the "Inconsistent Sea," because it was inconsistency that ruled the waves.

20

Sailing on the "Inconsistent Sea"

> *"Pelagic sealing should be prohibited in Bering Sea, the Sea of Ochotsk, and the adjoining waters during the months of May, June, October, November and December, which may be termed the 'migration periods' of the fur seal."*[1]

Captain Russell Glover, of the cutter *Wolcott*, returned to Port Townsend on September 22, 1890, after a 60-day leave of absence.[2] He switched from rest and relaxation to pressure in the blink of an eye. Immediately after he stepped off the boat on which he was a passenger a newspaper reporter asked him if it were true that he was being sent to Alaska to deal with seal poachers. Glover seemed caught off guard by the question: "I know absolutely nothing about the matter except what I saw in the Seattle papers this morning," he responded. "I don't know when I am going or where, and I am not even certain of going at all until I see what awaits me here."

Then, a Lieutenant Brosdeck handed the captain a batch of telegrams, which he scanned quickly. The reporter asked him if there was anything for the public in the telegrams. "No, sir, nothing," Glover said. "Besides, they contain strict orders from the department to keep the contents secret." That did not satisfy the reporter, who continued to question the captain beyond his limit of patience.

"I do not want to be rude," Glover said, "but you will oblige me by asking no more questions on this point, nor can I tell you anything at all. Yes, l am going to sail, but don't know whether today or tomorrow, and I can't tell you where I am going."

What was going on? Why all the secrecy? Above all, what was so important about a few seals? After all, despite Glover's reluctance to answer questions, people knew where he was going. All the information in his possession regarding the *Wolcott*'s future movements had been published in the previous day's newspapers. Despite the secrecy surrounding what was going on, which everyone allegedly was unaware of, outsiders knew as a matter of absolute fact that the *Wolcott* had been ordered to proceed to the Bering at once. They knew its agenda.

The cutter would stop at Sitka to join the *Rush* and the *Corwin*, whose commanders were awaiting the orders Captain Glover was carrying to them. They all understood that carrying out those orders could result in serious international complications. It all had to do with sealers, who were becoming an increasingly nagging problem in the region.

Two weeks earlier some of the sealers had entered ports with their vessels loaded to overflowing with prize sealskins. The owners had the audacity to brag to newspaper reporters how many skins they had taken and broadcast that they would try the patience of the United States by going out again that same season and obtaining more. The reporters naturally published the news. From the sealers' standpoint that was like announcing beforehand that they were going to assassinate a public figure and providing the details of where and when just to taunt anyone who wanted to interfere while knowing they couldn't do anything about it. It was an unforced error on their part.

Virtually anyone who knew that the sealing industry was getting out of hand and creating international tension recognized that the day was rapidly approaching when peaceful negotiations between concerned nations were on the brink of impossibility.[3] That apparently did not concern the increasingly brazen sealers. They were not satisfied with poaching during the regular season. They wanted to extend it. Besides, they were afraid that the increasing scarcity of seals would cause both Great Britain and the United States to prohibit for a time catching the animals by anyone. So, they determined to make one last haul before it was done.

U.S. State and Treasury Department officials resolved to take issues into their own hands while they prepared to open negotiations with any other nations. Their first step was to dispatch the *Wolcott* to the Bering Sea to reinforce the cutter complement already on scene. Glover's explicit instructions, which he carried to his commander counterparts, were to seize all sealers found operating there, nationality notwithstanding. What had set the crackdown in motion?

U.S. authorities in Washington D.C. had received information two weeks earlier that four sealers were fitting out for a winter cruise in Alaskan waters. The Victoria, British Columbia, newspapers had published the information, and United States Consul Myers was instructed to keep the government posted. Myers advised the authorities that the vessels left port together and were en route to the sealing grounds. No sooner had Assistant Secretary of the Treasury Spalding received the information than he ordered that the *Wolcott* be prepared to go to sea. Observers intimated from that order that the United States took the matter with the utmost seriousness.

Captain Glover joined the *Bear* and the *Rush* in the part of the Bering where the pirates were supposed to be poaching. Once they found them their orders were to send boarders onto those vessels. If the boarding parties found anything in the shape of skins or hunters' tools on the offending vessels, they were to seize the schooners in the name of the United States, deprive them of all steering apparatus, and bring them into the nearest American port. The key word there was "American."

A year earlier, when there were thirty or so sealing vessels in the region, Coast Guard commanders had seized offending ships, placed one crew member aboard as a "prize crew," and taken the vessel into a Canadian port in British Columbia, where the locals simply laughed at them.[4] The Americans learned a lesson from that. They vowed there would be no more nonsense like that.

If the poachers or authorities from another nation were not interested in protecting the seals, the Americans would take care of matters themselves. Besides, there were only four "pirates" this time and an equal amount of cutters. If the cutters seized them they could escort all four into Port Townsend Harbor. And the *Wolcott*, at least, was prepared to stay in the region for a long time. It carried 60 tons of coal, and by piling the decks with fuel it could carry 70 tons. The cutter also carried stores and ship chandlery for a two-month cruise. There was no doubt about the U.S. government's resolve to crack down on poaching this time.

The sealing problem was growing more and more complicated in the Bering region as commercial activities increased. Entrepreneurs had realized there was great wealth to be made in supplying the folks back home with the finest sealskins that were both fashionable and utile. There was no better way for consumers to stay warm and look chic at the same time.

More and more sealers appeared around the Pribilof Islands, which the U.S. owned. However, Russia claimed jurisdiction over the region of the Bering in which they were located, and had historically exercised "a very jealous care over the seals in Bering Sea."[5] The U.S. determined to carry on that tradition, even though it did not recognize Russia's claim to ownership of the sea after 1867. There was some question as to whether any country could claim ownership of an entire sea used by sailors from other nations for commercial purposes.

In 1891 there were 122 sealing vessels from different countries in the region. The sealers' catch numbers continued to increase concomitantly. The total reached 143,000 in 1894, when the sealers expanded their operations as far south as California. They weren't concerned about which seals they killed as long as they obtained skins.[6] Seal pups became collateral damage.

If a mother seal was killed and the pups died of starvation, so what? The popular belief among the less-than-environmentally-conscious sealers was that there was an inexhaustible supply of the animals. In 1896 alone there were 20,000 dead pups on the Pribilof breeding grounds. Prescient scientists, government officials, and assorted experts knew that the slaughter could not continue without extermination becoming a reality.

The U.S. government took the lead on seal protection, especially after officials of the North American Commercial Company, which held the only lease for sealing in the Pribilofs, complained because its annual catch there had dropped suddenly from 100,000 to about 20,000. That spurred the government to action.

U.S. warships and Coast Guard cutters began seizing sealing vessels regardless of country of origin. Many sealing ships operated under the Canadian flag. Since Canada was a part of the British Empire that created a problem. The British government was none too happy about the U.S.'s temerity. It threatened to retaliate. Fortunately, cool heads prevailed and the two countries reached an agreement aimed at curtailing the chaos that ruled in the region. Russia's concerns were not considered at the time.

According to the provisions of this treaty the two nations forbade their vessels to seal north of the 35th parallel during May, June, and July, and at all times within a zone of 60 miles around the Pribilofs. The use of steamers was forbidden completely, and no weapons other than sealing irons were allowed in the Bering Sea. The United States went even further and banned its citizens from engaging in the seal fisheries north of the 35th parallel.[7]

The treaty was a major step forward in protecting the seals, but there was a salient drawback. England and the United States were the only two countries that signed it. There were whaling ships from other countries operating in the region, such as Mexico and Japan. They did not have to abide by the treaty, except within the actual territorial jurisdiction of the United States. The Japanese did not always observe that limitation, and many vessels operating under the Japanese flag were actually American and British. Their captains simply changed flags to avoid the treaty obligations. That exacerbated enforcement problems for both the British and American governments.

"It is doubtful if the Bering Sea decision is one that either the Americans or British can afford to rejoice much over, because it is going to require both governments to maintain expensive fleets in Artic waters to prevent poachers from taking seals where and how they will, and that brings up the question whether the seals are worth all this trouble," one editor stated.[8] "The policy of spending the money of sixty five millions of people to protect game that can be enjoyed by a comparatively few aristocrats, and that is entirely beyond the reach of the masses, may well be open to objection."

Such opinions were none of Healey's or his cutter counterparts' concerns. Their mission was to stop poaching if they could until someone in authority told them not to. Enforcing anti-poaching laws became a top priority for the cutter crews for two primary reasons: there were fears among experts that seals and walruses in particular were on the brink of extinction and that the loss of the animals literally threatened the existence of the natives. That was not mere speculation, as Captain Healey demonstrated in an 1893 report after the *Bear* visited King's Island near the Siberian coast and sounded an alarm.[9]

About 200 natives inhabited the island. Healey found them short of provisions due to a bad hunting and fishing season. He reported that they were in actual danger of starvation. Healey left them enough food to bridge them over until sealing began. He realized that was a stopgap measure though, and that some government restrictions on the natives were hurting more than helping them.

The government forbid the natives from buying breech-loading arms, which would have facilitated their hunting. Instead they were restricted to antiquated weapons like spears with which to hunt the large animals that they needed for food, clothing, and other necessities of life, while poachers killed them by the thousands with sophisticated weapons. In his cruise report Healey called attention to the injustice of prohibiting the sale of those arms, especially as their lives depended on their hunting success. As he noted, the white men made seals and walruses so limited in numbers that the spears of the natives were no longer of any use. That explained in part why Healey had no use for poachers.

One reporter explained Healey's feelings.[10] "Captain Mike Healy of the revenue cutter *Bear*, who knows Bering Sea from the Aleutians to the Arctic, and is known to everybody in that region as the embodiment of Uncle Sam's power, usually stays about the seal islands later than anyone else, and the poacher who falls into Mike Healy's hands is likely to repent of his temerity," he wrote.

That rang true. Healey was a fair man who had the best interests of the natives at heart. Anyone who did them wrong was not his friend—and that included the poachers who had become a significant longstanding problem in the Arctic region. Because the area was so vast and communications were so slow it was difficult for authorities to enforce laws against poaching. The responsibility for enforcement fell on the shoulders of the Coast Guard crews. Therefore, the *Bear*'s crew was relentless in its pursuit of poachers, as were its counterparts on the other cutters in the region, often to no avail.

They worked in a pack to keep poachers off guard and in custody. Still, the question remained: was the anti-poacher mission cost effective or worth the effort? Essentially, the cutters were providing a government security and messenger service for a private company and risking a war in the process. Tension among nations with sealers known to engage in poaching was growing so high in 1890 that the Treasury Department put its cutter commanders on a full war preparation alert.[11]

A. C. Matthews, the department's first comptroller, traveled to Port Townsend to deliver orders personally for the commanders of the *Bear*, the *Rush*, and the *Corwin*, then returned immediately to Washington, D.C. The fact that a high ranking administrator would make that difficult journey just to deliver a message and then return at a time when travel was not easy highlighted how serious the poaching problem had become.

The commanders' orders were to patrol the Bering and seize all vessels they found with sealskins aboard or any other prima facie evidence that the vessels had been poaching. The crews were then to seize the captured vessels' papers and instruments and leave on board only a sufficient quantity of food to keep the crew until the vessel reached the nearest port. And, if any vessel resisted, it was to be fired upon and compelled to submit. That was serious business.

The commanders prepared immediately to sail to their assigned stations. Two or three British warships were doing the same, and U.S. authorities believed they were there to protect their sealers. Therefore, the Americans ordered their commanders to make sure that no British vessel was "outraged nor the British flag insulted."[12]

Healey was doing his part. He captured the sealer *Mattie Dyer* and ordered it to proceed to Sitka, where the case would be heard.[13] He ordered the ship's officers to be released. In November, Healey, who had been patrolling around the islands of St. Paul and St. George, was sailing south when he encountered the Coast Guard launch *Bertha*, which had instructions from the Treasury Department to sail to the seal islands and deter poachers. Healey did not think the *Bertha* was the right ship for the job.[14]

He believed that the *Bertha* was ill-equipped to cope with the icebergs and storms that were prevalent at that time of the year, so he took the instructions and sailed to the seal islands with a promise to carry them out until December 1. He was less concerned with poachers than he was with the bad weather the *Bertha* would be facing. Despite all the government warnings, diplomatic machinations, and statistical evidence contrary to predictions of extermination, Healey was not convinced that poaching was a significant problem in the Bering Sea region. He explained why when he returned to port. A reporter asked him whether he believed the seals there were being exterminated.[15]

> "Nobody can say unless thoroughly acquainted with the habits of the seals," he said. "I think there are probably as many seals as ever, but the bad weather this season may have caused the

small catch and confined the larger catches to only a few hunters." It must also be considered that it isn't the fault of the hunters if the seals are not almost exterminated, for the slaughter is indiscriminate and the nets, guns and spears used are the very best in modern, invention and American ingenuity. It should not be a matter of surprise if the seals refuse to herd as thickly as in former years.

Moreover, he noted, "Some captains told me that they have seen fur seals farther north this year than before. This may have been caused by scarcity of food or stormy weather." He added that he had not seen any evidence of poaching during his patrols. He even suggested that it was not worth their time to engage in the practice.

> I saw quite a number of suspicious vessels, but none of them were at work. I think it is a mistake to believe that poachers reap a harvest in the Bering Sea. You must know that at the present time the sealing vessels go south, some as far as the Mexican coast, and work their way north in search of seals. They arrange to reach Bering Sea by the middle of July, in time for the opening of the season there. By the middle of September, when the season closes, they return south.
>
> Now, if a poacher is caught with a big catch on board it is also altogether probable that the greater part of the cargo has been taken from the Pacific Ocean during the trip northward. You can then readily perceive that the poachers are not the principal exterminators of the seals. The modern appliances for killing and wounding the seals are to blame for the evil threatened.

He made it clear that this was his opinion, even if it didn't agree with other people's convictions. He complemented his discussion by giving a geography lesson:

> I have not been able to discuss with Alaskans the international difficulty over seal-hunting in Bering Sea. It was impossible to get very many men together at a given point on my cruise, and therefore I was unable to glean the ideas of the people up there on the subject.
>
> Why, in Western Alaska there are only 500 people, and that section of the country covers over 5,000 miles, so you see that any gathering of the residents would be very small. I learned nothing to determine me upon the views of the people on the international sealing troubles this season, and during my cruise little or nothing occurred to furnish me with anything new on the situation of affairs. The catch was small this season, the weather was very stormy, and there was but limited inducement for poaching anyway.

Despite his reservations critics wanted more protection for the seals. They pointed to the ongoing trouble over the poachers on St. Paul Island that emphasized the necessity of a better revenue cutter service in the surrounding waters, suggesting that a single crew of armed poachers could raid the island and cripple—if not destroy completely—the entire fur seal industry. That did not happen under Healey's watch, but it became a concern after the Japanese sealers grew more aggressive a few years later.

21

Five Killed, a Dozen Captured

> "*A large fleet of Japanese poachers operated near Alaska. In one encounter several of the Japanese raiders were killed, which demonstrated how bold and determined they were about killing the seals. Worse for the 'Coasties,' even when they apprehended some of the poachers the government just let them go after admonishing them not to do it again.*"[1]

Poaching was still a concern long after Healey was court-martialed and replaced. A new "villain" emerged as Japanese poachers started devastating operations in the region. That was not unexpected. Japan had just ended a victorious war against Russia in which its naval units were heavily engaged. After the war ended, and President Roosevelt brokered a peace treaty between the two belligerents, Japan's warships were freed to provide protection to Japanese commercial vessels if need be. Once again there were threats of war as a result. One particular incident set off fireworks.

Japanese poachers were threatening to the point that their government sent warships into the region to protect them even though Japan and the United States were allegedly on a friendly basis. The threat was not restricted to sealing though. The poachers were not above killing cattle and stealing farmers' and fishers' products to sustain themselves.

American and British farmers and fishermen who inhabited the 20 small, productive, Shumagin Islands, located in the Aleutians East Borough south of the mainland of Alaska, suffered great losses during the fishing season.[2] The poachers raided their pastures and killed cattle left grazing unattended on the island of Simeonoff. The farmers knew who killed the cattle, but since they couldn't identify the exact perpetrators or describe the precise vessels involved for the cutter commanders, there was nothing anyone could do except promise to provide more protection for the islands the following year. That was just one more task for the commanders.

Meanwhile, the *Bear*'s crew was assigned to conduct an official survey of the Northeast and Reef Points and forward charts with their findings to Washington, with Lieutenant Ward in charge of the survey. The government would adopt officially the soundings of the coast. Monitoring poachers' activities took priority over such tasks though, futile as it might have been at times.

In 1906 a fleet of Japanese vessels appeared near St. Paul. Captain Dunwoodie of the cutter *Perry* stopped the schooner *Tokwa Maru* on July 5, but there were no seals aboard, dead or alive.[3] The location of the stop showed how important the *Bear*'s Pribilof surveying activities were.

The topography was changing constantly. The *Perry* hailed the *Tokwa Maru* off a new volcanic island that had formed the previous March near Bogosloff, forty miles from St. Paul. New formations like that helped explain why so many cutters ended up on reefs or ran aground in places that changed from time to time and were uncharted. The stop raised Dunwoodie's suspicions about Japanese poachers in the area and he set sail immediately for the Pribilofs. His intuition was correct. The poachers had invaded the islands. They might not have if they knew how heavily armed the guards were.

The U.S. government protected the Pribilofs with more armaments than they did the nation's capital.[4] The guards, a corps of dedicated Aleut natives who were proud to serve their new country, were armed with the finest weapons of the time: Gatling (machine) guns, mountain howitzers, and Krag-Jorgenson rifles. Their firepower, combined with that carried by the cutters, formed a perimeter defense that seemed formidable enough to deter any poachers from raiding the rookeries. It didn't.

On July 17, 1906, four Japanese poaching vessels slipped through the fog to evade any cutters in the area and anchored off St. Paul Island.[5] Sealers went ashore, where native guards employed by the company shot and killed five of them, captured 12 more, two of whom were wounded seriously, and seized four of their boats. The raid was considered to be the most serious ever carried out on the rookeries there. It was certainly damaging for the Coast Guard, because the events left the islands unprotected and showed that no matter how many cutters it dedicated to patrolling two tiny islands it was not always enough.

The *Perry*'s cylinder pump broke on July 22 about a mile off shore and disabled the vessel. The *Thetis* was patrolling in the Arctic and the *Rush* was on duty at Nushagak, Bristol Bay. The *Bear* was not available at the time and the *McCulloch* had to transport the prisoners to Valdez. Critics had to wonder if the concentration on one small area in the vast coverage territory while depriving others was efficacious. They had cause for concern.

The lack of coverage notwithstanding, the *McCulloch* transported the captured poachers to the United States Court at Valdez, which was the venue for both the circuit and district courts. There they were indicted on August 18 for violation of the United States law enacted to protect fur-bearing seals.[6] U.S. officials hoped to throw the proverbial book at them, including a charge of piracy.

At best they would be charged with a violation of the United States Revised Statute forbidding the killing of any fur-bearing animal in the Alaskan Jurisdiction, which prescribed a penalty of not more than $1,000 and not less than $200 fine, or six months' imprisonment, or both, for each violation. The penalty for piracy would be more serious, but the Department of Justice ruled that it did not apply in this instance. Charges aside, the shootings occurred a little too late to help the seals.

The poachers had killed 200 of them—many of them pregnant females with nursing pups, who died of starvation—and carried away 120 skins.[7] It was determined later that the four vessels were part of a 12-ship fleet operating in the area despite the presence of cutters nearby. Apparently, the Japanese government was unaware of the incident for almost a month. Even when they found out about it, they did not seem too concerned about the killing of the poachers, treating it as a matter between civilians from two countries.

Therefore, it wasn't until August 9 that a representative appeared at a state department office for information about the slayings. Japanese government officials were not too happy about the shooting, but they had little recourse for complaint. According to international law seals were treated as property. Therefore, when Japanese nationals stepped on to American territory and captured seals they were considered thieves. Perhaps the guards were a bit overzealous in shooting the poachers, but they were within their rights. And the Japanese government was not party to any international treaty regarding sealing, so it had no standing in the matter.

Despite the fact that the law was on the Americans' side the Japanese did not accept that idea immediately. In August the Japanese government dispatched the third secretary of the Japanese legislation to Seattle, where he was picked up by the *Rush* and transported to Valdez to attend the trial of the Japanese poachers.[8] He was in for a circus.

The trial lasted for almost a week. The original indictments were quashed and a judge ordered the grand jury to return a corrected indictment. Five defendants pleaded guilty to avoid a trial and sentencing was deferred. Six more opted to undergo a trial by jury. The twelfth prisoner was scheduled for a standalone trial.

Three attorneys were appointed to defend the group of five, and they did an admirable job. A jury was selected, heard the evidence, and retired. They deliberated for almost a day, then said they could not agree on a verdict, so they were dismissed. A second jury was appointed. This one returned a verdict of guilty. The case against the one remaining defendant was turned over to the jury on August 30.

The outcome of the trials was not surprising. Eventually, even the Japanese government proved that the poachers' story was untrue.[9] The poachers had told government officials that they landed at St. Paul with no intention of hunting seals and the guards fired at them with no provocation. The Japanese investigators debunked that story. They determined that the sailors were in search of seals.

The truth was that the crew on one of the ships, the schooner *Toya Maru*, refused to work unless the captain would permit them to go ashore to club seals.[10] Once they got there and were detected they tried to escape. That is when they were shot. One of the four occupants of the boat that brought them ashore was shot in the chest and died soon afterward. His body was packed in salt and taken to Japan. Based on those findings the Japanese government determined that there was no cause for an international incident and let the matter drop. That did not put an end to Japanese poaching however.

There was a similar case in 1907 when a Japanese vessel named *Kaiwo Maru*, commanded by Captain Kadota, and 33 crew members were placed on trial for violating U.S. sealing laws.[11] Authorities alleged that they found two freshly killed seals, one a female, and a seal carcass still warm, in a boat 300 yards from shore at St. Paul Island. The defense admitted that the poachers had killed the seals but claimed they were shot outside the three-mile limit. The boat they were in near the shore had become lost in the fog trying to find the *Kaiwo*.

The trial was a waste of time. Even though some of the crew members were convicted and released, government officials ordered the authorities at Valdez to release the ship and the crew, but issued a stern warning that severe punishment would be meted out to the next poachers taken.[12] That had to make the cutter commanders wonder why they bothered enforcing the poaching laws. The government gave them cause to continue wondering.

The preponderance of sealers in the region the next year sailed under the Japanese flag. Cutter personnel boarded 30 vessels, 28 Japanese and two Canadian. There was only one land raid attempted. That was on July 22.[13] Two Japanese vessels closed in on Northeast Point near Saint Paul, the richest rookery in the islands, during a heavy fog and started taking seals within the three-mile American limit. Instead of seals they caught a *Bear*—or the *Bear* caught them. The *Bear* might not have been the fastest or most modern cutter on the seal watch, but it still caught its fair share of poachers.

A particularly good year was 1908 for the *Bear*, under the command of Captain E.P. Bertholf. One exciting chase in particular caught the nation's attention after the guards on St. Paul warned Bertholf of a threatened raid. Almost a year to the day after the 1907 incident that almost caused an international incident the guards spotted three daring—perhaps too daring—poachers from what was later identified as the *Kensei* (or *Hinser*),[14] with a crew of 32, nearing the island. The other was the *Saiki Maru*, with a crew of 27.[15]

The *Bear* happened to be patrolling nearby within the three-mile limit, so one of the guards rowed out and notified the captain that a raid might be imminent. He explained that for several days the guards had heard shots at regular intervals near the rookeries for some miles along the coast. They couldn't locate a ship because of

The Japanese sealing schooner *Kensei Maru*, seized by the *Bear* on July 21, 1908, for illegal sealing, at sea (USCG Historian's Office).

the fog. In fact, the guard said, they believed there was more than one vessel in the immediate vicinity. And, he theorized, if the three poachers they had seen close to shore were any indication, the crew of the unidentified sealer was preparing for an immediate raid on the island. That was all Bertholf needed to hear. The chase was on.

Bertholf dispatched Lieutenants Hinkley and Alexander and a few crew members in a small boat to find the sealer. They discovered a fishing boat with three Japanese aboard, who surrendered without resistance. The "Coasties" found two freshly killed seals in the poachers' boat. They took the poachers and the seals back to the *Bear*.

Bertholf set sail through the heavy fog in the direction from which the guards had reported the shooting. A half-hour later crew members heard several rifle shots coming from all directions and spotted half a dozen small boats directly under the *Bear*'s bow. They disappeared quickly into the fog, all going in one direction.

The *Bear* followed. The fog grew even denser, if that was possible. The crew noted that the small boats were scurrying to a schooner that was plainly visible from the *Bear*'s bridge. Surprisingly, the small boats took the *Kensei* in tow while the crew aboard unfurled sail and got into the wind which had just sprung up. They took aboard the boats one by one as the schooner gained speed under full sail, with the *Bear* close behind under full steam. Steam vs. wind: it was a battle of two technologies.

Kensei was a strange-looking vessel. It was painted in white in imitation of the cutter *Manning*. That didn't fool anyone aboard the *Bear*, since the *Manning* was in San Francisco at the time. The forward part of the ship was covered by papier-mâché. The disguise did not deter Bertholf.

He blew the *Bear*'s whistles frantically as a warning to the *Kensei* to stop. Not surprisingly, the fleeing target paid no heed. Bertholf barked orders from the bridge to load the *Bear*'s forward 10-pounder and aim it at the Japanese vessel. The crew held its fire as more whistles were sounded. The *Kensei* continued to sail into the fog. Bertholf was out of patience.

He ordered the gun crew to fire. Their first round whistled through the poachers' rigging. The *Kensei* finally got the message and stopped. The *Bear* captured its prize without further resistance. Then, the *Bear* took the *Saiki Maru* as a prize as well. Bertholf turned both vessels over to the cutter *Rush*, which escorted them to Unalaska. Government officials there took charge of the 60 poachers captured, the 600+ skins aboard the sealers, valued at $25 each, and the equipment aboard, worth $5,000. The government confiscated the vessels as well. It was a good day's work for Bertholf, but the story did not end there.

The poachers were not happy that they had been captured and held and lost their ships and equipment. They were placed under an armed guard in a church building while awaiting trial. None of them were manacled or restrained in any way. For the most part they were well behaved. That changed as time passed without a trial and some of the prisoners grew violent.

About dinner time on the evening of September 12, about twenty of them attempted to escape. Four prisoners attacked a guard named Butterworth and threw boiling tea into his face.[16] The guard fired his rifle and alerted the townspeople.

Twenty citizens picked up a variety of weapons, including iron bars from a blacksmith's shop adjoining the church, and raced to the guard's aid. They forced the prisoners back into the church before any of them could escape. That didn't work out well for the poachers. The government doubled the guard and there were no additional attempts at escape before the trial.

None of that concerned Bertholf. He was back at sea setting his sights on a Canadian poacher. He had sent a report to Washington on September 20 that Canadian fishermen had been engaged in seal poaching in Alaskan waters during the past summer. That, he emphasized, was in violation of the agreement between the United States and Great Britain.

Bertholf mentioned specifically the schooner *Thomas H. Bayard* as the alleged offender.[17] He said he had obtained the information from fishermen at Sanborn Harbor, Alaska. They alleged that the *Bayard* had 28 sealskins aboard in July that year. The allegations demonstrated that it was not only the U.S. government and the cutter commanders who were concerned about poaching. Citizens whose livelihoods were threatened were on board with enforcing the laws against it as well.

As for Bertholf, even though he did not apprehend the *Bayard*, he trusted that the Treasury Department would ask Great Britain to take action. But there was another wrinkle in the legal proceeding in the *Saiki Maru* case. Theoretically, what happened in the courts was of no concern to the cutter commanders. Their job was to capture the poachers and let the courts do theirs. But, the outcomes had to prey on the commanders' minds if they saw judges and juries negate their efforts with adverse decisions. The legal games with the *Saiki Maru* crew continued long after the *Bear*'s annual cruise ended in 1908.

Twenty-seven members of the ship's crew demanded their release from custody on Christmas Eve, the day after the 30 days provided for in their original sentence ended. They declared through their lawyer, H.S. Ritchie, that they were paupers.[18] Ritchie based the claim on Section 1,042, revised statutes of the United States. The section provided that where a person without money was sentenced to imprisonment, and fine, or to pay a fine in lieu of imprisonment, he could, after serving 30 days in excess of the fine imposed, avoid serving out the remainder of the fine and obtain his release by making an oath that he was a pauper. The court agreed to a hearing on the request.

The authorities agreed that there was no question that they were paupers under the law. In passing sentence on November 21, Judge Silas Reid had assessed a fine of $600 to $800 per defendant as a penalty in the case. In lieu of payment a financially limited defendant was sentenced to serve 300 days in jail at Valdez.[19]

The section of the statute under which the application was made was unequivocal, the only provisions being compliance with the specified form of procedure. The district attorney could resist the application. The only question at issue seemed to be one of jurisdiction. There was some doubt about whether or not a commissioner in Alaska had all the authority that went with the office in the states.

Notice of the application was served on District Attorney Crossley in Fairbanks, and it was expected that Assistant District Attorney Martin would be in Valdez in time to be present at a hearing set for January 11, 1909. That was the year two

Japanese armored cruisers were plying the waters in the vicinity of the Pribilofs, the location where most of the Japanese poachers apprehended were found. It was also the year when a federal judge officially signed an order approving of the forfeiture of *Kensei Maru* and *Saiki Maru*, which were sold at Unalaska by a U.S. marshal.[20] That, more than anything else, satisfied the cutter commanders whose role was vindicated.

The end of the poaching problem was fast approaching.

22

A Seemingly Hopeless Task

"We have expended millions in trying to save the seals on a rational basis, and thus far since 1890 we have been beaten and thwarted at every point."[1]

The *Bear* concentrated on apprehending seal poachers in 1909. There was, though, the occasional emergency to take Bertholf off his route—like providing taxi services for poachers and stranded workers. Side trips were diversions for the crew, but they took the *Bear* off its regular patrols. That was detrimental to the Coast Guard's anti-poaching duties.

On September 2, 1909, Seal Agent Judge apprehended six Japanese poachers in two boats off Walrus Island.[2] They had to be tried somewhere. The chosen site was San Francisco. The *Bear* was assigned to transport the poachers there for trial. It arrived in San Francisco in late September and returned quickly to its duty station. The *Bear* had barely started its patrols before it was diverted again. This new assignment was one of its most bizarre.

Bertholf was patrolling the Pribilofs in October when he received an urgent message to return to Nome. There were some men and women there who needed a ride back to Seattle. They were stranded in Nome after the Alaskan Development and Investment Company left them on their own.[3] The company had imported them from the states to work in its plant but then refused to pay them their season's wages. Somehow that became the Treasury Department's responsibility. That sounded like a simple mission. It was anything but.

Captain William V.E. Jacobs, the commander of the cutter *Manning*, who was at the Coast Guard office at Nome, volunteered the *Bear* to transport the workers back to Seattle. Communications were still a bit difficult between shore and sea, but Jacobs got a message to Bertholf via wireless and steamer that his services were required. That was timely.

The *Bear* and the *Thetis* had just been fitted with the Marconi system of wireless telegraph about the middle or latter part of May before returning to the Arctic for the summer cruise.[4] They joined many of the larger ships of the Coast Guard cutter fleet that now had wireless aboard. And, it was the Treasury Department's intention to equip all its vessels likewise in the near future. The *Bear* and its fleet partners were entering the 20th century communications-wise.

Bertholf returned immediately to Nome, but was surprised to learn that what sounded like a simple mission was a bit complex. On his arrival in Seattle, he discovered that the party he was transporting comprised 144 men and 12 women. That was too large a number for the *Bear* to accommodate under normal conditions. The inclusion of the women complicated matters. The innovative commander solved the problem quickly. He left the women behind under the care of the Nome city officials, who also supplied extra cooking and mess utensils for the unusual crowd on the cutter.

Then Bertholf set his industrious crew to work with hammers, saws, and nails. They constructed 61 bunks in the center of the ship and assigned two passengers to sleep in each of these by turns. The rest were furnished with hammocks. He left nothing to chance regarding safety either—and he did not intend to let everyone ride free if any of the passengers could afford to pay for the trip.

As the men boarded the *Bear* crew members searched them. Each individual's money was placed in an envelope with the owner's name on it, and each man received a receipt. The plan was to return their money when the *Bear* reached Seattle. The crew did not find anyone who had enough money to pay the passage, which was not surprising under the circumstances. After all the company had failed to—and could not—pay its workers.

To compound matters, three of them were physically challenged and unable to travel on the *Bear*. One of them was transferred to the *Thetis*. The other two, each with a fellow passenger to take care of them, were placed on board the *Manning*. Captain Jacobs' crew members apparently did a more careful search than the *Bear*'s. One of the sick men placed aboard the *Manning* was carrying $672.75, together with a watch, chain, and valuable papers. Another had $45.

Once everyone was settled the *Bear* set out from Nome to Seattle on October 9 via Unalaska, where it arrived on the 13th. The weather was bad there, so Bertholf decided to make the passage to Seattle through the Shelikoff Strait and then through the Inland Passage. That trip was no picnic either.[5] Even by taking this route the cutter was delayed two days by storms and severe gales. Nevertheless the party reached Seattle safely, no doubt happy to be back in the United States. It was a quick turnaround. Two weeks later the *Bear* captured a number of seal poachers on Walrus Island, one of the Pribilof group.[6]

According to a brief notice received at Treasury Department headquarters, several other poachers escaped in their boats. Those captured were taken to Valdez for trial, where they joined several Japanese poachers who had been snared by Special Agent Proctor Judge and transported by the *Perry*.[7] They were sentenced to three months imprisonment, $200 fines each, and deportation to Japan when their jail terms ended.

The episode once again triggered recommendations to the Treasury Department for more cutters to police the northern waters. But, since it was so late in the season the department deferred action for the time being. The request also highlighted a flaw in the patrol plan, which had plagued the service for years. Continually pulling cutters away from the islands to serve as water taxis was counterproductive. The system was not working.

There were too many sealers in the region for the Coast Guard to monitor. In

1908 there were 37 Japanese vessels alone. They were not fazed by the Coast Guard or even the U.S. Navy, which had dispatched the gunboat *Yorktown* to cruise the Bering to intimidate and apprehend sealers operating inside the restricted area. The Japanese were too coordinated to worry about the American Navy and Coast Guard enforcers.

The Japanese technique was simple.[8] Their 37 vessels, carrying a combined 210 small boats, formed a cordon through which breeding female seals had to pass when trying to reach the open sea in search of food. The seals could not bypass the cordon despite their great numbers since they were funneled into a trap by poachers in small boats.

Half a dozen Japanese schooners congregated near St. Paul and St. Matthew and lowered small boats which moved in toward the rookeries, using the fog as cover. When they got close to shore the poachers opened fire with shotguns. The noise spooked the seals, which stampeded into the water. The small boat poachers withdrew from the shore and waited until the fog lifted. When it did they slaughtered the seals at their leisure. The resulting losses were devastating—and unpreventable, since they took place in open water. U.S. government administrators recognized the folly of trying to stop the slaughter as time went on.

Secretary Oscar Straus of the Department of Commerce and Labor made that point clear in 1909 when he admitted that the date of extinction for the fur seals was approaching rapidly.[9]

> Long experience and painstaking investigation have demonstrated that pelagic sealing alone is responsible for the continuous diminution of this herd, and that no patrol, however great in numbers and active in duty, no measures of conservation, however wise and vigorous, can adequately avail for protection during the continuance of such destructive practice.
>
> The sixty-mile zone of exemption prescribed by the Paris convention was long ago found an insufficient safeguard, and since that safeguard has been swept aside by the intrusion of a new foe to the seal life the swift and certain extermination of this valuable animal, from a commercial standpoint, becomes a matter of near approach.

That was a startling admission. He didn't mention that pelagic sealing was only part of the problem caused by Japanese poachers that was draining Coast Guard resources. Other poachers were at work near Hawaii and the western Pacific islands exterminating birds to supply milliners in Europe and the United States with the feathers and plumes they needed to decorate fancy hats and dresses. That was as big a problem as pelagic sealing, and alleviating it fell under the Coast Guard's purview.

The service stationed a couple of cutters in the Hawaii region to deter the poachers. The *Thetis*, commanded by Captain W.V.E. Jacobs, had a modicum of success, but it couldn't do the job alone. The antiquated *Iroquois* was thrown into the effort, but it was of little help. The *Bear* was diverted to the islands to participate in the effort. That was quite a diversion for Captain J.G. Ballinger and his crew, who had to leave the frigid north and sail to a tropical environment located a seven-day voyage away.

The *Bear*'s reception was a bit disappointing. Locals were unhappy with one of the commander's decisions. Crew members uncovered a large cache of poached bird skins on one of the islands, but left it there.[10] Once the *Bear* left the scene the

Japanese had access to the skins, which the *Bear* was supposed to prevent. The *Bear* eventually returned to Alaska and resumed its normal patrol, with a new emphasis.

The cutter's new responsibility was to look out for walrus poachers.[11] A new law to prevent the destruction of walruses limited hunters to no more than one per year each. Walruses, like seals, were threatened with extinction by crews of poachers. Since the danger of extinction of birds in the Hawaiian Islands had passed and the thousands of birds on the heavily threatened Laysan Island were again nesting undisturbed by Japanese poachers due to U.S. enforcement efforts, the *Bear* returned to Alaska.

When he arrived Captain Ballinger found that the Japanese poachers hadn't gone anywhere, although they were posing less of a threat and the Japanese and U.S. governments were talking about a treaty to save the seals. A lot had happened during the *Bear*'s deployment to Hawaii to change the relationship between the U.S. and Japanese governments regarding the seal poaching situation. There was speculation that the Japanese government in particular was changing its usual stance of looking the other way when it involved protecting seals.

There was some suspicion that their government was subsidizing the Japanese poachers. Therefore, U.S. government and Coast Guard officers were worried that at some point there was bound to be trouble with the Japanese government over the sealing question. The *Manning*'s officers in particular were concerned about the suspected subsidies. They had spent the 1910 season cruising about the sealing grounds with the cutters *Perry*, *Bear*, and *Tahoma* to protect them from invasion by the Japanese. Dealing with poachers was one thing. Confronting the Japanese Navy for meddling on behalf of its citizens was another.

The Japanese positioned 25 schooners just outside the three-mile limit in 1910, along with one small boat and 816 men who were engaged in killing the unfortunate seals that swam away from the rookeries. They slaughtered an estimated 5,000 to 7,000 animals. Treasury Department officials were aware that the cutter commanders' responsibilities were limited to stopping the poaching. Dealing with the Japanese government had to be done at a much higher level. To everyone's relief several interested nations, including Japan, began negotiations to find a way to protect the seals.

The seal poaching situation spiraled out of control as more and more Japanese vessels reached the Bering. There needed to be a solution to the problem if any seals were to survive. Three solutions stood out. The poachers could continue their operations until they exterminated the animals. That would end the problem, but there would be no seals left to hunt. Or, they could voluntarily cease poaching and save the seals. That was not likely to happen, since its adverse economic impact would affect too many people, from hunter to end user.

The third, and most viable option, was for the countries most involved in protecting the seals to enter a treaty to stop the poaching. Door three was their final choice. Of course, that meant there was still a need of enforcement to make sure the poachers adhered to the terms of the treaty. That was the option the concerned countries chose.

The United States, Great Britain, Japan, and Russia concluded treaty negotiations on July 7, 1911, and set a date of December 15, 1911, for its implementation.[12] The formal adoption of the agreement marked one of the most important international conservation measures that had ever been effected up to that time. Moreover, it set a precedent for future pacts of its kind. Henceforth, it was hoped, the fur seals of the North Pacific Ocean would receive, for the first time ever, a form of protection that had become a necessity, rather than a wish. It provided a guarantee that the seals would be protected for the next fifteen years.

The agreement prohibited pelagic sealing completely. It placed the legitimate killing of surplus male seals on land under the direct control of the governments that signed the deal. The pact insured the rescue of the depleted fur-seal herds from commercial extinction and prohibited the citizens or subjects of the contracting powers from engaging in a wasteful, cruel occupation. Finally, hopefully, and perhaps most important, the treaty ended a lengthy interruption of international goodwill between and among some of the signatories. That part did not come to fruition, since several of them were at war on opposite sides three years later. The seals, however, had a respite. The poachers were a different story: they did not accept the terms of the treaty—or so it was suggested.

There were rumors in 1913 that a fleet of Japanese poachers was on its way to raid the coast of Alaska to make a clean sweep of the seals at various places along the coast.[13] No one was sure of where the rumors started, and not everyone believed them. One doubter said, "There seems to be no ground for the rumor that [*Thetis*] was sent north in a hurry to head off Japanese poachers. At least no further developments of that story have come."[14]

But one skeptic was not going to dissuade U.S. government officials from acting early. They were not taking any chances on their veracity. So, using the better safe than sorry defense, they prepared to head off the poachers if they materialized. It was a big "if." The *Thetis*, which was in Oakland for repairs, was ordered to sail immediately for Seattle. The overhaul could wait. Seattle would be the starting point from which it could intercept the poachers. The cutters already in Alaskan waters were placed on standby too. People along the Alaskan coast waited excitedly for the invasion—even though as of yet no one had accurate information about the source of the rumors.

Newspapers did nothing to quell the news. Instead, they fanned the flames. They declared that the raid was a certainty, and that the Japanese poachers had already started on their voyage from the Japanese coast. And, they announced, it was most likely that all the Coast Guard cutters available were sure to be sent to the Pribilof Islands. "If the reports as to the intentions of the Japanese are correct, they intend to make one grand raid," reporters claimed. "Their intention is said to have been discovered by agents of the United States who are stationed on the Japanese coast for the purpose."[15]

The reporters allowed that the Japanese government was undoubtedly doing its best in the spirit of international cooperation to prevent the raids and might even assist the U.S. government to capture the raiders. Rumors swirled and people waited in great anticipation for the poachers' arrival. They did not show up. Reports surfaced in August that the supposed Japanese poachers failed to materialize.[16]

Cutters *Northland* and *Unalga* tied up at dock in downtown Juneau, Alaska; note the government building visible on the hillside behind them (Alaska State Library Historical Collections).

Apparently they had been scared off by the presence of the cutters *Tahoma* and *Unalga*, which had been patrolling the Pribilofs for ten days. Their commanders reported that they had seen no evidence of any raid on the fur seal rookeries. Government officials speculated that word had been passed to the Japanese that an unusually elaborate campaign would be carried out against them during the season, which perhaps caused them to change their plans. Perhaps—but maybe they had never planned to come in the first place.

The great final showdown between poachers and seal protectors did not materialize and the crisis ended quietly. Finally, after a thirty-year struggle, the fur seal population was able to start rebounding from near extinction. The *Thetis*'s officers reported in 1913 the northern waters were remarkably free from poachers, and that the seals had been undisturbed for several years.[17] The seals were free to mate and the Coast Guard commanders and crew members were able to return to other duties, although they did not relax their oversight of the Pribilofs immediately.

Besides, there was another war looming to occupy the *Bear*'s operations. This one did not involve seals. First, there was another major rescue to complete.

23

The *Bear* and the *Karluk*

> "In August 1913, Karluk, a brigantine formerly used as a whaler, became trapped in the ice while sailing to a rendezvous point at Herschel Island. After a long drift across the Beaufort and Chukchi seas, in January 1914 the ship was crushed and sunk. In the ensuing months, the crew and expedition staff struggled to survive, first on the ice and later on the shores of Wrangell Island. In all, eleven men died before rescue."[1]

One of the *Bear*'s most celebrated missions involved its attempt to rescue the members of the crew of the schooner *Karluk* in 1914, although it played a minor role. The fact that it was involved captured the nation's attention. Just how involved was unimportant.

The *Karluk*, which had barely escaped being trapped in the ice at Point Barrow in 1897-98, was the wrecked flagship of an expedition led by Canadian explorer and anthropologist Vilhjalmur Stefansson to find a rumored polar continent, which was the "Holy Grail" for the numerous explorers in the region at the time to chart channels, explore islands for minerals, and study the natives. Its captain in 1897, A.H. McGregor, had left a significant portion of the ship's supplies at Point Barrow to help the stranded whalers survive the winter and then escaped to San Francisco. The ship would not be as lucky a second time.

After the *Karluk* was stranded in ice in 1914 Stefansson bought a new ship, the *Polar Bear*, and continued on his expedition, leaving half his party behind. No one knew where Stefansson was, let alone *Karluk*'s location. The latter was not surprising; it had been destroyed by ice and its crew and explorers were stranded. That set off a wide search in the northland.

It was not uncommon for ships to get trapped in the ice in the north in the late 1800s and early 1900s.[2] Some captains were prepared for that eventuality and laid in extra stores or escape mechanisms such as dog sleds and hunting equipment to tide them over until they were rescued or their ships were crushed by ice and sunk. Those who were less prepared put their crews and vessels at risk of death.

In any case, when a ship was at risk captains of various vessels and the Coast Guard felt a moral and ethical duty to send out rescue missions. That was not always easy even in 1914, since communications about stranded ships were still often as slow to travel as was a whaler in an ice field. Wireless radio was in its infancy and not all ships were equipped with communications gear. Relayed transmissions increased rescue times, hampered coordinated efforts, and heightened the dangers for trapped sailors of succumbing to hunger, disease, madness, or other conditions that meant death. There was no time to waste for rescuers, which was highlighted in the case of the *Karluk*.

Rescue efforts to save the 22 (some sources say 25) persons stranded on Wrangell Island were initiated as soon as word of the *Karluk*'s plight was received at various places in the region. The location made the effort difficult. Wrangell Island was surrounded at all times by grounded icebergs and landing was difficult, even in midsummer. That was not unexpected in the area—but it did not deter rescuers from carrying out their duty.

The *Bear* left Nome on September 5 to do what it could. The Russian steamer the *Taimyr* and the trading schooner *King and Wing* were already in the Arctic trying to take off the castaways.[3] A fourth ship, the former revenue cutter *Corwin*, was set to leave Nome the same day as the *Bear* to aid in the rescue. Jatfet Lindberg, a millionaire mining magnate and reindeer herd owner, had advanced the money to outfit and provision the *Corwin* as a rescue vessel. Captain Dick Healey, no relation to the *Bear*'s former commander Michael, was in command of its crew of specially selected personnel. The *Corwin* carried Eskimos, dogs, sledges, and skin boats.

The *Bear*'s newly appointed captain, Claude Stanley Cochran, known to most people simply as C.S., who had extensive experience in the Arctic region, released a report dated August 23, 1914.[4] In it he revealed that he had been at Point Barrow on July 30 and also had stopped at Cape Prince of Wales on his way to Nome without finding any trace or hearing any news of the explorers, nor had any of the other Coast Guard cutters searching in the region. The report didn't reach Washington, D.C., until September 17, by which time the party—or what was left of it—had been rescued.

"No vessel had passed Point Barrow from the eastward," Cochran reported. "And no news had been heard of the Canadian Arctic expedition nor Stefansson himself." At the time of the report the *Bear* was at Unalaska, which was 800 miles from Nome. It was not particularly safe at that point for ships to go north before the following spring, when the ice would break up in the Bering Straits. But the *Bear* was not just any ship. It was considered as good an ice boat as any that existed in the region, except for explorer Roald Amundsen's *Fram*, which had been built specially for Arctic exploration.

Soon, word was received that the party had been located by the crew of the *King and Wing*, captained by Olaf Swenson. The *Bear* was dispatched to pick the survivors up. There did not seem to be any rush. Friends of the persons marooned on Wrangell Island were sure they were safe and could wait a little longer for rescue. They had plenty of food, it was believed, since the great numbers of wild birds that should have arrived on the island were good sources of food that provided them with a change of diet. And, the friends surmised, even during the winter the explorers were able to travel about freely on their dog sleds to kill game. Captain Cochran took those suppositions into account as he prepared for his voyage to Wrangell Island.

He reckoned that as long as he was going there he might as well drop off some mail at Point Barrow. Normally, it took ten days to sail from Nome to Point Barrow, and there was no guarantee that any ship that made it there would make it out. A year earlier only eight ships, the *Bear* among them, had visited Point Barrow. Only one, the *Bear*, found its way back out into southern waters, and that was after it had been trapped in the ice for a few days.

Wrangell Island lay 675 miles northwest of Nome in a straight line. Cochran had no idea how long it would take for the *Bear* to reach the island. There were too many variables. He did not know the ice conditions, and the ice in the Arctic that summer was unusually bad. Worse, Wrangell Island was always surrounded by ice.

Before he set sail he took aboard Captain Robert Bartlett, former master of the *Karluk*, who had gained his knowledge of the Polar Regions while serving under Admiral Peary on the successful dash to the North Pole in 1911. Bartlett had left the camp on Wrangell Island the previous March and made his way to North Cape and across Siberia to the Bering with a dog team and an Eskimo companion to notify authorities of the party's plight and location.

Also aboard were Mr. Shields, of the United States Bureau of Education; the Rev. Mr. Hoare, a missionary headed for Point Hope; Mr. Train, a movie maker; and Mr. Hersey. Train and Hersey had been with the *Bear* since its departure from Seattle and went along for the ride to Wrangell Island. The *Bear* also carried two sled dogs. Bartlett and Cochran would meet again later under different circumstances.

Cochran was not taking any chances. The dogs would be helpful if he could not actually reach the island. As an extra precaution he planned to pick up other dogs in Siberia. He had sleds and every appliance he needed for a dash over the ice if a landing on the island from boats could not be made. As it turned out, it couldn't. Once everything was in place the *Bear* left Nome on July 25, 1914, and made the pick-up safely, although it did not have to go all the way.

The *King and Wing* had set out for Nome with the survivors on board. The *Bear* met it 75 miles away from the island. After Swenson gloated a bit about beating the *Bear* to Wrangell he agreed to transfer the survivors to the cutter since it had better medical facilities. And, to Cochran's surprise, Swenson added a cat to the mix.[5] The *Karluk*'s crew had "enlisted" it the previous year in Victoria, British Columbia. The cat had survived all the same hardships as the crew.

Cochran tried to contact the *Corwin* via his wireless set. The *Corwin* was reportedly still at Wrangell in the belief that the *Karluk* party was there. Cochran wanted to advise him that he had the survivors, but he could not get a message through. The *Bear* could hear the *Corwin* but the opposite was not true. Cochran gave up the attempt and continued on his way to Nome. En route he forwarded a terse report so the people there would know what to expect[6]:

> *Bear* is now returning to Nome with the following members of the Canadian Arctic expedition: Munro, Williamson, McKinley, Hadley, Ohaf, Templeman, Williams, Maurer, and Eskimo family.
> All doing well under care of the surgeon. Will arrive Nome Sunday [Sept. 13].
> Party was rescued by [the gasoline] schooner *King and Wing* on September 7. Transferred to *Bear* September 8. latitude 69 degrees, 55 minutes north. longitude 175 degrees, 30 minutes west.

> Malloch and Mamen died of nephritis. Brady accidentally shot. There are eight missing persons who never reached Wrangell Island. The *Bear* reached within 12 miles of Herald Island. Clear weather and heavy ice. Unable to land on the island, but no signs of life....

For Cochran and the *Bear* it was just another mission completed. He and his crew had made their last run north for the season and would head to Seattle. But, they would be back in the spring as the *Bear*'s cycle continued. That was its routine, which comprised missions that were anything but routine that it carried out year after year at or near the "Top of the World." There was some question, though, as to whether the *Bear* and the other ships involved in the rescue mission had been duped by Steffanson, who might have staged the entire affair[7]:

> Two years ago after the loss of the *Karluk* a man who is now on the staff of the Gateway wrote in an outside publication that the whole thing about the loss of Steffanson was a fake pure and simple, and also that Steffanson would come to life again after having disappeared long enough to advertise himself. That Steffanson is a faker is a belief shared by many other people who know the man....
>
> Anyone who knows anything about those coasts up around Herschel Island knows that Steffanson could have let it be known that he was alive long ago if he wanted to. As a matter of fact the whole expedition was a fiasco from beginning to end....
>
> After the blowing away of the Karluk Steffanson telegraphed outside that he left her on September 20 when he thought she was held safely in the ice for the winter, but any old-timer in those waters will tell you that any man who believed a vessel was securely held in the ice at that time of the year must have known nothing about it. If Steffanson did know it he could only mean that he deserted the ship and left his companions to their fate while securing his own safety....
>
> One had only to know Steffanson and his outfit to become mighty skeptical to say the least.

Whether those allegations were true or not was of no interest to Captain Cochran or his civilian counterparts when the initial call for help reached them. They had a duty to perform, and they did it. All they knew was that fellow seafarers' lives were at risk. Saving them was the primary mission. That was first and foremost in the minds of Cochran and his crew. The rescue of the *Karluk's* survivors was just one more testament to Semper Paratus.

24

The *Bear* and the Explorers

> "*I desire especially to commend Capt. Thomas Ross of this station for his gentlemanly and courteous treatment, coupled with his efficient management of this outpost coast guard service on the Bering Sea. Seafaring men generally appreciate the retention of this station, and are unanimous in its praise as a credit to the coast guard service.*"—Captain Raold Amundsen[1]

One major difference between the *Bear* and the *Northland*'s timelines was the era of exploration. The *Bear* operated during the "golden age" of Arctic exploration. In fact, the *Bear* had gone farther north than most of the noted explorers before they reached the North Pole, some of whom were on a first name basis with its captains. Between 1884 and 1921 the *Bear* had aided an estimated twenty explorers and countless miners.[2] By the time the *Northland* made its first voyage north, the golden era was all but over and exploration methods had changed due to upgraded technology.

Rescues by the *Bear* in particular were more likely to be spur-of-the-moment than those carried out by the *Northland*. One salient reason was the upgraded communications equipment installed on the newer cutter. News to and from the vessel was quicker, whereas the *Bear* often came upon folks in need of help either by accident or through news relayed from ship to ship, ship to shore and back to ship, or some other slow means. Lieutenant Jarvis effected one of the more notable rescues along those lines in the summer of 1898, at the height of the gold rush in Alaska.

The *Bear* was heading north to Point Barrow on its regular summer trip. During a stop-over at Cape Prince of Wales Jarvis learned of some awful destitution battering the flood of gold seekers at Kotzebu Sound.[3] The ship diverted there, where the crew found a devastating state of affairs. Men had died of starvation and scurvy, and by drowning. Jarvis obtained an initial list of 48 deaths, which by all accounts was nowhere near complete.

Jarvis learned that over 1,000 gold seekers had wintered at Kotzebu. The *Bear*'s crew relieved as much of the residents' distress as possible and left stores, lime juice, etc., for the survivors. They transported 82 of the survivors to St. Michael, and turned them over to the military authorities there. Jarvis noted in his July 30 report from St. Michael that he had left between 225 and 250 survivors at Kotzebu Sound. He informed headquarters that the *Bear* would continue its trip to Point Barrow and upon its return would go into Kotzebu and pick up anyone else who desired to return with him. His report read in part:

First Lieutenant Bertholf and Surgeon Hawley were sent to the camp at Hotham Inlet. They returned with 32 sick and convalescent attacked with scurvy. Some of these were in a very low condition and the chances are would not have survived many days without medical attention. From 225 to 250 people were still in the camp.

Some had plenty of food and means of paying their way out. Returning to the camp Lieutenant Bertholf and the surgeon brought off all those in a destitute condition or without means; 48 men, two women and an infant, making 53 persons in all taken from the camp.

It was not possible to take any more at that time, but assurances were given the people ashore that if they did not succeed in getting away before the vessel's return they would be taken out by the *Bear*.

There were plenty of provisions for the use of those remaining, many of them having a year's outfit. The only sick person remaining was Mrs. Smith, whose case was so serious that she could not be moved.

The bark *Alaska*, of San Francisco, was expected to arrive and the steamer *Townsend* passed in as the *Bear* left. The charterer of the *Townsend*, Mr. C.D. Lane, assured me that he would take out all who wished to go. Many, if not all, will be able to leave by these two vessels, but upon my return from the Arctic I will clean the beach of all who remain. The rush of people to Kotzebu Sound was a sad, deplorable affair.

Jarvis had seen a lot of suffering in his career in the Arctic region. This episode seemed to bother him more than most, however, because he felt that the miners had been duped by opportunists. Jarvis's closing reveals his sadness over the senseless loss of life:

Misled by false information and advertisements, 1,200 people, many totally unfitted to stand hard conditions and climate, rushed to the country during the open season of 1898, and during the winter no gold whatever was found, and in the spring they sought every means of escaping from the region. Many were drowned in the swift currents of the rivers in the fall of 1898, others lost their lives during the winter from the cold and, worst of all, in the spring scurvy broke out in nearly all the camps.

I enclose a list of 48 deaths. These are all that could be gathered from the people at Hotham inlet, but I have no doubt that many others occurred that were not recorded and could not be learned of. I apprehend also that many of those who started coasting along the shore for Cape Nome may have lost their lives.

It was a sad time for Jarvis and the *Bear*, but things would get better for visitors in Alaska as time passed and technology evolved. There were signs toward the end of the *Bear*'s service in the far north that the need for cutter rescues was diminishing. Nevertheless, the *Northland*'s designers took explorers into account. The cutter included a boom rigged for hoisting an airplane.[4] If any airborne explorer needed assistance at sea the *Northland* could pluck his aircraft from the water and carry it to land. Some explorers were not impressed.

The changes in methods were so noticeable that one famous explorer who had figured in one of the *Bear*'s adventures decided to quit exploring. Valhjalmur Stefansson, who had resurfaced after the *Karluk* incident, said in 1924 that he was quitting the business.[5] "Aircraft inventions have taken the joy out of the work," he said, noting that discovery in itself was not the sole lure of the men who braved the dangers of far places. "Modern inventions, bringing with them ease, safety, comfort and certainty of attainment, have made exploration and discovery more or less humdrum pursuits," he advised. But, Steffanson was appreciative of the new methods. He concluded that the dirigible airship *Shenandoah* would negotiate an upcoming proposed polar flight without mishap and add the "Arctics" to the world's map.

The veteran Norwegian adventurer Captain Raold Amundsen agreed with Stefansson about the future of exploration being conducted via aircraft, but he wasn't sure that dirigibles were the way to do it.[6] And, he added, he had no intention of using aircraft to explore. His belief that dirigibles would not work was prophetic. Amundsen said in 1927, about the same time Charles Lindbergh completed his historic solo flight from New York to Paris, that any future traveling he would do in the Far North would be with rod and gun. "Exploring will all be done from the air in the future," he predicted. "I am too old to take up flying and I do not intend to start anything which I cannot carry out myself." Then he made a startling admission. "My trip on the dirigible *Norge* over the Arctic Regions was a mistake," he allowed. "Commander Nobile was a flier and I am an explorer. We did not see things alike."[7]

He also commented on another Arctic plane expedition. "The Wilkins expedition was a mistake from the beginning and Wilkins should never have attempted to carry on flights from Fairbanks as a base. He should have used Point Barrow for a base. Wilkins was too obstinate." He was referring to a March 1927 flight in which the Australian Sir Hubert Wilkins and pilot Carl Ben Eielson explored the drift ice north of Alaska by plane, landing on it in the first land-plane descent onto drift ice.[8] They took soundings at the landing site that indicated a water depth of 16,000 feet, from which Wilkins hypothesized that future Arctic expeditions would take advantage of the wide expanses of open ice to use aircraft in exploration.

Wilkins also made an attempt to be the first to cross under the North Pole in a submarine. He failed in his attempt, but he proved that submarines were capable of operating beneath the polar ice cap. That discovery, too, paved the way for future successful missions and suggested that cutters like the *Bear* and the *Northland* would soon be out of the explorer rescue business.

Coast Guard cutter captains in the Arctic region were no doubt pleased to hear about the new trend in exploring, since it would mean less risk for them and their ships in the future. For the nonce, though, they did not have the option of quitting their efforts to aid explorers, whether they were on foot or in the air. If explorers insisted on exploring, cutter captains would have to keep coming to their aid, even if it meant losing their own crew members in the process, as the *Bear* had done in the past.

On June 6, 1891, four members of the cutter's crew drowned at a place called Icy Bay.[9] They were transporting members of a Mount St. Elias exploring party led by noted geologist Professor Isaac Cook Russell to land. Their boat capsized in the heavy surf in the bay. The drowned crew members were Lieutenant Robinson and Seamen Anderson, Nelson and Henry Smith. W.C. Moore, a member of the exploring expedition, also drowned. Lieutenant Robinson left behind a wife who lived at Port Townsend.

In October 1891 the crew of the *Bear*'s counterpart cutter *Corwin* visited Lieutenant Robinson's grave at Sitka before leaving port. The *Corwin*'s officers and crew made a headboard of Alaska cedar and placed it at Robinson's burial site. The inscription on the board read: "In memory of Lieutenant L.L. Robinson, U.S.R.M., drowned with a boat's crew at Icy Bay, Alaska, in the performance of his duty, June 6, 1891. Erected by the *Corwin*."

Once again the officer got the glory and the crew members' names were overlooked. Regardless, the tragedy demonstrated the perils Coast Guard members, officers and enlisted alike, faced while performing their duties. Death did not recognize ranks. Officers and crew members sometimes died, and their losses were felt keenly regardless of their ranks and ratings. Death was not always a certainty for "Coasties," but uncertainty was a way of life for them.

Explorers may have found new ways to chart the Arctic region, but they still faced one significant obstacle: uncertainty. The adventures of Raold Amundsen, who combined planes and ships to enhance his exploration expeditions, proved that. He had discovered the South Pole and conquered the Northwest Passage, and was determined to reach the North Pole regardless of the risks involved. He opted to incorporate airplanes in his new venture. In 1921 Amundsen, a pilot himself, purchased two planes to carry aboard his ship the *Maud*, which turned it into one of the first aircraft carriers, albeit non-naval. He hired two Norwegian aviators to assist him in his next effort to reach the North Pole and set out in the fall.

Amundsen's original plan was to drift aboard the *Maud* with the Arctic ice pack to the North Pole. That plan went awry quickly. Both of the ship's propellers were damaged by the ice off the Siberian coast.[10] The *Bear* was summoned in July to tow the *Maud* into the Bering. The cutter towed it into Whalen, Siberia, about 200 miles from Nome, until the weather moderated and then continued 100 miles south of St. Lawrence Island, from where the *Maud* sailed to Seattle under its own sails for repairs. That delayed the expedition by one year. Amundsen restarted for Nome in 1922.

It was a good thing for some mariners in the region that the *Bear* went to the *Maud*'s rescue. At about the same time, the cutter's crew discovered the wrecked American schooner *Gertrude* a few miles from East Cape, Siberia, where it was beached in a sinking condition.[11] The *Bear*'s crew rescued the *Gertrude*'s sailors. Then, for good measure, the *Bear* saved from St. Lawrence Island Dr. F.F. Bruning and Dell Bishop, who were shipwrecked there the previous fall after they had drifted about for days in a frail boat in one of the worst storms of the season. Bruning and Bishop had spent the entire winter on the island subsisting on food furnished by the natives.

These rescues were all made while the *Bear* was actively searching for the missing schooner *Ram*, which was ten days overdue on its voyage en route from Teller, Alaska, to Nome, with an unknown cargo and number of passengers aboard. The *Bear* apparently never located the *Ram*. The multi-tasking was all in a season's work for the *Bear*'s crew.

On June 28, 1922, Amundsen left Nome aboard the *Maud* to begin his long voyage across the North Pole, which he hoped to finish by plane. Amundsen was bound for Point Barrow, from where he hoped to fly over the North Pole to Spitsbergen or Grants Land, Norway. That was not going to happen.

It was a festive day for the people of Nome. They gave Amundsen a royal send-off.[12] There were ceremonies ashore before he left, after which the crew of the *Bear* led him to his ship. Every available craft in the area escorted him out of the harbor. Captain Thomas A. Ross, commander of the Nome Coast Guard station, was at the *Maud*'s helm for the first ten miles in a procession led by Captain Cochran and the *Bear*. It was not the last Cochran would see of Amundsen.

Keeping track of Amundsen was a difficult task. In July he boarded the schooner the *Holmes* and apparently reached Point Barrow some time before the *Bear* arrived there in August. Captain Amundsen said that he had definitely abandoned, for this year at least, his plan for the airplane flight. Instead, he planned to make it in 1923. His takeoff had been delayed by unfavorable ice conditions and the season was too far advanced to permit success. Besides, his plane and equipment were at Wainwright, 100 miles southwest of Point Barrow. Wainwright would be the base for his 1923 flight. He added a side note: the *Maud* was frozen in the ice near Wrangell Island, but he expected to rejoin it by airplane before then.

Trying to find a vessel frozen in the ice in the Polar Regions was akin to locating a message written in brown ink on a specific grain of sand in the Sahara Desert. Finding the *Maud* was not an easy task, even though it had a state-of-the-art (for the time) radio system installed. There was much to be learned about radio transmissions then, so no one could rely on them.

It was one of the oddities of radio, unexplained at the time, that a sending radio possessed during daylight hours only a fraction of the range that the same equipment had at night.[13] Transmissions from the *Maud*'s system, as up to date and efficient as it was, could not always be received with clarity across the wastes that separated it from civilization while the sun shone. That was a continual problem during the Arctic summer with its eternal sunshine.

By September 1923 the north Polar Regions were set to undergo their long period of night. That would make it easier for messages to get through, but it still didn't help Cochran find the peripatetic Amundsen. The last Captain Cochran knew Amundsen was back at Wainwright, according to a radio message he sent Ross in late August 1922. He and the *Bear* had better things to do than chase Amundsen all over the Arctic region. Besides, there was a limit to where the *Bear* could sail.

As promised, Amundsen set out once again for the North Pole in 1923. His plan was to fly to the pole and meet the *Maud*. Unfortunately, in October that year the *Maud* was reported stuck in the ice 400 miles from the North Pole with seven men and two years' worth of supplies aboard. This time the *Bear* could not come to its rescue, but its brushes with explorers continued.

More than likely Cochran was happy to hear Amundsen say in 1926 that "My work is fulfilled" in speaking about polar exploration. He could only agree with a reporter's comment that "[Amundsen] regrets that there are no more poles to be found."[14] If there were they were not going to be found with the help of dirigibles.

Fate stepped in and curbed the use of dirigibles for exploration. In 1925 noted explorer Donald MacMillan declared that big dirigibles were best for Arctic exploration.[15] He cited two of them, the U.S. Navy airships *Shenandoah* and *Los Angeles*, as the type of craft best suited to overcome the hazards that the Far North presented to explorers. They had one major drawback though: the continually drifting ice floes. MacMillan explained that their constant movement made it impossible for the heavier-than-air machines to land on them.

Then, in September 1925 tragedy struck. The *Shenandoah* crashed in a storm in Ohio, killing 14 of its crew members. The Navy moved immediately to halt dirigible operations pending an investigation of the crash. From that point on Arctic airborne explorations were carried out by airplanes. That was still a concern for the *Bear* and the *Northland* when it took over.

At just about the same time that MacMillan recommended the use of dirigibles, Amundsen announced that he had perfected his financial plans for a flight in the summer of 1926 from Spitsbergen, Norway, over the North Pole and the unknown Arctic and Alaska regions. It was a good thing neither explorer needed the services of the *Bear* that day. It had just arrived in Nome after having run aground on the shoals off the coast of Cape Prince of Wales a few days earlier.

Covell had sent a message to Captain Dodge informing him that the *Bear* had run aground, but had floated off the shoals at 2:15 a.m. on August 12, 1925.[16] The cutter had proceeded to Cape Prince of Wales, a small village, where it was anchored safely in seven fathoms (42 feet) of water. Damage to the vessel was minimal. It had lost a shoe under the keel, but there was no leaking. "As soon as weather moderates we will proceed to Nome," Covell said, as if the ship had sustained a flat tire. "I have sent a wire to the *Algonquin*, which is coming to our assistance, stating that she is not needed."

A passing freighter, the *Oduna*, which was 568 miles north of Akutan, wired authorities in Seattle on August 13, 1925, that the *Bear* had succeeded in getting back to deep water again. There was no need for any response from rescuers. The *Algonquin* returned to Unalaska, the *Oduna* continued to Seattle, and the *Bear* resumed its patrol. Nothing to see here!

Cochran had a passing acquaintance with the introduction of dirigibles as exploration vehicles. One of the passengers aboard the cutter when it left Seattle on May 15, 1924, for its annual summer cruise in Arctic waters was Robert Bartlett, the former master of the *Karluk*, which the *Bear* had aided ten years earlier.[17] He was going north to map the proposed route for the 1925 flight of the dirigible *Shenandoah* across the Polar Regions and into the unexplored territory of the north. He had a commission from the national geological society and the cooperation of the United States Navy in his work. He gained his knowledge of the Polar Regions while under Peary on the successful dash to the North Pole in 1911.

Lieutenant Commander Richard Byrd, a U.S. Navy aviator, made it clear that the end of land exploration of the Arctic regions was all but over on May 9, 1926, when he became the first person to fly over the North Pole.[18] He accomplished the feat during a 15-hour round trip from Spitsbergen. That marked a decided change in one phase of the Coast Guard cutters' duties in the Arctic. The explorers appreciated the cooperation the Coast Guard had provided over the years, which Amundsen addressed in a June 1922 letter to Commandant Captain Reynolds.[19]

Amundsen outlined specific instances where Coast Guard representatives had extended the expedition "many courtesies" and valuable service. He wrote:

24. The Bear and the Explorers

Being about to weigh anchor at this port upon a voyage of research and discovery across the north pole, and you have granted permission to Capt. Thomas Ross, boatswain of coast guard station No. 305 at Nome, Alaska, to accompany my vessel, the *Maud*, as far as Grant's Harbor. I take this occasion to express to you personally and to the coast guard service generally my deep appreciation for the many courtesies extended me in these northern waters.

Upon my arrival in Bering sea from the northwest passage, on September 1, 1906, in the schooner *Gjoa*, Capt. Ross of the Nome life guard service met us at sea and piloted us to the port of Nome; again, upon my arrival from the northeast passage on July 30, 1920, and my arrival again here on June 21, 1922, the Nome coast guard service has assisted me in every possible way, for which I am deeply grateful.

I desire especially to commend Capt. Thomas Ross of this station for his gentlemanly and courteous treatment, coupled with his efficient management of this outpost coast guard service on the Bering Sea. Seafaring men generally appreciate the retention of this station, and are unanimous in its praise as a credit to the coast guard service.

That was high praise for the service, but it was earned. Even though neither the *Bear* nor its crews were cited specifically, they deserved credit for their aid to explorers over the years, which finally ended in 1927, when the *Northland* took over the northern patrol. It was just as well. The *Northland* would soon have a much more important mission: to participate in a war, which the *Bear* had never done. The tide was turning for the two cutters as the transition from the "Old" to the "New" Coast Guard occurred.

25

The *Bear* Goes into Hibernation

> *"And mothering this busy brood is the veteran battler of Arctic ice, the* Bear. *The* Bear *is a name that many times has stirred the world with its exploits of daring."*[1]

There had been rumors afloat for years in Washington, D.C., that it was time to retire the *Bear*. Its lack of modern technology had caught up with it and there was no longer a need for a wooden-bottomed icebreaker in the fleet. The fact that it had survived as long as it did in the north land was a miracle in itself.

The *Bear* had not played much of a role in World War I. For that matter, neither had the Coast Guard. The most significant effect on the service was a loss of personnel who left for seagoing positions that paid more but posed more risk. Many "Coasties" who received higher wages paid for the change with their lives.

There was not much going on in Alaska during the war. The *Bear* was more likely to see walruses than enemy warships; they seemed to have returned to the Bering.[2] Officers of the *Bear* reported that an enormous herd of walruses was seen on the lower edge of the Arctic ice pack during a 1919 trip along the coast. They sighted thousands upon thousands of the huge animals, which was an unusual occurrence. But it had nothing to do with the war that had just ended.

About the most exciting thing the *Bear*'s crew did during the war was transport dogs and down. In 1916 crew members were still involved to some extent with the reindeer industry their predecessors had started years earlier. In June the *Bear* carried two white Scotch collies to Point Barrow.[3] The dogs were destined to herd reindeer up there. They were being transferred from a comfortable home in Wisconsin to the bleak stretches of the tundra around Point Barrow. Those two collies were the first dogs ever sent so far north from the states for reindeer herding, although there were several of their breed caring for government herds around Nome and St. Lawrence Island. It was fitting that they were riding on the *Bear*, which was a pioneer in Alaskan marine animal transport services. Ironically, a photo of the collies aboard the cutter was taken with Miss Frances Cochran, the daughter of Captain Cochran, at their side.

Another less-than-exciting service rendered by the *Bear* was the portage of 400 pounds of down from Point Hope to Juneau for use at the hospitals in France.[4] The Eskimos and non-natives at Point Hope were extremely patriotic and one of the few ways they could help the U.S. government was to produce material that would help the troops. Governor Riggs explained that Alaska supported twenty beds in the Red Cross hospital at Neuilly, France, all of which were named for Alaskan towns. Such were the contributions of the *Bear* to World War I operations. It was business as usual—but an essential business. At least Captain Cochran still had a crew to command.

In the early days of the war commercial maritime companies were desperately seeking experienced sailors to man their convoy and blockade-running merchant vessels. British and Scandinavian ships in particular were offering bonuses of $1,000 and more to men who could make officer grades. The lure of high wages enticed hundreds of Coast Guard members to leave the service to become mates, boatswains, engineers, quartermasters, etc., on boats converted from junk heaps and loaded with explosives, weapons, and other valuable military materiel that invited attacks from enemy warships and submarines.[5]

Many of these merchant ships, some of which were less than seaworthy to begin with, crossed—or tried to cross—the ocean alone without convoys or naval escorts. That made them extremely vulnerable targets, and many of them succumbed to enemy attacks. Sadly, large numbers of the ex–Coast Guard personnel never completed their voyages. Most of them ended up at the bottom of the North Sea or in the waters off the Irish coast.

A few survived, some of whom became masters of ships. Others returned to the Coast Guard and resumed their lives at isolated stations. Meanwhile, rumors about the *Bear*'s withdrawal from service began in earnest after World War I and grew more persistent as the early 1920s passed. "The story of the *Bear* is nearly complete," a reporter with a flair for romance wrote.[6] "After a career of 42 years, the old ship is on her next to the last voyage. Next year Father Time writes 'finis' at the end of the log, and the *Bear* will be no more." And its fate? "Perhaps dismantled and destroyed. Perhaps turned over to some coast city for a museum filled with Alaskan and Arctic relics. Seattle wants her for the museum and the wish may be granted."

None of that came to pass. But the *Bear*'s end as a Coast Guard cutter did. It was inevitable. Even the *Bear*'s most ardent supporters realized that romanticism and idealism were no substitute for pragmatism. When it arrived in Seattle in 1925 to take on supplies and coal for its 27th northern voyage, prognosticators were sure it was the last time anyone would see it. But, if that was the case, why had the Coast Guard given it a fresh coat of paint, placed iron bar sheathings on its sides, installed new propellers, and made general repairs? That seemed to be wasted money, especially after the *Bear* had experienced one of its worst trips ever in 1924, when it had fought heavy ice packs for 42 days in the Bering Sea and sustained serious damage to its propeller blades.

In early August that year the *Bear* had to cut its summer voyage short and return to San Francisco. The Arctic ice pack proved too heavy for the cutter and damaged the blades. Specialists made an unsuccessful attempt to repair them, which prompted the early return home. That disappointed Captain Cochran, who declared that the *Bear* was in just as good a condition as ever, otherwise. All he needed was sufficient money to rehabilitate the vessel. The Coast Guard ordered the *Mohave* to take the *Bear*'s place in the Bering Sea for the rest of the season.[7] That heightened rumors that the *Bear* was on its last sea legs.

Granted, the government had ordered a new vessel to replace it, one that would carry an airplane on its stern in a bow to new technology. And, it had assigned a new commander, Lieutenant Commander Lawrence C. Covell, to replace Captain Cochrane, who had been sent to San Francisco to oversee the service's fleet there. Covell was no stranger to the *Bear*. He had served aboard it twenty years earlier. Historically, the *Bear*'s commanders were aboard for many years, as was another fixture, the cutter crew's famous dog, Paddy. No change there.

Paddy was aboard for his fourth Far North tour.[8] Allegedly, he was the only being aboard who could refuse to take orders from Covell. Paddy was a wise, little, old dog, which Captain Cochran had rescued from the Oakland pound four years earlier. "I'm entirely outclassed when it comes to Paddy," Covell admitted. "Paddy does just as he pleases at all times and he seems to get a real thrill out of bossing the ship."[9] In truth, Paddy was more loyal than some of the crew members. The *Bear* was short three seamen and one radio man for this cruise, so ship's officers remained aboard to take applications to fill those billets before the cutter set sail. Other than that, it was business as usual.

"We have the usual heavy list of mail for Point Barrow and other distant points, medical supplies and provisions," Covell revealed. "Two interesting passengers are on their way here now from Wisconsin. They are two collie dogs, which we will take to Archdeacon Goodwin at Point Hope."[10] Also aboard were 11 Eskimos who had survived a tragic adventure on Wrangell Island a year earlier, and Professor George Haley of the University of California, en route to the Pribilofs for scientific research. The Eskimos were being transported to their homes near Nome. It was a normal manifest for the *Bear*. But was it the last one? No: it had two more in its future under the guidance of Covell, who was scheduled to have the honor of being its last commander. That did not turn out to be the case. At least he was the first to lead a "mothership" into a new venture for the service.

Early in 1926 the Coast Guard transferred a group of eight speedy "rum chasers" from the Eastern Seaboard to interdict smugglers along the West Coast, along with two Navy destroyers and seaplanes.[11] It was the midpoint of the Prohibition Era in the U.S. and the Coast Guard was ordered to intercept sea craft trying to import alcohol into the country illegally as the government introduced a new approach to curbing the problem. Covell was given full responsibility for stopping the flood of illegal beverages that were so plentiful they provided serious marketing competition for legitimate distillers ashore. The mother ship assignment was temporary; so was Covell's time as the *Bear*'s commander, as it turned out.

In February 1926 the Treasury Department announced that it had reassigned him to take charge of Section Base 17 at San Pedro, California, and replaced him with Captain Cochran. That was one of two major disclosures. The other was that headquarters wanted the names of any warrant or enlisted personnel who had experience in photography.[12] The Coast Guard was taking a major step forward in joining the other uniformed services to "tell it with pictures." Photos were in; the *Bear* was out. Finally, in 1927 the venerable old cutter was sent into hibernation after 43 years of service. Time, tides, and transitions wait for no one. The *Bear* went out as proudly as it came in. Little had changed in its four decades of service as a log of its final tour suggested.[13]

At the start of its cruise the *Bear* took on board eight destitute Eskimos and transported them to their homes in northern Alaska. After reaching Nome, Captain Cochran duly qualified as United States Commissioner for the Second Alaska District. The *Bear* sailed to the native village of Savoonga. The cutter had to force its way through a dangerous field of loose ice to get there. The mission was to investigate the fatal shooting of a native, which was determined to be accidental. The next stop was the village of Campbell, where the medical staff rendered medical services to the natives, one of whom was taken aboard for transportation to Nome for hospital treatment. The *Bear* traveled from there to several other native communities on welfare checks to make sure their inhabitants were in good condition and progressing satisfactorily.

The voyage was not bereft of the usual Bering Sea hazards. After continuing its tour the *Bear* weathered a severe storm and encountered some dangerous ice fields that required skillful navigation to get through. Finally, the *Bear* anchored off the village of Shishmaref, which was for the most part deserted. Most of the natives were away hunting reindeer. While they were there crew members investigated reported immorality on the part of the young natives of the village. The investigators determined that the conditions weren't any worse than in other native villages of the same size. They did, however, warn the natives that disciplinary action would be taken if any further transgressions occurred. That done, the *Bear* continued on its way.

The cutter battled heavy ice for the next few weeks as it went from village to village. Finally, it put into Reindeer Station on July 5 and took aboard 50 orphaned Eskimo children. The crew treated them to a "Fourth of July party" and gave them presents of candy from the officers and crew. The rest of the voyage consisted of the usual functions, such as visiting other villages, warning mariners of dangerous ice and other obstacles to navigation, and transporting government employees, teachers, and missionaries from post to post.

Finally, the long voyage ended. The *Bear* docked at Seattle on October 1, having cruised 11,468 miles, examined five vessels and rendered medical aid to 70 persons, besides inspecting hundreds of others. The *Bear*'s long career in the north land was over.

The news was not totally unexpected in Alaska, but there was a bittersweet undercurrent in residents' reactions when definite word reached them that the *Bear* would be retired from duty there. They could take some solace in the news that the *Bear* would continue to serve as a receiving ship, but not in Seattle. A Nome newsman reported the story almost as if it was the obituary of a lost friend[14]:

GRATEFUL TO COAST GUARD.
The historic *Bear* has earned her release from strenuous duty, but she will not he "retired" to sink into oblivion or suffer from disuse. Like the famous Constitution, she has many ardent admirers. From the West came a protesting cry at the first suggestion of scrapping the old cruiser. Acceding to urgent requests it was decided by the Coast Guard authorities to send her to the California coast where she will cruise in the waters of the Pacific, serving as a training

ship for Coast Guard men. Her flag will not be furled nor her storm-scarred masts dismantled. She will bear herself proudly in her old age, a ship apart, cherished by those whom she has faithfully served.

"Another year and she is done with howling blizzards and the white seahorses that pound their heels against her shock-proof prow," another wrote. "A vessel costing one million dollars and capable of four times her speed is to be constructed for service up north."[15]

The Alaskans' disappointment at learning about the *Bear's* dismissal was widely shared elsewhere—especially among Coast Guard veterans. They simply refused to believe that the *Bear's* Bering Sea duties were a thing of the past when it returned to Seattle in September 1926 after its "absolutely final voyage to the Arctic." That was evident in a newspaper article published after the *Bear's* return.

> The *Bear* has been making annual "farewell" trips to the icy Alaskan coast so long that her record rivals that of outstanding operatic idols of past and present. Furthermore, if her impresario, otherwise known as Coast Guard Capt. W.H. Cochrane [*sic*], has his way she will continue her annual voyages up among the fur seals, breaking ice and Eskimos for a number of years longer, call them farewell tours or what you will.
>
> If the staunch little cutter could express the feelings pent up in her stout heart as she rides at dock here she probably would not be jealous of the Diesel-engined electric-drive modern steel cutter *Northland*, now nearing completion at Newport News, to become her successor next spring. Still confident of the strength in her seasoned pickled oak keel, heavy ribs and hull that have successfully plowed through ice season after season for half a century, she more likely would be disdainful than jealous.

There was a strong note of anthropomorphism in the writer's tone. Even Cochrane could not believe the *Bear's* career was at an end. After all, there were a number of steel ships in the Bering patrol, but none ventured as far north or took such chances with ice and rough seas as the veteran *Bear*. He was convinced after his return in 1926 that it would be the *Bear*, not the *Northland*, going to Point Barrow in 1927.

There was a glimmer of hope that it would. As late as February 1927 there were reported delays in the *Northland* construction program that suggested Cochrane could get his wish. The captain was so confident, in fact, that he was overhauling his ship for the expected journey to the north in May. Why not? The Coast Guard had still not released any definite sailing instructions for either the *Bear* or the *Northland* to head to the Bering. Nevertheless realists in the *Bear's* service area knew the end was finally at hand and started preparing the local people for it in May 1927.[16]

Cochrane adamantly remained dubious of a steel cutter's ability to replace the *Bear's* old wooden hulk, which he pointed out had weathered so many ice jams in northern waters. He was so loyal to the *Bear* that he had pushed headquarters in Washington to allow him and his cutter to rescue the *Northland* "when she gets into trouble in the Arctic."[17] His tenacity knew no bounds, nor did his memories.

No one could fault Cochrane for a bit of reminiscing as the *Bear's* final voyage ended—if it was indeed its final voyage. He had been assigned in the spring of 1921 to take the *Bear* on its "final voyage" to the lonely trading stations of the north. Here it was five years later and he was still doing the same thing. But there were plans in 1926 for him to take charge of the patrol station at Unalaska and to retire his favorite cutter. The retirement plan did not sit well with him. "I think she should be kept in service," he said. "She's too sound to be condemned. I don't believe they can build a steel ship that will stand what she will go through even yet."[18]

Worse, as far as he was concerned, it had been rumored that the *Bear* would be placed in salmon carrying or some similar service after retirement, Cochrane was repulsed at the idea. He, too, spoke anthropomorphically, as did so many other people when discussing the *Bear*, when he declared unequivocally that the *Bear*'s pride was not to be lowered to that extent. He preferred that it become a training ship if condemned for further service in the north. In that he got his wish.

Later in 1926 Cochrane met with some of his old friends from Alaska for a luncheon engagement.[19] He discovered that he was not alone in his fondness for the *Bear* and the old days up north. Before they dined, Cochrane, at that point the oldest captain in point of service in the Coast Guard, sat down aboard the *Bear* with three men he had known well in Alaska: Charles D. Brower, manager of the Cape Smythe Whaling Co., who had spent 12 years in Alaska, his co-worker Thomas Gordon, and the explorer Vilhjalmur Stefansson, who had done more to make the public aware of what was going on in Alaska than any other explorer. Gordon had lived three miles north of Point Barrow, where Brower had his headquarters.

The four men sat in almost complete silence, just as they had done so often during their respective activities in the territory. That was partly because they were so isolated, often with no one other than Eskimos who didn't speak English for company. Silence was a way of life for them, and if it hadn't been for a reporter and photographer at their meeting it might not have been broken aboard the *Bear*.

"Alaska lonely?" Gordon growled. "Why, I never was so lonely in my life as I've been right here in San Francisco." Brower chimed in. "We think Alaska is overpopulated and spoiled. There's a white man every hundred miles up there now. We used to think when there was one every 400 miles it was plenty." Stefansson could only smile. "When I met these two boys in 1908 they were complaining. They're still at it," he said.

That's when Cochrane joined the conversation. "When I first went into Alaska on the *Bear*—that was in 1896—I found Gordon and Brower there fussing about the number of white men who were taking possession of the country," he recalled. "Brower was at it before I was. When I came ashore at Point Barrow I found Brower sitting in the trading station there. And the first thing he mentioned was the over-population of the district."

At that point Stefansson looked whimsically at Captain Cochrane. All four men glanced at one another with looks of genuine admiration. There was nothing more to be said. Four of the human veterans of the Arctic life that was disappearing, sitting aboard a ship that had played a large role in their lives, had nothing more to say. It was time for them to go to lunch and for the *Northland* to take center stage.

It was a shame they couldn't take the *Bear* with them. Cochrane could, in memory at least. He was the last of a long line of storied commanders of the *Bear*. He gave way to Captain J.F. Hottel, the first commander of the *Northland*. It would be up to Hottel and his notable successors, e.g., E.D. Jones, Stanley V. Parker, William K. Scammel, Frederick A. Zeusler, and R.W. Butcher, to carry on the tradition of the Coast Guard's service in the Arctic region. They were all planks in the bridge between the *Bear* and the *Northland*—and all legends in their own times.

26

The Great Walrus Hunt

> "*Cutter Bear Given to Oakland as Museum—The House passed and sent to the Senate the Cutter Bill, authorizing the Secretary of the Treasury to give the Cutter* Bear *to the City of Oakland, California, for use as a free museum.*"[1]

The mood aboard the U.S. Coast Guard cutter *Northland* under the command of Captain J.F. Hottel was jovial on June 9, 1927, as the service's newest and most technologically advanced vessel made its maiden voyage (the *Bear*'s replacement still had auxiliary sails to help when—or if—they were needed. They weren't removed until 1936.)

The *Northland* had a long trip ahead. The ship was heading for the Arctic Circle—the "Top of the World"—to replace the antiquated 54-year-old cutter *Bear*, which had become the unofficial United States government in northern Alaska. The venerable *Bear*, which for more than 40 years had carried law, health, education, religion, protection and thrills to Xotzetu, Tin City, Aniyak, and a dozen more remote villages, was on reduced commission to serve as a receiving ship, training ship, barracks ship, or to perform some other menial service which fans considered beneath its dignity.

The *Bear* had furnished disaster relief, carried teachers to their stations, toted the mail and towed the skin boats of the King's Island natives with their season's catches of fish. Its captains had married and divorced the natives, handled disorders, and dispensed justice. The *Bear*'s ship surgeons and dentists had cared for hundreds of Alaskans and trained them to deal with the sicknesses and epidemics that would afflict them during its absence. That era had ended. Reporters pointed out that

> Here's June almost gone and the special little barkentine *Bear* hasn't pointed her jib boom into the harbor of Nome. North along the Alaskan coast native villagers are awaiting the *Bear*, waiting to bring their wives, children, dogs and chickens aboard and remain there until the *Bear* puffs on toward her next port of call.
> It's long past time for the *Bear* to load up with medicine and other supplies for the natives and heave away, but the *Bear* has sailed north for the last time and the ship that was built to replace her, the *Northland*, is proceeding down through the canal to follow the annual course of the *Bear* through the Bering Straits and up the coast to Point Barrow.[2]

It had quite a legacy to replicate, but Hottel and the crew were eager to get on with the job. All they had to do to was drop off the *Northland*'s passengers at Mount Vernon for their return to Washington aboard the cutter the *Apache*. Then the ship and crew, including Lieutenant-Commander F.J. Gorman, executive officer; Lieut.

L.O. Hammarstrom, navigator, seven other commissioned officers, six warrant officers, and 86 enlisted men, would move on to perform the numerous and various assignments for which the personnel were trained—and that was a lot.

The crew was unique. Each member was hand-picked. Many of them had served on the *Bear*. Reportedly, some of those old-timers had paid their own way to the East Coast to obtain placement.[3] Eleven first-class seamen shipped as mess members just to serve on the *Northland*. The officers were a select group as well. They had authority to prosecute and try cases involving the administration of justice, heal the physical ills of the natives in the operating room and dental clinic, perform marriage ceremonies, bury the dead, and distribute mail and supplies to ports that were ice bound most of the year, many of which never saw any other harbinger of civilization. A reporter acknowledged:

> To many an isolated colony of Eskimos the coming of the *Northland*, as was the case with the *Bear*, will represent the event of the year. She will bring to them medical and dental attention, a court of law, supplies when necessary, and other practical aids representative of organized government. She will be a floating government, carrying those with power to execute the functions of government, the furthermost northern representative of the United States.
>
> Of such will be the duties of the *Northland*. She will encounter all of the perils of the old *Bear*, but will be better equipped to combat them. The *Bear*, for instance, was once caught in an ice floe for 42 days, literally frozen in the ice, with supplies running dangerously low. The *Northland* is so constructed as to be able to smash through most ice fields and is equipped to maintain herself for eight months.[4]

Certainly nobody wanted to see if that was true. But, the ship had to get to Alaska first to prove it was. The crew had a long voyage ahead of them, down Chesapeake Bay, through the Panama Canal, and up the West Coast, unaware of the disappointment they would cause among the people in Nome and farther north when they discovered the *Bear* had been retired. Hottel didn't seem to in a hurry to get to Alaska. He had to showcase the *Northland* first.

The cutter arrived in San Francisco on August 3 and reached Seattle on August 8. From there it sailed north via the inside passage and visited most of the towns on the coast. The people in the communities to the north would just have to wait. The *Northland* stopped at Ketchikan for two days, where residents gave a dance and reception in the crew's honor. The cruise continued with another two-day layover in Juneau, including an "open house" for visitors from 1 o'clock until 5 o'clock one afternoon.

Next, the *Northland* sailed for Skagway, then Cordova, and the far west. Finally, after a two-and-a-half month voyage, the *Northland*, "trim as a yacht and equipped with every facility for the particular and peculiar service she is to render in Far Northern Alaskan waters,"[5] arrived in Nome on the afternoon of August 23. The late arrival meant that many of the communities Coast Guard crews had visited in previous years would be bypassed for one season.

Since it was so late in the year, Hottel said he did not know how far the ship would be able to go. But, he promised, he would proceed as far north as the ice would permit, perhaps as far as to Point Hope, and the *Northland* would not leave the Bering until after the last commercial vessel had sailed from Nome. Some people in the region, at least, would get to see the *Bear*'s replacement.

The 1,000-horsepower diesel-electric engine driving *Northland* was a technological marvel for its time. It had a cruising radius of 11,000 miles, the distance of its normal cruise, if necessary. (The *Bear*'s last cruise, in 1926, covered a distance of 11,648 miles. Overall, according to Coast Guard officers' estimates, the *Bear* traveled some one million miles during the nearly 50 years she was in service in Arctic waters.[6]) That the *Northland* could stay at sea that long without refueling was important: there was only one oiling station in its area of operation, which was not always easy to reach due to the heavy seas and thick ice that were common in its path.

Certainly, the *Northland*'s steel frame was a step forward in battling the elements. Its designers wanted to eliminate the need for miracles. Science and technology allowed them to do that. They constructed the *Northland* from steel. (See Appendix A for a list of the *Northland*'s features and specifications.) Of course, the inclusion of steel was no guarantee that the *Northland* could not be damaged by ice. Engineers understood that. So, they installed 16-inch "I" beams only two feet apart along with a hull of steel plate 1¼ inches thick to help the ship withstand the pressure of the ice the ship would encounter. That was notable. But what attracted the attention of the naval engineers and architects aboard the *Northland* as it moved down the Potomac was the revolutionary magnetic clutch embedded in the propeller shaft.

The propeller shaft provided added protection to the entire driving mechanism of the ship when it entered the ice fields. The clutch consisted of two great plates inserted in the propeller shaft. The plates were constructed so their magnetism could be increased or decreased from controls on the bridge. In heavy ice the magnetism was reduced barely to the point where it would drive the ship. That way, when the propeller struck ice the clutch slipped and saved the propeller blades.

Steel, diesel-electric engines, innovative propeller shaft ... all for less than a million dollars—maybe. The total cost reported in June 1927 was $925,000 (which would be around $14,772,250 in 2023), although the price tag went up to $1,000,000 by August 24, 1927, according to one newspaper reporter, who included that figure in an article heralding the ship's arrival in Juneau.[7] Even by government standards that $75,000 price hike in two months was an inflationary record leap.

Government officials touted the low cost and maintained that the *Northland* would save many times its value in shipping and in property protected and conserved from the rigors of the north. Regardless of the real cost the figure was considered a lot of money for what many Americans thought was just a mail boat. The crew might have felt otherwise, especially in light of their specialties and diverse assignments.

Yes, the ship delivered mail and supplies to ports that were icebound most of the year, where the inhabitants never saw any other harbinger of civilization. But, it also carried officers with authority to prosecute and try cases involving the administration of justice, who could heal the physical ills of the natives in the operating room and dental clinic, perform marriage ceremonies, and bury the dead. No one could put a price on what they did.

The *Northland*, like the *Bear* before it, was more than a mail boat, as the report of a typical year's cruise proves. What it showed was what members of any Bering Sea patrol cutter had learned: the road to hell is paved with good intentions. The way to Point Barrow was paved with ice, which made sailing through it hard as hell but less than easy for the crew. The cutter may have been a step up from the *Bear* from a technological standpoint, but that did not mean the people it served had enjoyed similar advances to make their lives easier. They still faced hardships in their attempts to survive in the harsh northern climate, and the *Northland*'s crew members had to adapt to it as well on their behalf, as one classic 1938 event demonstrated.

The worst advice one walrus could give another around Wainwright, Alaska, in the late 1930s was to, as humans might say in fun, "go with the floe"—especially if the *Northland* was in the area and people needed food. There was plenty of it moving about on ice floes in the form of walruses who were easy targets for hunters such as the *Northland*'s crew members. Many of them were able hunters who welcomed the chance to try their skills against walruses, but out of necessity, not just for the sport of the hunt—especially if local residents were to survive. Hunting walruses and seals was just another job crew members had to do. Significantly, it provided them with an opportunity to show political dignitaries how versatile and necessary they were in Alaska.

On one occasion, 12 Alaska natives were forced to escape from a herd of 18 enraged walruses which charged their frail crafts while U.S. Senator R.R. Reynolds (D-NC) and Dr. Thomas G. Thompson watched from a small boat nearby that had been launched from the *Northland*. Reynolds and Thompson, head of the Oceanography Department at the University of Washington, were cruising aboard the *Northland* on its voyage into the Arctic Oceans. They were allowed to accompany Coast Guardsmen and the natives on a walrus hunting expedition twenty miles out from Wainwright. The expedition led to more excitement than anyone expected, as Zeusler described it.

> A shortage of walrus meat this season prompted [trader] Jim Allen of Wainwright to request the commanding officer of the *Northland*, anchored off that village, for aid in killing as many walrus as possible for the coming winter supply. The ice being 20 miles offshore and there being considerable work in the village, the commanding officer dispatched a Coast Guard launch in charge of Lieutenant Commander Sarratt and a crew of eight with rifles. Allen acted as the guide. Three large Eskimo skin boats and twelve natives formed the remainder of the expedition.
>
> Permission was granted Senator Reynolds and Dr. Thompson to accompany the expedition. Loose ice was found eight miles off, but the main pack where many walruses were found was about 20 miles out. In making the approach to the main pack, a lone bull was sighted and Senator Reynolds was given first chance to kill. Two skin boats were cast adrift and they approached the ice from leeward until within range. One shot was fired by the senator at 20 yards. It went true and the bull toppled over. The bull fought bravely to escape, but another shot killed him.
>
> The walrus weighed about 3,000 pounds, tusks measured 32 inches. The natives immediately dissected the animal and loaded it into the towed skin freight boat. It was not long thereafter before the main pack was sighted and many of the floes had walrus on them. A flat floe of ice was selected on which there were about 25, three of them being cows with pups. The two skin boats approached the floes as before at different angles and the hunters were directed to pick certain bulls for slaughter.
>
> Five bulls and two pups were killed. Two cows and one bull were wounded. They ran for the water and headed toward the boats which were making for the ice floe. Evidently the

wounded cows had lost their pups and smelled the blood. About 15 other walruses charged the boats with the wounded walruses. The crews paddled desperately for the ice floe and as their boats struck the ice a wounded walrus hooked its tusk over the gunwale of one boat, nearly capsizing it.

Most of the crew got out on the ice. One native used an ax on the entangled walrus tusk, while a member of the *Northland*'s crew fired a shot into the neck of one of the fighting walruses. The shot killing the entangled walrus scared the others away. In all cases Jim Allen directed the firing to avoid unnecessary loss of walrus. About 46,000 pounds of walrus meat were provided to the native village.

Only one wounded walrus was lost, which had slid off the ice. As the three skin boats again arrived at the village 18 hours later, the natives were there to greet them with a cheer. The hunters gave Allen all the credit for the success of the expedition. Senator Reynolds enthusiastically gobbled up a piece of still warm blubber given to him by one joyful native after the killing was over.

The Coast Guard cutter *Northland* left a number of pieces of salted seal shoulders to assist in alleviating any possible distress due to shortage of food during the coming winter. During the hunting expedition the *Northland* was in radio communication with the ship's launch.[8]

It may have been an exciting experience for Reynolds and Thompson, but just another typical day in the lives of the *Northland*'s crew members. They added one more entry in their book of services to the people in need of help along their route. That was routine for them, just as it had been for their predecessors aboard the *Bear*. That's what made life aboard the *Northland* exciting, despite the tedium.

27

Routine, but Challenging

> "It will be the duty of the Northland to uphold the traditions of service established by the Bear, traditions which are the pride of Coast Guardsmen everywhere."[1]

Life aboard the *Northland* during an Arctic cruise may have sounded adventurous, exciting, and romantic for people following its activities from afar. It was less so for the crew members, whose leisure activities were limited. There were no radio, TV, cell phones ... none of the entertainment electronics so rife today. So what did the crew members do on their "adventure?" They read adventure stories, at least in 1929, one of the rare years in which the *Northland* reached Point Barrow without much difficulty.

The trip was uneventful that year because the Arctic Ocean ice was mostly on the Siberian coast. There were three or four ships at Point Barrow that were experiencing delays in rounding the sand spit to the east due to the Arctic ice pack hugging the shore line, but eventually they succeeded in getting through. The *Northland* left the community for Nome without problems.

On the return voyage the vessel carried the standard eclectic list of passengers and cargo.[2] Mrs. A.W. Newhall, wife of Dr. Newhall, who died the preceding winter while awaiting a plane to bring him to the Nome hospital. She was going back to the states. Dr. von M. Zesch, a dentist in Nome, was returning to his home city. Ted Scroggins, a magazine solicitor, was also aboard, as was a Mr. Vincent, who had erected the school house at Point Barrow in the fall of 1928. Life may have been difficult at times in Point Barrow, but sales reps went to great lengths to get there and sell their wares. Two scientists named Collins and Brandt were along for their ride in company with Archdeacon F.W. Goodman, who had spent the past four years at Point Hope doing missionary work and acting as U.S. Commissioner. Goodman was en route to St. Michael and ultimately to the states via the Yukon River.

Of course, no *Northland* taxi ride was complete without its ark component. Two polar bear cubs joined the human and animal menagerie aboard. Their presence was somewhat symbolic. They were destined to be tourist attractions to draw visitors to Alaska in the same year one of the oldest bear attractions—the old cutter, the *Bear*—was named by the U.S. Congress to be a museum for the same purpose. The polar bears were consigned to President Standard of the Alaska Steamship Company. He was going to present them to Woodland Park in Seattle, where they would be used as

27. Routine, but Challenging

The *Northland* officers on June 10, 1928. Left to right standing: D.F.A. deOtte; W.J.B. McAuliffe, USPHS; S.J. Woyciehowsky; P.E. Clement; H.B. Berg; J.C. Urquahart; E.A. Standon. Seated—R.E. Wood; F.J. Gorman; J.F. Hottel, Captain; W.C. Maglathlin and A.J. Maclean (USCG Historian's Office).

lures to the "North Country" for potential visitors. They were better off than some of their other animal kin. At least they were still alive.

Most notably, the *Northland* was carrying a significant mail consignment, much of which consisted of furs. The cutter was scheduled to stay in Nome for a day or two, then leave for St. Michael and St. Lawrence Island. That was simply standard operating procedure for the *Northland*. That year's 14,000-mile cruise was routine, at least for the peripatetic crew. Among the highlights that year they:

> Rescued between 15 and 20 shipwrecked sailors from the Norwegian fishing schooner *Elisif* who were stranded and on the brink of death on Little Diomede Island, one of the two bleak Diomede Islands located in the middle of the Bering Strait between the United States Far Northwest territory and the Russian Far East the Siberian coast.[3] They had reached the island in four small boats after a 250-mile trip from the Siberian coast where *Elisif* had beached on August 10. The ship and cargo were a total loss, amounting to $300,000. At the time the *Northland* reached the castaways, they had only two launches, the clothes on their backs, two gallons of drinking water, and a limited amount of provisions to sustain them. Their ordeal had lasted three weeks when the *Northland* wired authorities on August 31 that it was transporting the sailors to Nome—just in the nick of time.

> Saved two Russian White Army soldiers who were starving on one of the Diomede Islands.

> Retrieved the damaged schooner *Dorothy* and towed it 100 miles from Nome to Teller, Alaska, for repairs.[4] The *Dorothy* was chartered as part of a field museum expedition from Chicago. The ship's rudder was damaged by ice off Kolyuchun Bay, Siberia, which made the steering unmanageable. Temporary repairs allowed the ship to reach Nome, but that was as far as it could go without a tow from the *Northland*.

Rescued the starving trader Jim Allen and thirty Eskimos at Wainwright and took them to the walrus fields, where they launched skinboats and shot walruses for food (a skinboat is an easy-to-make type of prehistoric craft built by covering wood or skeletons with animal hides, which were dried, stretched, and specially treated).

Rescued an Alaskan commercial plane service pilot named Bennett whose plane had crashed on an island

When the cruise ended and the *Northland* reached home at Oakland, reporters asked Commander Edward D. Jones what the crew members did in their off-duty time. That's when he revealed that they read adventure magazine "to get thrills."[5] It's not like they didn't get enough of their own while doing their jobs. What other people may have defined as thrills were apparently just everyday tasks to the crew members of the *Northland*. They were just doing their job, which was an attitude that ran through the entire Coast Guard as its members did whatever they could to alleviate the hardships of northern living for residents and visitors alike.

Living in Alaska was not easy for the natives or people ranging from medical professionals, missionaries, and teachers to "do gooders" who lived there or the folks who made sure they were as well looked after as possible. If it weren't for the valiant sailors of the ships and smaller crafts that traversed the territory hauling supplies and professionals to administer services they might never have seen an outsider. And none of them depended on any entity more than on the Coast Guard.

The service's diverse assignments were vital to the lifeblood of the territory. Yet, it had significant limitations, not all of its own making, primarily adverse weather. That was demonstrated through the contents of the *Northland*'s August 1937 Arctic cruise to Point Barrow, furnished by Commander Zeusler, who had served aboard the *Bear* under Captain Cochrane.[6] Ironically, even though it was intended as a voyage to Point Barrow, the *Northland* did not reach its destination. Sometimes the *Northland* showed no improvement over the *Bear*. The 1937 cruise was atypical even by Coast Guard standards.

The *Northland* left Nome on July 31. Its proposed itinerary called for visits to all the villages in the Arctic area as far as Point Barrow, making oceanographic surveys, checking existing harbor surveys, rendering medical and dental aid, inspecting the villages, providing such assistance to boats and persons as necessary, and performing the other duties required of the Coast Guard—which were just about everything.

The cutter was loaded with stores, considerable mail, and personnel representing many branches of endeavor, such as the Hubbard Expedition, Point Barrow Expedition, and nurses. Zeusler was optimistic that the voyage would go well. He had received word from Point Barrow that the ice was clear, so it was his intention to sail directly to Point Barrow and then work very slowly to the southward.

The *Northland* made a short stop at King's Island to unload stores, but quickly ran into trouble afterwards. It entered the Arctic Ocean where, on August 1, the ship encountered a strong southwest breeze that quickly shifted to the northwest. Such wind shifts were not uncommon in the region, but the resulting rough seas made the *Northland* and everyone aboard, including the seasoned crew members, very uncomfortable. Late that evening the cutter reached Point Hope, where the crew off-loaded mail and supplies. The ship's medical, dental, and inspecting officers went ashore to start their work.

The inspectors quickly discovered a problem. The Point Hope lighthouse had been undermined by the heavy seas and needed repairs. Crew members spent valuable time building a new foundation and relocating the light. There was no rush to complete the project. The *Northland* could not go anywhere anyway. A northwest gale blew most of the time it was in port, so it was unable to sail until the afternoon of August 4 because of the heavy onshore seas. The *Northland* was only five days into its cruise and the early optimism was already fading.

Conditions did not get any better the next day. In fact, they grew worse. The following morning the *Northland* encountered heavy ice about 20 miles south of Icy Cape. The crew searched for some time for leads to open water but gave up and returned to Point Lay, where the 42-year-old merchant schooner *C.S. Holmes* was anchored. Like the *Northland*, the *Holmes* made an annual trip to Point Barrow. Zeusler always got a feeling of comfort when he encountered the *Holmes*.

By the time the *Northland* got back to Point Lay the seas had calmed down. The inspecting party went ashore at that village and performed its needed duties. While in port Zeusler received some happy news. The *Nanuk*, a trading vessel from Nome, had recently been to Point Barrow and its captain reported seeing very little ice except off Point Belcher and the Sea Horses. Zeusler was too experienced to jump for joy.

That had been a short while before, but even less experienced sailors knew ice could form almost while they were looking at clear water. That's what happened to the *Northland*. Seven days later practically solid ice was encountered at a point twenty miles south of Icy Cape, which reached well beyond Point Barrow. The westerly and northwesterly winds had closed in the leads which had permitted the *Nanuk* to negotiate a quick and safe passage to Point Barrow and return.

To make matters worse, unfavorable winds were blowing again. The *Northland* did not proceed again until early in August, after making several attempts to negotiate the ice without success. Finally, the *Northland* and its faithful "old sailing companion, the *Holmes*," as Zeusler put it, started north together.[7]

"From that day on until 15th of August, *Northland* and the *Holmes* punched their way through the ice until they arrived at Wainwright," he reported. "During that period of time native hunters of Wainwright, Icy Cape and Point Lay spent considerable time in the ice, killing many walrus and birds."

The *Northland* took on the role of a traveling seaborne auto club as it moved north. The crew provided assistance to a number of smaller craft that had engine troubles, bent propellers and bent shafts, as a result of the solid ice encountered, and other aid. At the same time they conducted scientific observations in regard to currents, tides, and types of ice. Their versatility was on full display.

A significant event occurred on August 13 when the *Northland* moored to an ice pan to take on board fresh water. The process marked a departure from the *Bear*'s capabilities in the "old Coast Guard" to the "new." The *Northland* used for the first time a gasoline pump provided that threw a stream of about 30 gallons of water per minute on board. In the course of two and a half hours the crew took on board 3,700 gallons of water.

On August 15 the *Northland* reached Wainwright, 80 miles southwest of Point Barrow, but spent very little time there. Zeusler received a report that Point Barrow was open. The ship cast off quickly and headed north. But, its lifesaving duties slowed the ship down. While en route during the afternoon crew members detected a distress signal among the ice floes about 25 miles northeast of Wainwright.

The *Northland* sailed in that direction and found a skin boat with an outboard motor attached. It was manned by two missionaries, one from Point Barrow and the other from Wainwright, headed from Wainwright to Point Barrow. They had started on a trip 30 hours earlier but had broken down. Some of the *Northland*'s crew members humorously referred to the rescued party as "Arctic hitchhikers."

As the *Northland* continued on its way the ice became heavier. Progress grew slower and slower, then ground to a halt. Nine miles northeast of Sea Horses, the Arctic ice pack, an impenetrable barrier, was grounded on shore. The *Northland* was only 20 miles from Point Barrow. A mirage silhouetted the distant houses of that place in plain view. That was frustrating for the crew. Zeusler could only say, "Thou shalt not pass could well have been the slogan of nature for that day and for some days to come." The crew attempted to sail through near the shore to 12 miles offshore without success. The *Northland* had to turn back.

Zeusler intended to stop at Point Franklin on the way back to Wainwright. But, another shift of wind prevented the *Northland* from anchoring in the vicinity of the community. The trip was turning into a fiasco. If it was any consolation, the *Northland* wasn't alone in failing to reach Point Barrow.

Prior to the cutter's departure from Wainwright the gas screw *Trader of Nome* had arrived there, stayed for a few hours, and set sail in the direction of Point Barrow. The *Northland* punched heavy ice all the way back to Wainwright. When it arrived early in the morning, the *C.S. Holmes* was anchored in ice near shore in what had been open water just ten hours earlier. The water was almost a closed roadstead by the time the *Northland* showed up. The cutter started to clear the ice.

Then a report arrived that the *Trader* was locked in Pearl Bay as a result of heavy ice to both the north and the south. Ice notwithstanding, Zeusler made another dash on August 19 for Wainwright and Point Barrow. The *Northland* could not get past the first ice barrier. Even if it had, the ship might have run into trouble. Its water supply was getting very low. The *Northland* had to divert to Cape Lisbourne, where it took on board by means of boats 25,000 gallons of water in about 12 hours. Undeterred by the ice and other delays, Zeusler determined to make another attempt to reach Point Barrow.

On August 21 the *Northland* returned to Wainwright to be near enough to Point Barrow to take advantage of any leads that might be open to it. While en route to Wainwright the *Northland* passed the Russian ice breaker *Krassin*, which had successfully punched its way to a point about ten miles west of Point Barrow. The *Krassin* was carrying planes, a heavy load of supplies, and gasoline, none of which helped it get any closer to Point Barrow due to the heavy ice pack. The ice was so thick the *Krassin* had to clear its position, since it was in danger of being pinched in it, an embarrassing situation for an ice breaker.

The *Northland* made another attempt to reach Point Barrow, getting as far as

Point Lay, to wait for a lead to Point Barrow via the in-shore route. The cutter was able to work through the ice to a point about 14 miles northeast of Sea Horses on August 22 and 23. But, heavy ice and dense fog prevented further progress, so the *Northland* returned to Wainwright, passing the *Holmes* about 25 miles northwest of Wainwright. No ship was going anywhere, it seemed.

The ships' inability to reach Point Barrow was an imposition to the people there, but it was a boon for the folks at Wainwright. Upon their arrival back there the medical, dental, and inspecting parties aboard the *Northland* continued the work they had started at two previous visits. And it didn't look like they were going to leave anytime soon. The *Holmes* returned to its anchorage at Wainwright and reported that the ice was again coming fast. All was not lost though.

Since the *Northland* had landed its passengers, freight, and mail at Wainwright, Zeusler did not see any point in spending more time trying to reach Point Barrow. The passengers and stores had been transported there by skinboat, through inshore leads. Zeusler's decision was sound. The crew had already devoted approximately 21 days to punching the ice and the cutter's work to the south was suffering, so the captain decided that no further attempts would be made to reach Point Barrow. After all, there was no guarantee the *Northland* would get there. The weather conditions at that time were 50–50 for opening up or closing. By the time those odds improved the *Northland* was long gone from Wainwright.

Three days after it departed, as a result of a strong east wind, a lead opened off the Sea Horses through which the *Krassin* and the *Holmes* sailed successfully to Point Barrow. Such was the caprice of the Arctic weather.

All was not lost for the *Northland*. It sailed southward to Point Hope Kotzebue, Kivalik, Kivalina, Deering, Shismaref, and King's Island. Stores were landed, inspections were made, and necessary services were performed in each location. Finally, after a harrowing month, the *Northland* returned to Nome on the morning of August 29, about a week later than usual. Zeusler was still able to list a number of successes on the voyage:

> During the time while to the northward of the Bering Straits, the cutter was able to make a number of running surveys of harbors and thoroughly check the inner channel off Icy Cape and rebuild the signals ashore at that point, so as to make it possible to negotiate the channel without going some ten miles off shore.
>
> The tidal and current observations were made and soundings taken by fathometer, all extremely valuable to the oceanographer, cartographer, and navigator.
>
> Three investigations were made in the villages and much information of value was obtained with reference to the Eskimos.
>
> The Commanding Officer of the cutter *Northland* devoted considerable time to discussing legal matters and matters pertaining to the welfare of the natives with the mayors and councils of the various villages.
>
> On the return trip *Northland* had on board the members of the Hubbard Expedition, the outcoming school teacher from Wainwright, and 16 natives and their belongings. Zeusler landed them all at Nome.
>
> The cutter devoted the remainder of the time in inspection work, completing oceanographic research which would take the vessel to St. Lawrence Island, St. Lawrence Bay, Ugelen, Wales, Teller, King's Island, and Nome, and would stand by and be of assistance to vessels and persons requiring aid.

Commander Zeusler's final entry in the August 1937 report was indicative of his resolve, which was endemic to all the cutter personnel in the territory. "Later on another cruise to the Northward will be made," he said. The words may have been written, but their tenor was unmistakable. He was going to do his job come what may. The *Bear*, the *Northland*, old Coast Guard, new Coast Guard, Captain Healey, Commander Zeusler. They all had a job to do and they did it, as they had for 150 years.

28

Sailing Toward War

> *"Bob Wheeler's home has been the coast guard cutter* Northland *which, next to the cutter* Bear, *is probably the most famous vessel of the entire coast guard fleet."*[1]

The *Northland* received a respite as America's political and military leaders became more and more convinced that the country would be dragged into World War II. *Itasca*, a non–ice breaker, had replaced the *Northland* in 1939.[2] The *Northland* was out of commission and had been turned over to the maritime training service. That assignment ended quickly and its crew became familiar with a place called Greenland.

One of them, Seaman First Class Bob Wheeler, from Tacoma, Washington, was among them. He typified his comrades. Wheeler had served aboard several other cutters around the Northwest before joining the *Northland* at San Francisco for a cruise to Boston and eventually Greenland in 1940. In May that year the *Northland* entered the New York Navy Yard to be outfitted for special survey duty in Greenland, for which it embarked on August 20 on what some folks suggested was more than a pleasure cruise. The announcement it was being deployed there raised a few eyebrows.[3] There was really no mystery about the assignment to people who paid attention to the United States' military strategies.

Greenland was important strategically for the United States and its allies.[4] Therefore the U.S. launched an effort in 1940 to initiate an emergency Coast Guard survey of accessible terrain and harbors on the vast ice-capped Danish island. At the same time the government began to move personnel and materials there to construct bases and limited port facilities. It wasn't keen on publicizing the cruise or why the *Northland* was heading there.

Reporters who asked about the *Northland*'s mission drew blank stares from military authorities. There were rumors afloat that the cutter had been assigned to go to Greenland as soon as it left the West Coast, but Coast Guard officials denied them. Even when the cutter reached the Brooklyn Navy Yard and the hammers began ringing, the welding torches started blazing, armor plated its deck, and ordnance specialists increased its armament to three guns—the officials remained noncommittal about why.

Curious people pieced together what was happening. They concluded the cutter was off on a scouting or observation cruise. They solved part of the puzzle after learning that the United States Army—or possibly the Navy—was operating a radio station in Greenland, presumably controlled by either one of those services, or maybe both. Reporters theorized, then, that the *Northland* had been ordered to contact the operators there and probably make a survey of the southern coast of Greenland from the standpoint of Western Hemisphere defense. They were right in their assumption. That didn't stop the guessing games however.

People were not sure of what the *Northland* was carrying to Greenland. The lack of publicity convinced people that this voyage—whatever it was—was no ordinary Bering patrol. After all, the *Northland* followers said, the Coast Guard is primarily what its name implies, a coastal patrol, and Greenland is not part of the United States' coast. And, with the exception of the recently established weather observation patrols in the Atlantic and iceberg patrols in the North Atlantic, the U.S. Coast Guard seldom operated far from American shores.

Newspaper staff members in Nome, where the *Northland* had a history, had a foreboding about the cutter. They wrote what sounded almost like an obituary as it headed away from Alaska and toward New York. Of course, they treated the new assignment as just another Bering voyage, but there was a tinge of sadness and nostalgia in their words, as if they knew they would never see the *Northland* again[5]:

> The Greenland junket will be just another leaf in the log of one of the most famous of the U.S. Coast Guard cutters. For some summers, the *Northland* has been in the Bering Sea patrol. Following the ice floes north in the spring along the coast of Alaska, the boat would cut west along the Aleutians and visit the ports of those sparsely populated stepping stones to within hailing distance of Russia. The reason is that these islands, with their tiny Eskimo communities, are isolated throughout the year and have no other contact with the outside world than the annual cruise of the Coast Guard.

No wonder the residents referred to the *Northland* by endearing nicknames. They seemed to have had more nicknames for the cutter than it had crew members. It was known alternately as "the Eskimo marrying boat," "the law west of Seward," and "The Angel of the Arctic." Whatever they called it, they had learned to rely on its sporadic appearances and services. A reporter explained:

> The captain of the *Northland* (or of whatever cutter might be making the cruise now) thus became, ex-officio, the only justice of the peace ever to visit the islands. And it became his duty to bless with legal matrimony all those couples who, by tribal custom, had united in marriage during the winter. It wasn't unheard of for the captain to marry couples who had, as witnesses, offspring a few months old. The *Northland* also carried a doctor and dentist and the boat tied up for days at these little Eskimo villages while the natives came aboard for examinations and treatment.

The implication was that the good folks of Alaska were going to miss that. Sure, another cutter might be assigned to take over, but the losses of the *Bear* and the *Northland* marked the end of an era. The upcoming war would exacerbate the process.

Certainly, the Greenland cruise wasn't unprecedented, but it was unusual enough to make headlines in the annals of the U.S. Coast Guard—and to make ordinary Americans suspect that there was something a bit nefarious afoot. How accurate that was became evident when the news that Greenland had been folded into the U. S.'s "protective custody" via an agreement signed by the Danish Minister Henrik De Kauffman was made public on April 10, 1941, twenty months into World War II.[6]

Anonymous authorities explained that American-built landing fields in Greenland for the use of military planes en route to Britain were one of the objectives of the agreement. American bombers were able to fly nonstop from Newfoundland to Britain, but fighter planes, which had a much shorter flight range, had to be transported in cargo vessels that could be sunk, resulting in losses of badly needed ships and planes at the same time.

Landing fields on Greenland would allow the fighter planes to take off from Newfoundland, refuel at Greenland, fly to Iceland, and then finish the journey to the British Isles. The longest hop in the flight would be less than 1,000 miles, which most fighter planes could easily complete without refueling. Authorities also believed that establishing bases on the island might be a prelude to convoys from southern Greenland, from which ships and planes could police the northern Atlantic sea lanes, including Iceland.

The plan was to establish bases on Greenland's south and west coasts. The U.S. already maintained a consulate in Godthaab on the western coast, which was a likely base site. Other points on which the Coast Guard reported favorably, particularly for ship bases, were Sukkertoppen and Paeringerhaven. Both, like Godthaab, were usually ice-free the year round. None of that could be done without the Coast Guard's involvement. The surveys were conducted by its cutters *Ouyaga* and *Northland* from June to December 1940.[7] That was the beginning of the *Northland*'s extraordinary service in the Greenland area during the war.

The cutter visited harbors in order to determine the best location for patrol forces. The information compiled contributed to the composition of a Greenland pilot volume as well as new charts. The charts were subsequently utilized in the formal organization of the Greenland Patrol, after the agreement between the United States and exiled rulers of Nazi-held Denmark was signed. That agreement incorporated Greenland in the United States' system of cooperative defense of the Western Hemisphere. The ensuing "cultural tour" of the *Northland* was an eye-opener for Wheeler and his crew mates. There was no hint of the hard days of battle to come.

The Greenland Eskimos they encountered during the voyage were described as "the politest and smelliest people in the world."[8] The territory known as the "home of the icebergs" was a Greenland glacier slightly larger than four miles wide and 600 miles long. It was a strange place. Huge pieces of ice would fall off a glacier at the blast of the ship's whistle, but explosives like TNT and gun fire did nothing more than chip off tiny pieces.

If the crew members were looking for female companionship on their liberty stops they were sadly disappointed. There were no non–Eskimo women in Greenland. The population comprised about 500 Danish miners and a few thousand Eskimos with names every bit as jaw-breaking as the words which were included in every mention they made of Greenland. Liquor was cheap, which was good for people who whiled away their hours drinking. The only other forms of recreation were hunting, fishing, and skiing.

Whatever their preferences, the crew did a lot of exploring ashore. And there was one bit of excitement to break the monotony. A German raiding party attacked an isolated radio station on the island and escaped successfully. The *Northland*

Five members of the *Northland* crew in caps and uniforms sitting on railing of dock during leisure time (Alaska State Library Historical Collections).

prowled the adjacent waters for several days afterwards but did not catch the raiders. The incident was a harbinger of alarms to come. Despite the lack of recreational opportunities, Wheeler said he would enjoy another lonesome long voyage in Arctic waters. His chance came sooner than he anticipated.

His tour aboard the *Northland* started and ended in Boston, consuming some 30,000 miles and six months. He survived it unharmed—until he returned to Boston. Almost immediately he emulated Captain Michael Healey and fell off the wharf. Subsequently he spent two weeks in the hospital with flu. While he recovered the *Northland* underwent extensive remodeling. So did the crew.

The officers reduced the crew to about two-thirds its regular size. They hand-picked the ones they wanted. Wheeler made the cut and was rewarded with a lengthy leave with orders to report back in the middle of February 1941.[9] He headed across country to Tacoma at once.

There were well-founded rumors circulating that the *Northland* was scheduled to attempt a two-year voyage through the Northwest Passage. If it took place, Bob Wheeler and some of his crew mates would be among the very few men in the world to encircle the North American continent in a ship. Even if it did not Wheeler could still claim a fancy certificate proving that he had crossed the Arctic Circle four times. That would have to do.

The *Northland* sailed again on April 7, 1941, on a two-month cruise to assist in the South Greenland Survey Expedition. While conducting this survey the crew searched for victims of ships sunk in the North Atlantic. The South Greenland Patrol was organized with the cutters *Modoc*, *Comanche*, and *Raritan* and the former Coast and Geodetic Survey ship the *Bowdoin*.

A month later the Northeast Greenland Patrol was organized with the cutter *Northland*, the former Interior Department ship the *North Star*, and the *Bear*, with overall command falling on Coast Guard Captain Edward H. ("Iceberg") Smith. Everyone was well aware that the ships might be pulled away for other purposes at any time. That happened quickly, and gave the *Northland* some moments in the sun.

The two patrols were consolidated on October 25, 1941, and the number of ships rose to 37 by 1943. Smith, who was promoted to Rear Admiral, adopted the *Northland* as his flagship. A month before that occurred, on September 12, the *Northland* sighted the German-controlled Norwegian sealer *Buskoe* and sent a boarding party to investigate. The *Northland* escorted the *Buskoe* to Mackenzie Bay, on the Greenland coast. That was a signal moment. The *Buskoe* earned the honor of becoming the first vessel captured by American forces prior to the U.S.'s entrance into World War II.[10]

The *Northland* had good reason to stop the *Buskoe*. Authorities believed the sealer had been sending weather reports and information on Allied shipping to the Germans. The apprehension had a collateral benefit. It led to the discovery of a German radio station about 500 miles up the Greenland coast from Mackenzie Bay. A night raiding party from the *Northland* captured three Nazis at a place named Peter Bregt, with equipment and code, as well as German plans for other radio stations in the far north.

The *Northland* engaged in another significant event on June 18, 1942, when lookouts spied and attacked a submarine in Davis Strait. The presence of oil and bubbles indicated possible hits from the cutter's depth charges, but German records did not indicate that a submarine had sunk in this area. That may or may not have been true. But, the incident proved to Bob Wheeler and his shipmates that life aboard the *Northland* was getting more exciting. Ensuing events bore out that feeling.

29

World War II's Weirdest Battle

> *The cutter* Storis *beat off a Nazi bombing attack while the* Northland *was pursuing the enemy trawler. A twin-motored [plane] sped in on the* Storis, *but just as it came within ack-ack range it veered off.... The* Northland, *meanwhile, was in difficulties. She had smashed her rudder in maneuvering through the ice pack.*[1]

U.S. military planners in the opening months of 1940 did not have to be geniuses to figure out that the chances of America's getting involved in the ongoing war scorching ever-wider parts of the globe were high—and growing. Americans were reading stories in their newspapers about German troops advancing in Greece, cleaning up Yugoslav and Serbian resistance, pursuing British troops in Libya.... Germans seemed to be fighting—and winning—everywhere they went. Alaska and other northern territories figured into their plans. The *Northland* would have to stay close to home.

The reasoning was simple. The United States had to support Great Britain by supplying it with necessary material. The supplies would have to be shipped via convoys through a northern route which was susceptible to German attacks. That, in turn, would lead to a U.S. declaration of war on Germany and Japan.

Leaders from those two countries agreed that if war started in the Atlantic Ocean, Japan would do what it could to help Germany by harassing allied shipping in the Pacific region and conducting nuisance attacks on the West Coast of the U.S. Such operations would affect Alaska, which was at the northern end of the U.S. Navy's first line of defense in the Pacific running south to Samoa. The United States lacked defense bases in this northern territory and was rushing to complete some, but that would take years.

A direct attack on Alaska would force an undermanned Navy to defend the north land with only a handful of Army troops to back it up. Military planners considered that scenario unlikely. They believed, however, that if the U.S. entered the war, allied ships around Alaska would require protective convoys to protect them from nuisance attacks. That was something the Coast Guard could—and did—do.

The aggressive Germans had established a blockade against Great Britain that included Iceland, just about 3,100 miles from Alaska. That was dangerously close to U.S. shores, the planners believed. Astute Americans inferred that it was only a matter of time before the U.S. got involved against them. "What was the American government going to do about Germany?" they wondered. One of the first steps was to call on the U.S. Coast Guard and the crew of the *Northland*.

Whether it was coincidence, or that top-level Coast Guard administrators were prescient, or some other reason, the *Northland* was relieved of its Arctic duties early in 1938 and reassigned to the Maritime Training Station, Government Island, Oakland, California, for training merchant marine seamen. The cutter was decommissioned and practically stripped of its crew. Commander Zeusler was assigned to the *Spencer*, Executive Officer Sarratt went to the *Haida*, and all but ten crew members were sent elsewhere. Only Lieutenants Morrison, Hahn, and Stephens remained with the *Northland*.

No one was sure if the vessel would ever return to the Arctic station for which it was designed. In June 1939, it was recommissioned and transferred to Boston, Massachusetts, to prepare for the second Byrd Antarctic Expedition, on which it would have been paired with the *Bear*. But, with the eruption of war in Europe in September, the *Northland* was withdrawn from the expedition and returned to Alameda, California. Next stop: Greenland.

By August 1940 newspaper reporters were picking up on increased activity around Coast Guard headquarters in Washington, D.C. But, no one there would answer their questions about the activity. "Getting any inside information on what is going on in any national defense work these days is like trying to pull jaw teeth with eyebrow tweezers," columnist Jack Stinnett wrote.[2]

The *Northland's* assignment to the Greenland Patrol was anything but boring. The area may have been frigid and desolate, but the action was hot. Greenland was where Europe's weather originated, so the Germans coveted the area as a base for secret weather stations and air and sea raider bases. The allies were determined to keep them away, and the *Northland* was a vital cog in the effort.

The 5-inch rifle and lesser armament of the *Northland* constituted Greenland's principal insurance against invasion in 1940. (Naval historians considered the 5"/38 gun the best intermediate-caliber dual purpose naval gun of World War II, especially as it was usually under the control of the advanced Mark 37 Gun Fire Control System, which provided accurate and timely firing against surface and air targets.) When the *Northland* returned to base for fuel or provisions another cutter relieved it on the Greenland patrol. That was a lot of responsibility for one ship, but Coast Guard officials believed the *Northland* and its partner cutters could handle it.

U.S. Navy leaders insisted that one ship was adequate as long as the British fleet and the Canadian occupation force on nearby Iceland remained intact. If they didn't, the newly created United States Atlantic fleet unquestionably would deploy to the defense of Greenland and perhaps Iceland. Maintaining a hold over those islands was critical for the allies, since they were the steppingstones for any summer air attack from Europe upon Canada's Maritime Provinces, New England, or New York. In winter, Greenland was almost wholly covered by ice, which reduced the chances of German attacks. The *Northland* patrolled in all types of weather.

The famed cutter was often in the right place at the right time. Early in 1942 allied shipping losses from the U.S. to England were beginning to mount. That dictated a change in the maritime policy.

In mid–July 1942 a flight of P-38s and a B-17 bomber en route from Greenland to Iceland on its journey to England were forced to crash land on the treacherous ice cap that covered seven-eighths of Greenland. The trapped fliers transmitted their location to their base via a jury-rigged radio. The folks at the base sent a rescue party via small boat through choppy seas to a spot on the coast that was near the downed planes. The *Northland*, loaded with aviation and gasoline supplies, was dispatched as well.[3]

When the small boat reached a fjord that allowed the rescuers access to their spot, they found that their progress was stopped by thick ice. Fortunately, the *Northland* showed up at the right moment and overtook the boat. The cutter broke the ice, which allowed the rescue boat to reach its landing site. Eventually the downed airmen were rescued, partly because the *Northland* was in the right place at the right time. That was not the last time.

The Americans had established dog sledge patrols operated by Danish nationals and Eskimo drivers to detect German operations in the area. The Germans had killed members of the patrol, including one named Eli Knudsen, and captured two others and their dogs. Despite that, the Danes reported the discovery of the radio station. That prompted them to seek help from the Americans—and revenge. There was plenty of help available.

Four cutters, the *Northland*, the *Storis*, and two new vessels on their maiden voyages, the *Southwind* and the *Eastwind*, were assigned to keep the Danes supplied and confront the Germans whenever possible. The discovery of the radio station gave them all a great opportunity to provide the Danes with help and a modicum of revenge in what was termed World War II's "weirdest battle," although the confrontation ended the *Northland*'s participation in the war.[4]

This was the second time a German radio station had been built in the Greenland area. The first was in September 1941. The rebuilt station demonstrated how desperate the Germans were to maintain such an establishment in that area to obtain weather data necessary for the operation of its aircraft and submarines in the North Atlantic. It was evident that the Germans planned to remain permanently at the base, which was small but solidly built. The facility included a radio station, power house, emergency generator, radio transmitter, defensive machine gun emplacements, and food caches. A small ship in the harbor had telephone communications with all principal shore points.

The Americans learned of the base's presence in July when the *Northland* and another cutter, the *North Port*, fought their way through the ice fields off Northeast Greenland on a mission to supply the sledge patrol's stations.[5] Crew members learned from the patrol's captain that he had spotted a well-fortified German station on Shannon Island, engaged in battle with enemy soldiers, and escaped. Shortly thereafter Coast Guardsmen and a U.S. Army combat team arrived to reinforce the Danish as they prepared to attack the German station.

It wasn't the first time in recent memory that Coast Guard sailors had been utilized as "infantry." Only a few years earlier the *Bear* had sent crew members ashore in Siberia during the Russian Civil War as part of a limited expedition involving U.S. military personnel.[6] The Siberian intervention, or Siberian expedition, of

1918–1922 was the deployment of troops of the Entente powers to the Russian Maritime Provinces as part of a larger effort by the Western powers, Japan, and China to support White Russian forces and the Czechoslovak Legion against Soviet Russia and its allies during the Russian Civil War. The Imperial Japanese Army continued to occupy Siberia even after other Allied forces withdrew in 1920. However, "Coasties" were not normally deployed as infantrymen unless it was necessary—as it became in Greenland.

Landing parties went inland to attack the Germans from the rear. They fought through heavy melting snow, sleet, and broken country, but encountered nothing more than disappointment. The Germans had destroyed their radio and meteorological equipment, gasoline, food, and ammunition, abandoned the outpost, and fled. The raiders returned to the *Northland*.

They soon received an unexpected surprise. They discovered that Germans had been chased away from their 155-foot armed trawler, believed to be the *Coberg*, which they had set on fire and dynamited in an ice field off the coast when they learned the *Storis* and the *Northland* were approaching. Apparently they had been rescued by a German aircraft that flew from Norway. That was the last contact between the *Northland*, under the command of R.W. Butcher, and the Germans for a few weeks. The crew's disappointment did not last long.[7]

About September 1 the *Northland*'s lookout spotted a German trawler about seven miles away off Great Koldewey Island. The German commander took evasive action and the trawler disappeared into the ice pack in the tricky dawn light as he tried desperately to reach open water. The trawler tried to circle behind some icebergs, but it could not elude the *Northland*, which gave chase along with the *Storis* for seven-and-one-half hours. The trawler was faster than the cutters, though, and

Whaling boat lowered from *Northland* (Alaska State Library Historical Collections).

it maintained a steady lead of about 10,000 yards. That did not faze the *Northland*'s crew. The seventy-mile pursuit began in earnest as the ships cut south through the ice field. Every time the trawler was exposed the *Northland*'s gunners fired on it.

The *Northland* closed the distance by cutting corners. For some reason the German captain tried altering course suddenly. Butcher countered the move. The trawler veered sharply again. The *Northland* sped straight ahead, gaining ground. Its shells dropped closer to the German vessel. Unexpectedly the German ship stopped because of a large finger of ice in its path. The *Northland* sailed directly for it, all guns firing.

The cutter's deck gunners homed in on the trawler and the Germans appeared to panic. Suddenly, the trawler shook from explosions fore and aft. The scuttled ship began quickly to sink. Eight German officers and 20 enlisted men pulled away from it in three lifeboats and surrendered to the *Northland*'s crew. One of the Germans was a full commander. In an elegant military gesture he handed his sword to Butcher. Eventually the sword was mounted on the *Northland*'s wardroom wall as a memento of the crew's bravery. The crew had escaped the chase unscathed. Unfortunately, the *Northland* did not.

While the *Northland* concentrated on the trawler a German Focke-Wulfe twin-motored bomber attacked the *Storis*, which fought off the plane. The *Northland*'s rudder was smashed during the action. The *Storis* stood by to cover the *Northland* while Commodore Earl G. Rose, commander of the Greenland patrol, radioed for reinforcements. Meanwhile, the damaged cutter's crew tried to repair the rudders as twenty-foot waves battered the vessel. Simultaneously, the eponymously nicknamed Rear Admiral Ed (Iceberg) Smith, Coast Guard commander of a task force positioned near Newfoundland, ordered the *Eastwind* and the *Southwind* to report to the scene. The *Northland* would be going home.

Repairing the rudder was next to an impossible task for the freezing crew members. But they had more to worry about than making repairs. They had to be on the alert for German U-boats and planes that might attack them as they worked. No attack materialized however. Regardless of the obstacles, the crew managed to jury rig the rudder, which allowed the helmsman to steer the vessel despite a large number of breaks in the cable lines.

The Coast Guard tender *Evergreen* was dispatched to tow the *Northland* to Boston, some 3,000 miles away, for repairs, much to the joy of the "Coasties" aboard. Temporary jubilation notwithstanding, the return marked an ignominious ending for the legendary cutter in its battle against enemy forces near Greenland. Butcher earned the Legion of Merit medal, a military award of the United States Armed Forces that is given for exceptionally meritorious conduct in the performance of outstanding services and achievements. It was not a medal for valor, but it was high praise for a member of the Coast Guard, which rarely received such recognition. Nevertheless, it was a victory for the allied forces—and for public relations for the Coast Guard.

Columnist Aycock Brown, after recounting Butcher's feat for his readers, wrote[8]: "The foregoing is published as a reminder of the important role the Coast Guard had in World War II. The Coast Guard seldom gets the publicity for its activities that other military forces receive and that is why, when this column can recall some Coast Guard incident, it always puts in a plug for that wartime/peacetime service. There is seldom a day that passes when some new achievement of the Coast Guard is not in the making."

That September battle marked the end of Germany's activities in the area. The *Northland*'s rudder was merely damaged. The Germans were completely rudderless around Greenland. That was a profitable tradeoff for the *Northland* and the entire Coast Guard—and the end of an era.

Epilogue

The Bear *Goes to the Bottom;* the Northland *Ends Life on the Scrap Heap*

> "*Cutter Northland Awaits Buyer*—The 216-foot Coast Guard cutter Northland, which did valiant duty in Greenland waters during World War II under command of Lt. Cmdr. R.W. Butcher, is one of 24 vessels on which the Maritime Commission opened buyers' bids for yesterday."[1]

> "*CUTTER 'BEAR' SETS PATROL TRIP RECORD*—The famous Coast Guard cutter 'Bear' set a record when she made 42 patrol trips to the Bering Sea, during which she sailed almost 700,000 nautical miles in treacherous, ice-filled waters. Once the cutter arrived at its destination, fires, fish and seal poachers, and Eskimo weddings were all in the day's work."[2]

Such were the epitaphs for arguably the two most storied cutters in Coast Guard history. The *Bear* and the *Northland* headed in dramatically different directions after 1927. The *Northland* became the Coast Guard's "go to" ship in the Arctic, and then Greenland. The *Bear* came out of hibernation and headed for the South Pole as part of Rear Admiral Richard Byrd's 1933–1935 Antarctic Expedition. The Coast Guard may have lost faith in the *Bear*; Byrd did not.

Byrd was familiar with the *Bear*'s capabilities. Terms like "useful economic life" meant little to him. He purchased the former cutter for $1,000 in 1932 specifically for his expedition and moved it from San Francisco to Boston.[3] The voyage consumed 22 days, but the *Bear* arrived for duty in Boston on the night of August 10.

It was certainly still seaworthy. The trip was so successful the government dragged it out of retirement again in 1939 to accompany two other ships in another of Byrd's expeditions, one of which was scheduled to be the *Northland*.[4] How ironic that would have been: the links between the "old" and "new" Coast Guards working together for the first time. But it was not to be.

World events intervened, and the *Northland* was diverted to Greenland while Byrd and the *Bear* were going "way down under" to claim lands for the U.S. that he had already charted with the aid of a trans-Atlantic flyer. At least the announcement of the *Bear*'s new mission gave reporters a chance to brush up on their flowery phraseology.[5]

> A barnacle smudged old barkentine was being dandied up today to take a man with "itching feet" back to the frozen Antarctic where he cheated death in the polar darkness. She's the

Bear of Oakland, rugged veteran of the icefields, which the United States Government has commissioned.

She's no beauty, as ships go. But she's still fit, despite almost 70 years of punishment as a sealer, a watchdog of the Coast Guard among the ice packs and, most recently, the running mate of the flagship Jake Ruppert during Byrd's last expedition to the South Pole in 1933–35. Where workers flock her masts today, armed with paint pots, weather-roughened sealers once scanned the icy wilderness and yelled above the smashing of the floes: "White coats ahead!"

The *Northland* was returned to the Treasury Department on January 1, 1946, and remained on weather patrol duty. It sailed into Boston on February 1, 1946, with 40 Greenland veterans aboard, then was decommissioned on March 27.[6] A reporter glowingly described its return: "But it reached Boston, its decks filled with cheering American soldiers and sailors, its hold heavy with the remains of Hitler's disastrous effort to establish a weather empire on the roof of the western hemisphere."

Then it continued its service as the first warship of the new Israeli Navy. The *Northland* was sold for $50,000 to an American firm surreptitiously for the Israeli "underground," sailed for the Mediterranean in 1947, underwent conversion work, and took the new name of *The Jewish State*. The Israeli government got its money's worth.[7]

The former cutter ran the British blockade of Palestine a number of times to transport Jewish immigrants. It took on a new name, *Matzpen*, after the creation of the State of Israel in 1948. The name may have changed but the missions didn't.

The ship engaged Egyptian forces that attacked Israel by sea, shelled Tira and Tyre, served as a training vessel, and became a tender to the Israeli motor torpedo boat fleet. Finally, it was designated an accommodations ship for the port command at Haifa. Sadly, its usefulness disappeared. The 35-year-old old cutter was decommissioned from the Israeli Navy in February 1962 and sold for scrap. The *Bear* lived on, but not for long.

It was almost as if the wooden vessel heard about the *Northland*'s demise and decided to go with it. A year later the *Bear* was being towed to Philadelphia to be converted into a floating restaurant. The *Bear* escaped the tow about 90 miles south of Cape Sable, Nova Scotia, and 260 miles east of Boston, sank, and remained undisturbed at the bottom of the ocean for almost sixty years. Explorers detected its position in 2019. Two years later Coast Guard and National Oceanic and Atmospheric Administration officials declared that they were reasonably sure the wreck was the *Bear*.

Ironically, they made the announcement the same day the U.S. Coast Guard Cutter *Healey*, named after the *Bear*'s former captain, arrived in Boston. The *Healey*, an icebreaker commissioned in 1999, had recently completed a voyage through the Arctic Northwest Passage.

William Thiesen, the Coast Guard Atlantic Area's official historian, briefly highlighted *Bear*'s accomplishment during its Arctic career[8]: "During *Bear*'s 40-year career in Alaska, the cutter performed some of the most daring and successful Arctic rescues in history," he recounted. "When malnourished Native Americans needed food, *Bear* brought it. When stranded whalers needed rescue, *Bear* saved them. One hundred years ago, when thousands of Alaskans contracted the Spanish flu during the pandemic, *Bear* brought doctors and medicine."

The *Bear* lets go of its tow line and heads for the bottom (USCG Historian's Office).

That last mission demonstrated another similarity between the crew members of the *Northland* and the *Bear*. They were willing to risk their own health to help others. The *Northland*'s crew got its chance in 1928 when a chickenpox epidemic broke out in Nome, Alaska. Well, almost.[9]

Coast guard physicians and territorial doctors dispelled the rumor quickly. They said about twenty Eskimos had been stricken with chickenpox, but the cases were not serious. Nevertheless, Admiral Billard in Washington, D.C., had ordered the commander of the *Northland* to give all aid possible. No Coast Guard commander needed orders to do that, especially those on the *Northland* and the *Bear*.

It was a sad time for Coast Guard officials when the *Bear-Northland* era ended. "*Bear* had served in various capacities for nearly 90 years, a remarkable record for a ship built of wood," Thiesen said. The *Northland* may not have lasted that long, but its record was every bit as exemplary.

No wonder the links between the "old" and the "new" Coast Guards both became legends in Coast Guard history—and the public's eye.

Appendix A

Technical Specifications/ Features (the *Northland*)[1]

The *Northland* was a mechanical marvel for its time, although it did not mark a complete break between the old and the new technologies. Designers hedged their bets. The *Northland* was a brigantine, i.e., a two-masted sailing vessel with a fully square-rigged foremast and at least two sails on the main mast: a square topsail and a gaff sail mainsail. The main mast is the second and taller of the two masts. In accordance, *Northland* was rigged with a square rig on the foremast and fore and aft on the mainmast.

Here are some of the ship's most significant characteristics:

The Northland

- had a boom rigged for hoisting an airplane aboard and was spaced for carrying its own plane, although it was not equipped for one on its first voyage
- carried its own moving picture machine, and its large after deck gave plenty of room for the audience
- featured a completely outfitted hospital and dentist office on board to be used for treatments at out of the way places along the ship's course
- included a high-powered radio outfit
- offered passenger space for natives, with six spare cabins for government officials and guests
- was 216 feet in length, with a 39-foot beam
- displaced 2,050 tons
- was powered by two 600 H.P. Diesels with 1,000 horsepower capable of driving her at 11½ knots an hour
- had a maximum cruising radius of 16,000 miles while at slow speed
- was protected from the ice by welded and riveted steel plates, covering the boat 1¼ inches in thickness
- had a blunt and gradually sloped bow for breaking through ice fields
- employed all the latest instruments in its wheelhouse, including a radio compass, electric fathometer, automatic log register, and course recorder
- was equipped with Diesel electric drive, single screw

- was steered with an electric hydraulic steering gear
- carried an auxiliary power engine and seven life boats, three of which were equipped with engines
- was armed with four mounted guns: two 4-inchers forward, two 6-pounders aft, and machine guns

Appendix B

How *The Call* Has Outfitted the *Bear*[1]

SEATTLE, Nov. 25.—Outfits have been furnished by *The Call* to the following officers of the *Bear* and members of the overland relief expedition:

Captain F. Tuttle.

First Lieutenants J, H. Brown and David H. Jarvis.

Second Lieutenants C.H. Cochrane, John C. Berry (*The Call* correspondent), B.H. Camden (Examiner correspondent), H.G. Hamlet (Chronicle correspondent), E.V. Bertholf (*The Call* correspondent)

Chief Engineer H.W. Speer.

First Assistant Engineer H.N. Wood (*The Call* photographer).

Second Assistant Engineers H.K. Spencer and J.I. Bryan.

Surgeons:—Dr. S.J. Call, Dr. E.H. Woodruff (*The Call*'s surgeon).

Steward William Boundy.

Explorer F. Koltzschoff.

Each man was furnished with the following articles: Eskimo dog skin parkie and breeches, dog skin boots, silk mitts, buckskin gloves, silk hoods, fur cap, half-dozen silk socks, half-dozen Arctic socks, duck vest, two suits silk underwear, suit chamois-skin underwear.

In addition, the members of the overland expedition were supplied with sleeping blankets, duck parkies, wolfskin robe, field glasses, rifle, knives and complete outfit.

A library of over 200 bound volumes and book and sheet music was also furnished for the wardroom of the *Bear*. Extra provisions for the crew were furnished by *The Call* and shipped from San Francisco. The stores, including groceries, provisions, wines and cigars for the wardroom mess, were procured in Seattle.

The whole amounted in value, for which cash was paid to various firms, to $7,069.78.

The complete cost breakdown reflected the fact that *The Call* spared no expense to buy the best supplies it could, even going as far as Paris, France for some items:

The following is a complete list of the bills paid by the management of *The Call* for the outfit furnished to the *Bear* Relief Expedition:

IN SAN FRANCISCO.
William Cluff & Co., provisions and canned goods.. $695.70
Dodge, Sweeney & Co., provisions.. $484.57
Wieland Brewing Company, beer… $3000
Freight on above paid to Seattle $79.27
Total $1,289.54

IN SEATTLE.
M. M. Windmiler, fur clothing $452.50
City of Paris, fur clothing, gloves, mitts, blankets, wolfskin, robes, socks, etc. $353.00
Minor W. Bruce, silk hoods $18.75
The Famous Clothing Company, duck vests, fur caps, silk socks…. $90.00
J. Redelscheimer & Co., silk and chamois underwear $861.00
Lawman & Hanford, books and magazines $43.85
Winter & Harper, book and sheet music $11.40
Graham & Moore, field glass $25.00
Seattle Hardware Company, skin boots, rifle, knives $92.00
J. Baillargoon & Co., silk socks…. $45.50
Washington Rubber Company, oil coat $2.75
Fisher Bros., groceries, meats, canned goods, etc. $2,980.37
F. A. Buckland & Co., wines, ales, beers, etc. $486.00
Fisher Bros., cigars and cigarettes. $307.62
Calvert Company, books $4.50
Expressage, rubber stamps, etc…. $6.00
Total $5,780.24
Grand total, $7,069.78

Chapter Notes

Introduction

1. https://brainyquote.com/quotes/steve_backshall_1169830
2. San Francisco, CA, *Call*, Aug. 1, 1897
3. Richmond, VA, *Times Dispatch*, June 1, 1914, p. 7
4. http://www.fdca.org.uk/Stephens_Whalers.html
5. https://en.wikipedia.org/wiki/Lady_Franklin_Bay_Expedition
6. Stamford, CT, *Daily Advocate*, Thursday, June 23, 1927, p. 17
7. *Ibid.*
8. https://www.history.uscg.mil/Browse-by-Topic/Assets/Water/All/Article/2082164/bear-1885/
9. Wichita, KS, *Daily Eagle*, Oct. 1893, p. 6
10. New York, NY, *Herald*, Sept. 3, 1922, SECTION TWO, p. 2
11. Philadelphia, PA, *Evening Public Ledger*, Aug. 17, 1922, Sports Extra, p. 15
12. Douglas, AZ, *Daily Dispatch*, June 23, 1927, p. 2
13. Imperial Valley, CA, *Press*, June 10, 1926

Chapter 1

1. Stamford, CT, *Daily Advocate*, July 14, 1932, p. 8
2. San Francisco *Chronicle*, Aug. 8, 1927, p. 25

Chapter 2

1. "O Captain! My Captain!" an 1865 poem by Walt Whitman about the assassination of U.S. president Abraham Lincoln.
2. Nome, AK, *Nugget*, Aug. 9, 1930
3. San Francisco, CA, *Call*, Nov. 18, 1897
4. Nome, AK, *Nugget*, June 10, 1933, p. 4
5. Cordova, AK, *Daily Times*, June 27, 1922
6. Nome, AK, *Nugget*, Aug. 10, 1929, p. 2
7. Nome, AK, *Nugget*, July 1, 1938
8. Washington, D.C., *Evening Star*, July 9, 1933, p. A-2
9. Juneau, AK, *Daily Alaska Empire*, July 10, 1933

Chapter 3

1. "News from Alaska," Seattle *Post-Intelligencer*, May 19, 1891, p. 7
2. Juneau, AK, *Alaska Daily Empire*, Nov. 8, 1913
3. Anaconda, MT, *Standard*, Oct. 9, 1899, p. 2
4. Birmingham, AL *Age-Herald*, Aug. 25, 1899
5. https://alaskashipwreck.com/shipwrecks-by-area/west-central-alaska-shipwrecks-2/west-central-alaska-shipwrecks-g/
6. Nome, AK, *Daily Nugget*, Nov. 5, 1912
7. Skagway, AK, *Daily Alaskan*, Apr. 22, 1909
8. San Francisco, CA, *Call*, Dec. 13, 1908, p. 4
9. Skagway, AK, *Daily Alaskan*, Oct. 22, 1909
10. Washington D.C. *Evening Star*, Dec. 1, 1912, p. 9
11. Seattle, WA, *Post-Intelligencer*, May 19, 1891
12. Skagway, AK, *Daily Alaskan*, Mar. 14, 1922, p. 2
13. Nome, AK, *Nugget*, June 5, 1934
14. Seattle, WA, *Post-Intelligencer*, May 19, 1891, loc. cit.
15. Seattle, WA, *Post-Intelligencer*, June 4, 1891, p. 12
16. Los Angeles, CA, *Herald*, Aug. 5, 1892

Chapter 4

1. https://www.brainyquote.com/quotes/mark_twain_141773
2. Helena, MT, *Independent*, Nov. 2, 1892, Morning, p. 5
3. Cordova, AK, *Daily Times*, Apr. 8, 1915
4. Seattle, WA, *Post-Intelligencer*, May 19, 1891
5. Valdez, AK, *Alaska Prospector*, Apr. 17, 1902
6. Valdez, AK, *Alaska Prospector*. Apr. 17, 1902
7. *Ibid.*
8. *Ibid.*
9. San Francisco, CA, *Call*, Mar. 6, 1895, p. 6
10. Seattle, WA, *Post-Intelligencer*, May 19, 1891
11. Honolulu, HI, *Pacific Commercial Advertiser*, June 20, 1896, p. 5
12. *Ibid.*
13. New York, NY, *Sun*, Jan. 26, 1896, p. 6

Chapter 5

1. Virginia City, MT *Madisonian*, Dec. 14, 1895
2. https://www.history.uscg.mil/Browse-by-Topic/Notable-People/All/Article/1848494/captain-michael-a-Healey-usrcs/ (New York *Sun*)
3. https://www.history.uscg.mil/Browse-by-Topic/Notable-People/All/Article/1848494/captain-michael-a-Healey-usrcs/
4. Portland, ME, *Daily Press*, June 1, 1886, p. 4
5. Las Vegas, NV, *Review-Journal*, June 13, 1982, p. 85
6. Sitka, AK, *Daily Sentinel*, Oct. 26, 2006, p. 3
7. Atlanta, GA, *Journal*, Oct. 4, 1973, p. 31
8. Fairbanks, AK, *Daily News Miner*, Oct. 16, 1982
9. "Indians seek apology from U.S. Navy for attack," Las Vegas, NV, *Review-Journal*, June 20, 1982, p. 62
10. Sacramento, CA, *Daily Record Union*, Apr. 13, 1886
11. Healey biographical information, loc. cit.
12. San Francisco, CA, *Call*, Dec. 3, 1895, p. 8

Chapter 6

1. Author.
2. Tucson, AZ, *Weekly Citizen*, Dec. 14, 1895
3. Portland, OR, *Oregonian*, Jan. 30, 1896, p. 2
4. San Francisco, CA, *Call*, Nov. 15, 1895, p. 9
5. San Francisco, CA, *Call*, Jan. 31, 1896, p. 14
6. Portland, OR, *Oregonian*, Jan. 28, 1896
7. San Francisco, CA, *Call*, Dec. 2, 1895, p. 12
8. San Francisco, CA, *Call*, Jan. 24, 1896, p. 7
9. "Back from the Arctic," San Francisco *Call*, Nov. 15, 1895, p. 9
10. San Francisco, CA, *Call*, Dec. 2, 1895, p. 12
11. *Ibid.*
12. "Back from the Arctic," San Francisco *Call*, Nov. 15, 1895, p. 9
13. *Ibid.*
14. New York, NY, *Tribune*, Dec. 2, 1895, p. 1
15. San Francisco, CA, *Call*, Dec. 2, 1895, p. 12
16. Salt Lake, UT, *Herald*, Dec. 20, 1895, p. 2
17. "Along the waterfront," San Francisco *Call*, Dec. 19, 1895, p. 7
18. Logansport, IN, *Daily Pharos*, December 6, 1895, p. 1
19. San Antonio, TX, *Daily Light*, Dec. 5, 1895
20. Salt Lake, UT, *Herald*, Dec. 12, 1895, p. 2

Chapter 7

1. San Francisco *Call Bulletin*, Dec 3, 1895, p. 9
2. Elmore, ID, *Bulletin*, Jan. 15, 1896
3. Wichita, KS, *Daily Eagle*, Jan. 28, 1896, p. 7
4. "Never drunk while on duty," Wichita, KS, *Daily Eagle*, Jan. 28, 1896, p. 7
5. https://hakaimagazine.com/article-short/true-blue/
6. *Ibid.*
7. Portland, OR, *Oregonian*, Jan. 25, 1896, p. 2
8. San Francisco, CA, *Call*, Jan. 29, 1896, p. 8
9. "Antics in the Arctic," San Francisco *Call-Bulletin*, Jan. 29, 1896, p. 9
10. "Antics" loc. cit.
11. "The accused on the stand in his own behalf," Portland, OR, *Oregonian*, Jan. 30, 1896, p. 2
12. Portland, ME, *Daily Press*, Feb. 10, 1896, p. 5
13. Washington D.C. *Evening Star*, Feb.8, 1896, p. 2
14. San Francisco, CA, *Call-Bulletin*, Feb. 9, 1896, p. 20
15. Portland. OR, *Oregonian*, Feb. 21, 1896, p. 2
16. "Sharp's stories scored," San Francisco *Call*, Feb. 22, 1896
17. *Ibid.*
18. *Ibid.*
19. *Ibid.*

Chapter 8

1. Author unknown
2. Reno, NV, *Weekly Nevada State Journal*, Mar. 28, 1896, p. 2
3. Washington D.C. *Evening Star*, March 17, 1896
4. San Francisco, CA, *Chronicle*, Mar. 29, 1896, p. 19
5. San Francisco, CA, *Call*, Mar. 27, 1896
6. Honolulu, HI, *Pacific Commercial Advertiser*, June 18, 1896, p. 2
7. Seattle, WA, *Daily Times*, Apr. 16, 1902, p. 9
8. Little Falls, MN, *Weekly Transcript*, July 17, 1900
9. Skowhegan, ME, *Somerset Reporter*, Dec. 5, 1901, p. 6
10. San Francisco, CA, *Call*, Apr. 9, 1896, p. 11
11. Seattle, WA, *Daily Times*, Apr. 10, 1902, p. 5
12. Valdez, AK, *Alaska Prospector*, Sept. 17, 1903
13. Seattle, WA, *Post-Intelligencer*, Apr. 28, 1896, p. 2
14. Honolulu, HI, *Pacific Commercial Advertiser*, May 21, 1905, p. 10

Chapter 9

1. "Our little 'White Navy,'" Dearborn, MI, *Independent*, Jan. 8, 1921, p. 6
2. Washington D.C. *Evening Star*, May 7, 1933, p. A-9
3. Nome, AK, *Nugget*, Aug. 3, 1938, p. 4
4. San Diego, CA, *Union*, Mar. 2, 1930, p. 40
5. Perth Amboy, NJ, *Evening News*, Nov. 26, 1909, Last Edition
6. https://www.history.uscg.mil/Browse-by-Topic/Notable-People/All/Article/1762503/commodore-ellsworth-p-bertholf/
7. Providence, RI, *News*, Nov. 12, 1897
8. Seattle, WA, *Post-Intelligencer*, Oct. 11, 1891
9. San Francisco, CA, *Call*, Nov. 17, 1897, p. 2
10. San Francisco, CA, *Call*, Nov. 18, 1897

11. San Francisco *Call,* Nov. 17, 1897, p. 2
12. San Francisco, CA, *Call*, Nov. 20, 1897

Chapter 10

1. San Francisco, CA, *Call,* Nov. 20, 1897
2. San Francisco, CA, *Call,* Nov. 8, 1897
3. Ibid.
4. Ibid.
5. San Francisco, CA, *Call*, Nov. 11, 1897, p. 6
6. San Francisco, CA, *Call*, Nov. 10, 1897, p. 2
7. Los Angeles, CA, *Herald*, Nov.9, 1897, p. 2
8. San Francisco, CA, *Call*, Nov. 8, 1897
9. Ibid.
10. Topeka, KS, *State Journal*, Nov. 9, 1897, p. 3
11. San Francisco, CA, *Call*, Nov. 17, 1897, p. 2
12. San Francisco, CA, *Call*, Nov. 9, 1897
13. San Francisco, CA, *Call*, Nov. 9, 1897
14. San Francisco, CA, *Call*, Nov. 14, 1897

Chapter 11

1. San Francisco, CA, *Call*, Nov. 22, 1897
2. San Francisco, CA, *Call*, Nov. 12, 1897
3. Marietta, OH, *Daily Leader*, Nov. 20, 1897
4. San Francisco, CA, *Call*, Nov. 17, 1897, p. 2
5. San Francisco, CA, *Call*, Nov. 27, 1897
6. Ibid.
7. San Francisco, CA, *Call*, Nov. 17, 1897, p. 2
8. Ibid.
9. San Francisco, CA, *Call,* Nov. 20, 1897
10. Marietta, OH, *Daily Leader*, Nov. 20, 1897
11. San Francisco, CA, *Call,* Nov. 20, 1897
12. San Francisco, CA, Call, Nov. 27, 1897
13. Ibid.
14. Providence, RI, *News*, Nov. 12, 1897
15. San Francisco, CA *Call*, Nov. 22, 1897
16. San Francisco, CA, *Call*, Nov. 17, 1897
17. San Francisco, CA, *Call*, Nov. 27, 1897
18. San Francisco, CA, *Call*, Sept. 13, 1898

Chapter 12

1. "Captain of the Bear," Wichita, KS, *Daily Eagle,* Oct. 5, 1893, p. 6
2. Ibid.
3. San Francisco, CA, *Bulletin*, Oct. 3, 1891
4. Wailuku, HI, *Maui News*, December 31, 1904
5. Ibid.
6. Wailuku, HI, Maui *News,* Dec. 31, 1904
7. Skagway, AK, *Daily Morning Alaskan*, Aug. 4, 1901

Chapter 13

1. Astoria, OR, *Morning Astorian*, Sept. 6, 1900
2. San Francisco, CA, *Call*, May 6, 1900
3. New York, NY, *Sun*, Apr. 6, 1900, p. 4
4. St. Louis, MO, *Republic*, May 8, 1900, p. 13
5. Butte, MT, *Daily Inter Mountain*, June 18, 1900
6. Astoria, OR, *Morning Astorian*, Apr. 11, 1900
7. Indianapolis, IN, *Journal*, Apr. 4, 1902
8. Raleigh, NC, *News & Observer*, Apr. 04, 1902
9. Seattle, WA, *Post-Intelligencer*, May 6, 1900, p. 12
10. San Francisco, CA, *Call*, June 27, 1900
11. Honolulu, HI, *Republican*, July 6, 1900
12. St. Louis, MO, *Republic*, Sept. 9, 1900, p. 3
13. Astoria, OR, *Morning Astorian*, Sept. 6, 1900
14. Marshalltown, IA, *Evening Times-Republican,* July 12, 1900
15. L'Anse, MI, *Sentinel*, Sept. 1, 1900
16. Potosi, MO, *Journal*, Nov. 7, 1900
17. New York, NY, *Tribune*, July 12, 1900, p. 4
18. Americus, GA, *Times-Recorder*, July 12, 1900
19. New Haven, CT, *Daily Morning Journal and Courier,* July 12, 1900
20. Washington D.C. *Times*, July 6, 1900, p. 7
21. Norfolk, VA, *Virginian-Pilot*, August 12, 1900
22. Astoria, OR, *Morning Astorian*, Sept. 6, 1900
23. Maysville, KY *Daily Public Ledger*, Sept. 6, 1900, p. 3
24. Waterbury, CT, *Evening Democrat*, Sept. 6, 1900, p. 4
25. Condon, OR, *Globe*, Sept. 13, 1900
26. Stamford, CT, *Daily Advocate*, Nov. 5, 1900, p. 6
27. L'Anse, MI, *Sentinel*, Sept. 1, 1900

Chapter 14

1. Honolulu, HI, *Hawaiian Star,* Feb. 2, 1905, SECOND EDITION
2. Honolulu, HI, Hawaiian *Star*, May 11, 1905, SECOND EDITION, p. 5
3. Honolulu, HI, *Pacific Commercial Advertiser,* Feb. 25, 1905, p. 10
4. Honolulu, HI, *Pacific Commercial Advertiser,* Jan. 24, 1905, p. 7
5. Honolulu, HI, *Hawaiian Star*, Mar. 30, 1905, p. 5
6. Honolulu, HI, *Hawaiian Star*, Feb. 2, 1905
7. Honolulu, HI, *Hawaiian Star*, Feb. 14, 1905
8. Honolulu, HI, *Hawaiian Gazette*, Feb. 17, 1905, p. 8
9. Honolulu, HI, *Evening Bulletin*, Feb. 16, 1905
10. Honolulu, HI, *Hawaiian Star*, Feb. 15, 1905, p. 5
11. Honolulu, HI, *Pacific Commercial Advertiser*, Feb. 26, 1905
12. Honolulu, HI, *Pacific Commercial Advertiser*, Mar. 5, 1905
13. Honolulu, HI Pacific *Commercial Advertiser*, Mar. 2, 1905, p. 10
14. Honolulu, HI, *Hawaiian Star*, Apr. 3, 1905, p. 8
15. Honolulu, HI, *Evening Bulletin*, June 6, 1905
16. Ibid.

Chapter 15

1. Honolulu, HI, *Hawaiian Star*, Nov. 15, 1905, SECOND EDITION, p. 7
2. San Francisco, CA, *Call*, Nov. 4, 1905, pp. 1–2
3. Douglas City, AK, *Island News*, Sept. 13, 1905
4. Skagway, AK, *Daily Alaskan*, Nov. 13, 1905
5. San Francisco, CA, *Call-Bulletin*, Jul. 18, 1905, p. 3
6. Nome, AK, *Tri-weekly Nugget*, Dec. 2, 1905
7. Shore Whaling was undertaken from a fixed facility on land known as a "Station" or "Fishery. The men lived on shore and left the bays and beaches during the whaling season in "whaling gangs" to row out to the sea adjacent to the coast in order to hunt migrating Southern Right Whales or Tohorā. Following their capture the dead whales were towed by whaleboats back to the station. The carcasses were then hauled up on sheers (also known as sheer legs) and processed using shore based facilities. (http://whalerswahine.com/)
8. San Francisco *Call-Bulletin*, Nov. 7, 1906, p. 11
9. Rampart, AK, *Yukon Valley News*, Aug. 01, 1906
10. Spokane, WA, *Press*, Sept. 11, 1906
11. San Francisco, CA, *Call-Bulletin*, Nov. 18, 1906
12. San Francisco, CA, *Call*, Sept. 4, 1907, p. 9
13. Manning, SC, *Times*, Nov. 6, 1907
14. *Ibid*.
15. Nome, AK, *Semi-weekly Nugget*, Aug. 12, 1905

Chapter 16

1. Washington D.C. *Evening Star*, Dec. 1, 1912, p. 9
2. Norwich, CT, *Bulletin*, Aug. 3, 1910
3. Chickasha, OK, *Daily Express*, Sept. 13, 1910, p. 2
4. Los Angeles, CA, *Daily Herald*, Sept. 16, 1889, p. 2
5. Ogden, UT, *Evening Standard*, Nov. 11, 1911, p. 14
6. Washington D.C. *Evening Star*, Nov 8, 1910, p. 2

Chapter 17

1. "Uncle Sam's seals," Holbrook, AZ, *News.*, Jan. 13, 1911
2. Wakarusa, IN, *Tribune*, Dec. 1, 1910
3. Washington D.C. *Evening Star*, Dec. 19, 1909, p. 8
4. Las Vegas, NV, *Age*, Jan. 14, 1911, p. 2
5. Madison, SD, *Daily Leader*, Feb. 10, 1910
6. Holbrook, AZ, *News*, Jan. 13, 1911
7. Walla Walla, WA, *Evening Statesman*, Dec. 31, 1909 p. 6
8. *Ibid*.

Chapter 18

1. About Us | Alaska Commercial Co.—NWC
2. Ketchikan, AK, *Miner*, Aug. 7, 1909
3. Los Angeles, CA, *Herald*, Aug. 8, 1891
4. Wilmington, DE, *Evening Journal*, Dec. 8, 1890
5. *Ibid*.
6. Skagway, AK, *Daily Alaskan*, Nov. 23, 1909
7. Washington D.C. *Evening Star*, Dec. 10, 1909, p. 20
8. Worcester, MA, *Daily Spy*, May 7, 1893, Worcester, MA, p. 9
9. New York, NY, *Tribune*, Aug. 9, 1906, p. 2
10. Canton, OH, *Repository*, May 6, 1893, p. 7

Chapter 19

1. Ketchikan, AK, *Miner*, Aug. 7, 1909
2. San Francisco, CA, *Morning Call*, May 27, 1890, p. 4
3. Waterbury, CT, *Evening Democrat*, Sept. 22, 1890
4. Sacramento, CA, *Daily Record-Union*, June 13, 1890
5. *Ibid*.
6. San Francisco, CA, *Morning Call*, June 12, 1890
7. Los Angeles, CA, *Herald*, Mar. 30, 1892
8. New York, NY, *Tribune*, Jan. 12, 1889, p. 6
9. San Francisco, CA, *Morning Call*, May 27, 1890, p. 4
10. Saint Paul, MN, *Daily Globe*, Feb. 23, 1888
11. *Ibid*.
12. Los Angeles *Herald*, Aug. 16, 1893, p. 2
13. *Ibid*.

Chapter 20

1. Los Angeles, CA, *Herald*, July 24, 1890
2. Seattle, WA, *Post-Intelligencer*, Sept. 24, 1890
3. Waterbury, CT, *Evening Democrat*, Sept. 22, 1890
4. Seattle, WA, *Post-Intelligencer*, Sept. 24, 1890
5. Los Angeles, CA, *Daily Herald*, Sept. 9, 1889, p. 2
6. River Falls, WI, *Journal*, Aug. 24, 1893
7. Seattle, WA, *Star*, May 9, 1914, p. 15
8. River Falls, WI, *Journal*, loc. cit.
9. Seattle, WA, *Post-Intelligencer*, Oct. 11, 1891
10. Bridgeton, NJ, *Pioneer*, May 18, 1893
11. St. Paul, MN, *Daily Globe*, July 3, 1890, p. 8
12. Waterbury, CT, *Evening Democrat*, July 3, 1890
13. New York, NY, *Herald*, Sept. 25, 1890, p. 7
14. Seattle, WA, *Post-Intelligencer*, Nov. 20, 1890
15. San Francisco, CA, *Morning Call*, December 1, 1890, p. 4

Chapter 21

1. Author.
2. San Francisco, CA, *Call*, Dec. 3, 1908, p. 8

3. Honolulu, HI, *Hawaiian Star*, Dec. 19, 1906, SECOND EDITION, p. 10
4. St. Louis County, MN, *Virginia Enterprise*, May 27, 1910, p. 5
5. Bemidji, MN, *Daily Pioneer*, Aug. 9, 1906
6. Bon Homme Count, SD, *Citizen-Republican*, Aug. 23, 1906, p.3
7. Newport News, VA, *Daily Press*, Aug. 9, 1906
8. Valdez, AK, *Alaska Prospector,* Aug. 30, 1906
9. Seward, AK, *Weekly Gateway*, Oct. 20, 1906
10. Ibid.
11. Salt Lake *Herald,* Sept. 5, 1907, Page 2
12. Douglas City, AK, *Island News*, Sept. 11, 1907
13. San Francisco, CA, *Call*, Dec. 13, 1908, p. 4
14. Lincoln, NE, *State Journal*, Aug. 16, 1908, p. 2
15. San Francisco, CA, *Call*, Dec. 3, 1908, p. 8
16. Coeur d'Alene, ID, *Evening Press*, Sept. 30, 1908, p. 4
17. Heppner County, OR, *Gazette*, Oct. 1, 1908
18. Valdez, AK, *Prospector*, Dec. 24, 1908
19. Albuquerque, NM, *Citizen*, Nov. 28, 1908
20. Topeka, KS, *State Journal*, Oct. 8, 1909, p. 3

Chapter 22

1. Washington D.C. *Evening Star*, Dec. 10, 1909, p. 20
2. Vernon County, WI, *Censor*, Sept. 29, 1909, p. 7
3. Bismarck, ND, *Daily Tribune*, Oct. 8, 1909
4. Washington D.C. *Evening Star*, Mar. 21, 1909, p. 12
5. Perth Amboy, NJ, *Evening News*, Nov. 26, 1909, Last Edition
6. Skagway, AK *Daily Alaskan*, Oct. 22, 1909
7. Deseret, UT, *Evening News*, Sept. 28, 1909
8. Washington D.C. *Evening Star*, Jan. 3, 1909, p. 14
9. Ibid.
10. Honolulu, HI, *Hawaiian Star*, Jan. 26, 1910
11. Washington D.C. *Times*, May 20, 1912, LAST EDITION, p. 7
12. Elbert County, CO, *Tribune*, Apr. 5, 1912
13. Nome, AK, *Daily Nugget*, June 4, 1913
14. Nome, AK, *Daily Nugget*, Aug. 7, 1913
15. Nome *Daily Nugget*, June 04, 1913
16. Valdez, AK, *Daily Prospector*, August 5, 1913
17. Honolulu, HI, *Star-Bulletin*, Sept. 18, 1913, p. 2

Chapter 23

1. https://en.wikipedia.org/wiki/Last_voyage_of_the_*Karluk* (incident synopsis)
2. Richmond, VA, *Times Dispatch*, June 1, 1914, p. 7
3. Denver, CO, *Rocky Mountain News*, Sept. 6, 1914, p. 8
4. Ogden, UT, *Standard*, Sept. 17, 1915, City Edition
5. San Jose, CA, *Mercury News*, Sept. 15, 1914, p. 1
6. Portland, OR, *Oregonian*, Sept. 14, 1914, p. 5
7. Seward, AK, *Gateway*, Sept. 18, 1915

Chapter 24

1. Washington D.C. *Evening Star*, Aug. 31, 1922, p. 13
2. Seward, AK, *Gateway*, March 18, 1921
3. Birmingham, AL, *Age-Herald*, Aug. 25, 1899
4. Wrangell, AK, *Sentinel*, Sept. 15, 1927
5. Washington D.C. *Evening Star*, Jan. 19, 1924
6. Juneau, AK, *Daily Alaska Empire*, June 10, 1927
7. Ibid.
8. https://en.wikopedia.org/wiki/Hubert_Wilkins
9. Seattle, WA, *Post-Intelligencer*, Oct. 11, 1891
10. New York, NY, *Tribune*, Oct. 12, 1921, p. 4
11. Washington D.C. *Evening Star*, July 19, 1921, p. 13
12. Cordova, AK, *Daily Times*, June 28, 1922, p. 8
13. Seattle, WA, *Star*, Sept. 25, 1923
14. Juneau, AK, *Alaska Daily Empire*, Aug. 12, 1926, p. 4
15. Kusko, AK, *Times*, Aug. 22, 1925
16. Seward, AK, *Daily Gateway*, Aug. 13, 1925
17. Riverside, CA, *Imperial Valley Press*, May 15, 1924, p. 6
18. Watauga, NC, *Democrat*, May 13, 1926
19. Washington D.C., *Evening Star*, Aug. 31, 1922, p. 13

Chapter 25

1. Seward, AK, *Daily Gateway*, Jan. 15, 1926, p. 2
2. Cordova, AK, *Daily Times*, Oct. 10, 1919
3. Nome, AK, *Daily Nugget*, June 7, 1916, p. 8
4. Juneau, AK, *Alaska Daily Empire*, Dec. 3, 1918, p. 5
5. Philadelphia, PA, *Evening Public Ledger*, Aug. 17, 1922, Sports Extra, p. 15
6. Seattle, WA, *Star,* May 12, 1925, p. 2
7. Juneau, AK, *Daily Empire*, Aug. 4, 1924
8. Seattle, WA, *Star*, May 12, 1925, p. 2
9. Ibid.
10. Seattle, WA, *Star,* May 11, 1925, p. 7
11. Seward, AK, *Daily Gateway*, Jan. 15, 1926, p. 2
12. Washington D.C. *Times*, Feb. 25, 1926, p. 8
13. Washington D.C. *Evening Star*, June 5, 1927, p. 14
14. Nome, AK, *Nugget*, Oct. 8, 1927, p. 5
15. Seward, AK, *Daily Gateway*, Jan. 15, 1926, p, 2
16. Juneau, AK, *Daily Alaska Empire*, May 12, 1927
17. Washington D.C. *Times*, Feb. 2, 1927, p. 8
18. Washington D.C., *Evening Star*. Sept. 26, 1926, p. 10

19. Juneau, AK, *Daily Alaska Empire*, Dec. 23, 1926, p. 2

Chapter 26

1. Douglas, AZ, *Daily Dispatch*, June 23, 1927, p. 2
2. *Ibid.*
3. Seward, AK, *Daily Gateway*, Sept. 2, 1927
4. Washington D.C. *Evening Star*, June 5, 1927, p. 14
5. Seward, AK, *Daily Gateway*, Sept. 2, 1927
6. Wrangell, AK, *Sentinel.*, September 15, 1927
7. Juneau, AK, *Daily Alaska Empire*, Aug. 24, 1927, p. 8
8. Wrangell, AK, *Sentinel*, Sept. 23, 1938, p. 3

Chapter 27

1. Washington D.C. *Evening Star*, June 5, 1927, p. 14
2. Nome, AK, *Nugget*, Aug. 10, 1929, p. 2
3. LaCrosse, WI, *Tribune and Leader Press*, Aug. 31, 1929, p. 1
4. Oakland, CA, *Tribune*, July 18, 1929
5. Dubuque, IA, *Telegraph-Herald and Times-Journal*, Nov. 27, 1929
6. Nome, AK, *Daily Nugget*, Sept. 2, 1937
7. *Ibid.*

Chapter 28

1. Tacoma, WA, *Times*, Feb. 19, 1941, p. 6
2. San Diego, CA, *Evening Tribune*, May 23, 1939, p. 4
3. Nome, AK, *Nugget*, Aug. 23, 1940, p. 2
4. Detroit, MI, *Evening Times*, Jan. 14, 1941, NIGHT EDITION, p. 2
5. Nome, AK, *Nugget*, Aug. 23, 1940, p. 2
6. Mount Clemens, MI, *Daily Monitor*, Apr. 12, 1941
7. Waterbury, CT, *Democrat*, Apr. 11, 1941, p. 6
8. Tacoma, WA, *Times*, Feb. 19, 1941, p. 7
9. *Ibid.*
10. Washington D.C. *Evening Star,* Nov. 30, 1947, p. 29

Chapter 29

1. Mount Clemens, MI, *Daily Monitor Leader*, Dec. 14, 1944
2. Nome, AK, *Nugget*, Aug. 23, 1940, p. 2
3. Wichita Falls, TX, *Times Record News*, Mar. 18, 1944, p. 2
4. Augusta, GA, *Chronicle*, Dec. 15, 1944, pp. 1 & 6
5. Waterbury, CT, *Democrat*, Nov. 9, 1943, p. 4
6. Philadelphia, PA, *Evening Public Ledger*, Aug. 17, 1922, Sports Extra, p. 15
7. Washington D.C. *Evening Star*, Dec. 24, 1944, p. B-5
8. Greensboro, NC, *Daily News*, Nov. 23, 1946, p. 7

Epilogue

1. Staten Island, NY, *Advance*, Nov. 26, 1946, p. 7
2. Nome, AK, *Nugget*, Oct. 23, 1944, p. 2
3. Wrangell, AK, *Sentinel*, Sept. 2, 1932, p. 3
4. Washington D.C. *Evening Star*, July 8, 1939, p. A-4
5. Washington D.C. *Evening Star*, July 30, 1939, p. C-12
6. Waterbury, CT, *Democrat*, Feb. 1, 1946, p. 2
7. Cleveland, OH, *Plain Dealer*, Nov. 26, 1946, p. 11
8. https://abcnews.go.com/U.S./wireStory/coast-guard-wreck-found-atlantic-storied-cutter-Bear-80589510
9. Indianapolis, IN, *Times*, Aug. 16, 1928, p. 13

Appendix A

1. Juneau, AK, *Daily Alaska Empire*, Aug. 24, 1927, p. 8

Appendix B

1. San Francisco, CA, *Call*, Nov. 27, 1897

Bibliography

Newspapers/Magazines

"The accused on the stand in his own behalf," Portland, OR, *Oregonian*, Jan. 30, 1896, p. 2
Albuquerque, NM, *Citizen*, Nov. 28, 1908
"Along the waterfront," San Francisco *Call*, Dec. 19, 1895, p. 7
Americus, GA, *Times-Recorder*, July 12, 1900
Anaconda, MT, *Standard*, Oct. 9, 1899, p. 2
"Antics in the Arctic," San Francisco *Call-Bulletin*, Jan. 29, 1896, p. 9
Astoria, OR, *Morning Astorian*, Apr. 11, 1900
Astoria, OR, *Morning Astorian*, Sept. 6, 1900
Atlanta, GA, *Journal*, Oct. 4, 1973, p. 31
Augusta, GA, *Chronicle*, Dec. 15, 1944, pp. 1 & 6
"Back from the Arctic," San Francisco *Call*, Nov. 15, 1895, p. 9
Bemidji, MN, *Daily Pioneer*, Aug. 9, 1906
Birmingham, AL *Age-Herald*, Aug. 25, 1899
Bismarck, ND, *Daily Tribune*, Oct. 8, 1909
Bon Homme Count, SD, *Citizen-Republican*, Aug. 23, 1906, p.3
Bridgeton, NJ, *Pioneer*, May 18, 1893
Butte, MT, *Daily Inter Mountain*, June 18, 1900
Canton, OH, *Repository*, May 6, 1893, p. 7
"Captain of the Bear," Wichita, KS, *Daily Eagle*, Oct. 5, 1893, p. 6
Chickasha, OK, *Daily Express*, Sept. 13, 1910, p. 2
Cleveland, OH, *Plain Dealer*, Nov. 26, 1946, p. 11
Coeur d'Alene, ID, *Evening Press*, Sept. 30, 1908, p. 4
Condon, OR, *Globe*, Sept. 13, 1900
Cordova, AK, *Daily Times*, Apr. 8, 1915
Cordova, AK, *Daily Times*, June 27, 1922
Cordova, AK, *Daily Times*, June 28, 1922, p. 8
Cordova, AK, *Daily Times*, Oct. 10, 1919
Denver, CO, *Rocky Mountain News*, Sept. 6, 1914, p. 8
Deseret, UT, *Evening News*, Sept. 28, 1909
Detroit, MI, *Evening Times*, Jan. 14, 1941, Night Edition, p. 2
Douglas City, AK, *Island News*, Sept. 11, 1907
Douglas City, AK, *Island News*, Sept. 13, 1905
Douglas, AZ, *Daily Dispatch*, June 23, 1927, p. 2
Dubuque, IA, *Telegraph-Herald and Times-Journal*, Nov. 27, 1929
Elbert County, CO, *Tribune*, Apr. 5, 1912
Elmore, ID, *Bulletin*, Jan. 15, 1896
Fairbanks, AK, *Daily News Miner*, Oct. 16, 1982
Greensboro, NC, *Daily News*, Nov. 23, 1946, p. 7
Helena, MT, *Independent*, Nov. 2, 1892, Morning, p. 5
Heppner County, OR, *Gazette*, Oct. 1, 1908
Holbrook, AZ, *News*, Jan. 13, 1911
Honolulu, HI Pacific *Commercial Advertiser*, Mar. 2, 1905, p. 10
Honolulu, HI, *Evening Bulletin*, Feb. 16, 1905
Honolulu, HI, *Evening Bulletin*, June 6, 1905
Honolulu, HI, *Hawaiian Gazette*, Feb. 17, 1905, p. 8
Honolulu, HI, *Hawaiian Star*, Apr. 3, 1905, p. 8
Honolulu, HI, *Hawaiian Star*, Dec. 19, 1906, Second Edition, p. 10
Honolulu, HI, *Hawaiian Star*, Feb. 14, 1905
Honolulu, HI, *Hawaiian Star*, Feb. 15, 1905, p. 5
Honolulu, HI, *Hawaiian Star,* Feb. 2, 1905, Second Edition
Honolulu, HI, *Hawaiian Star*, Jan. 26, 1910
Honolulu, HI, *Hawaiian Star*, Mar. 30, 1905, p. 5
Honolulu, HI, Hawaiian *Star*, May 11, 1905, Second Edition, p. 5
Honolulu, HI, *Hawaiian Star*, Nov. 15, 1905, Second Edition, p. 7
Honolulu, HI, *Pacific Commercial Advertiser*, Feb. 25, 1905, p. 10
Honolulu, HI, *Pacific Commercial Advertiser*, Feb. 26, 1905
Honolulu, HI, *Pacific Commercial Advertiser*, Jan. 24, 1905, p. 7
Honolulu, HI, *Pacific Commercial Advertiser*, June 18, 1896, p. 2
Honolulu, HI, *Pacific Commercial Advertiser*, June 20, 1896, p. 5
Honolulu, HI, *Pacific Commercial Advertiser*, Mar. 5, 1905
Honolulu, HI, *Pacific Commercial Advertiser*, May 21, 1905, p. 10
Honolulu, HI, *Republican*, July 6, 1900
Honolulu, HI, *Star-Bulletin*, Sept. 18, 1913, p. 2
Imperial Valley, CA, *Press*, June 10, 1926
Indianapolis, IN, *Journal*, Apr. 4, 1902
Indianapolis, IN, *Times*, Aug. 16, 1928, p. 13
"Indians seek apology from U.S. Navy for attack," Las Vegas, NV, *Review-Journal*, June 20, 1982, p. 62
Juneau, AK, *Alaska Daily Empire*, Aug. 12, 1926, p. 4
Juneau, AK, *Alaska Daily Empire*, Dec. 3, 1918, p. 5
Juneau, AK, *Alaska Daily Empire*, Nov. 8, 1913

Juneau, AK, *Daily Alaska Empire*, Aug. 24, 1927, p. 8
Juneau, AK, *Daily Alaska Empire*, Dec. 23, 1926, p. 2
Juneau, AK, *Daily Alaska Empire*, July 10, 1933
Juneau, AK, *Daily Alaska Empire*, June 10, 1927
Juneau, AK, *Daily Alaska Empire*, May 12, 1927
Juneau, AK, *Daily Empire*, Aug. 4, 1924
Ketchikan, AK, *Miner*, Aug. 7, 1909
Kusko, AK, *Times*, Aug. 22, 1925
LaCrosse, WI, *Tribune and Leader Press*, Aug. 31, 1929, p. 1
L'Anse, MI, *Sentinel*, Sept. 1, 1900
Las Vegas, NV, *Age*, Jan. 14, 1911, p. 2
Las Vegas, NV, *Review-Journal*, June 13, 1982, p. 85
Lincoln, NE, *State Journal*, Aug. 16, 1908, p. 2
Little Falls, MN, *Weekly Transcript*, July 17, 1900
Logansport, IN, *Daily Pharos*, December 6, 1895, p. 1
Los Angeles *Herald*, Aug. 16, 1893, p. 2
Los Angeles, CA, *Daily Herald*, Sept. 16, 1889, p. 2
Los Angeles, CA, *Daily Herald*, Sept. 9, 1889, p. 2
Los Angeles, CA, *Herald*, Aug. 5, 1892
Los Angeles, CA, *Herald*, Aug. 8, 1891
Los Angeles, CA, *Herald*, July 24, 1890
Los Angeles, CA, *Herald*, Mar. 30, 1892
Los Angeles, CA, *Herald*, Nov. 9, 1897, p. 2
Madison, SD, *Daily Leader*, Feb. 10, 1910
Manning, SC, *Times*, Nov. 6, 1907
Marietta, OH, *Daily Leader*, Nov. 20, 1897
Marshalltown, IA, *Evening Times-Republican*, July 12, 1900
Maysville, KY *Daily Public Ledger*, Sept. 6, 1900, p. 3
Mount Clemens, MI, *Daily Monitor Leader*, Dec. 14, 1944
Mount Clemens, MI, *Daily Monitor*, Apr. 12, 1941
"Never drunk while on duty," Wichita, KS, *Daily Eagle*, Jan. 28, 1896, p. 7
New Haven, CT, *Daily Morning Journal and Courier*, July 12, 1900
New York, NY, *Herald*, Sept. 25, 1890, p. 7
New York, NY, *Herald*, Sept. 3, 1922, SECTION TWO, p. 2
New York, NY, *Sun*, Apr. 6, 1900, p. 4
New York, NY, *Sun*, Jan. 26, 1896, p. 6
New York, NY, *Tribune*, Aug. 9, 1906, p. 2
New York, NY, *Tribune*, Dec. 2, 1895, p. 1
New York, NY, *Tribune*, Jan. 12, 1889, p. 6
New York, NY, *Tribune*, July 12, 1900, p. 4
New York, NY, *Tribune*, Oct. 12, 1921, p. 4
Newport News, VA, *Daily Press*, Aug. 9, 1906
"News from Alaska," Seattle *Post-Intelligencer*, May 19, 1891, p. 7
Nome, AK, *Daily Nugget*, Aug. 7, 1913
Nome, AK, *Daily Nugget*, June 4, 1913
Nome, AK, *Daily Nugget*, June 7, 1916, p. 8
Nome, AK, *Daily Nugget*, Nov. 5, 1912
Nome, AK, *Daily Nugget*, Sept. 2, 1937
Nome, AK, *Nugget*, Aug. 10, 1929, p. 2
Nome, AK, *Nugget*, Aug. 23, 1940, p. 2
Nome, AK, *Nugget*, Aug. 3, 1938, p. 4
Nome, AK, *Nugget*, Aug. 9, 1930
Nome, AK, *Nugget*, July 1, 1938
Nome, AK, *Nugget*, June 10, 1933, p. 4
Nome, AK, *Nugget*, June 5, 1934
Nome, AK, *Nugget*, Oct. 23, 1944, p. 2
Nome, AK, *Nugget*, Oct. 8, 1927, p. 5
Nome, AK, *Semi-weekly Nugget*, Aug. 12, 1905
Nome, AK, *Tri-weekly Nugget*, Dec. 2, 1905
Norfolk, VA, *Virginian-Pilot*, August 12, 1900
Norwich, CT, *Bulletin*, Aug. 3, 1910
Oakland, CA, *Tribune*, July 18, 1929
Ogden, UT, *Evening Standard*, Nov. 11, 1911, p. 14
Ogden, UT, *Standard*, Sept. 17, 1915, City Edition
"Our little 'White Navy,'" Dearborn, MI, *Independent*, Jan. 8, 1921, p. 6
Perth Amboy, NJ, *Evening News*, Nov. 26, 1909, Last Edition
Philadelphia, PA, *Evening Public Ledger*, Aug. 17, 1922, Sports Extra, p. 15
Portland, ME, *Daily Press*, Feb. 10, 1896, p. 5
Portland, ME, *Daily Press*, June 1, 1886, p. 4
Portland, OR, *Oregonian*, Jan. 25, 1896, p. 2
Portland, OR, *Oregonian*, Jan. 28, 1896
Portland, OR, *Oregonian*, Jan. 30, 1896, p. 2
Portland, OR, *Oregonian*, Sept. 14, 1914, p. 5
Portland. OR, *Oregonian*, Feb. 21, 1896, p. 2
Potosi, MO, *Journal*, Nov. 7, 1900
Providence, RI, *News*, Nov. 12, 1897
Raleigh, NC, *News & Observer*, Apr. 04, 1902
Rampart, AK, *Yukon Valley News*, Aug. 01, 1906
Reno, NV, *Weekly Nevada State Journal*, Mar. 28, 1896, p. 2
Richmond, VA, *Times Dispatch*, June 1, 1914, p. 7
River Falls, WI, *Journal*, Aug. 24, 1893
Riverside, CA, *Imperial Valley Press*, May 15, 1924, p. 6
Sacramento, CA, *Daily Record Union*, Apr. 13, 1886
Sacramento, CA, *Daily Record-Union*, June 13, 1890
St. Louis County, MN, *Virginia Enterprise*, May 27, 1910, p. 5
St. Louis, MO, *Republic*, May 8, 1900, p. 13
St. Louis, MO, *Republic*, Sept. 9, 1900, p. 3
St. Paul, MN, *Daily Globe*, July 3, 1890, p. 8
Saint Paul, MN, *Daily Globe*, Feb. 23, 1888
Salt Lake *Herald*, Sept. 5, 1907, Page 2
Salt Lake, UT, *Herald*, Dec. 12, 1895, p. 2
Salt Lake, UT, *Herald*, Dec. 20, 1895, p. 2
San Antonio, TX, *Daily Light*, Dec. 5, 1895
San Diego, CA, *Evening Tribune*, May 23, 1939, p. 4
San Diego, CA, *Union*, Mar. 2, 1930, p. 40
San Francisco *Call Bulletin*, Dec 3, 1895, p. 9
San Francisco *Call-Bulletin*, Nov. 7, 1906, p. 11
San Francisco *Chronicle*, Aug. 8, 1927, p. 25
San Francisco, CA *Call*, Nov. 22, 1897
San Francisco, CA, *Bulletin*, Oct. 3, 1891
San Francisco, CA, *Call*, Apr. 9, 1896, p. 11
San Francisco, CA, *Call*, Aug. 1, 1897
San Francisco, CA, *Call*, Dec. 13, 1908, p. 4
San Francisco, CA, *Call*, Dec. 2, 1895, p. 12
San Francisco, CA, *Call*, Dec. 3, 1895, p. 8
San Francisco, CA, *Call*, Dec. 3, 1908, p. 8
San Francisco, CA, *Call*, Jan. 24, 1896, p. 7
San Francisco, CA, *Call*, Jan. 29, 1896, p. 8
San Francisco, CA, *Call*, Jan. 31, 1896, p. 14
San Francisco, CA, *Call*, June 27, 1900
San Francisco, CA, *Call*, Mar. 27, 1896
San Francisco, CA, *Call*, Mar. 6, 1895, p. 6

San Francisco, CA, *Call*, May 6, 1900
San Francisco, CA, *Call*, Nov. 10, 1897, p. 2
San Francisco, CA, *Call*, Nov. 11, 1897, p. 6
San Francisco, CA, *Call*, Nov. 12, 1897
San Francisco, CA, *Call*, Nov. 14, 1897
San Francisco, CA, *Call*, Nov. 15, 1895, p. 9
San Francisco, CA, *Call*, Nov. 17, 1897, p. 2
San Francisco, CA, *Call*, Nov. 18, 1897
San Francisco, CA, *Call*, Nov. 18, 1897
San Francisco, CA, *Call*, Nov. 20, 1897
San Francisco, CA, *Call*, Nov. 22, 1897
San Francisco, CA, *Call*, Nov. 27, 1897
San Francisco, CA, *Call*, Nov. 4, 1905, pp. 1–2
San Francisco, CA, *Call*, Nov. 8, 1897
San Francisco, CA, *Call*, Nov. 9, 1897
San Francisco, CA, *Call*, Sept. 13, 1898
San Francisco, CA, *Call*, Sept. 4, 1907, p. 9
San Francisco, CA, *Call-Bulletin,* Feb. 9, 1896, p. 20
San Francisco, CA, *Call-Bulletin*, Jul. 18, 1905, p. 3
San Francisco, CA, *Call-Bulletin*, Nov. 18, 1906
San Francisco, CA, *Chronicle*, Mar. 29, 1896, p. 19
San Francisco, CA, *Morning Call*, December 1, 1890, p. 4
San Francisco, CA, *Morning Call,* June 12, 1890
San Francisco, CA, *Morning Call*, May 27, 1890, p. 4
San Jose, CA, *Mercury News*, Sept. 15, 1914, p. 1
Seattle, WA, *Daily Times*, Apr. 10, 1902, p. 5
Seattle, WA, *Daily Times*, Apr. 16, 1902, p. 9
Seattle, WA, *Post-Intelligencer*, Apr. 28, 1896, p. 2
Seattle, WA, *Post-Intelligencer*, June 4, 1891, p. 12
Seattle, WA, *Post-Intelligencer*, May 19, 1891
Seattle, WA, *Post-Intelligencer*, May 6, 1900, p. 12
Seattle, WA, *Post-Intelligencer*, Nov. 20, 1890
Seattle, WA, *Post-Intelligencer*, Oct. 11, 1891
Seattle, WA, *Post-Intelligencer*, Sept. 24, 1890
Seattle, WA, *Star,* May 11, 1925, p. 7
Seattle, WA, *Star*, May 12, 1925, p. 2
Seattle, WA, *Star*, May 9, 1914, p. 15
Seward, AK, *Daily Gateway*, Aug. 13, 1925
Seward, AK, *Daily Gateway,* Jan. 15, 1926, p, 2
Seward, AK, *Daily Gateway*, Sept. 2, 1927
Seward, AK, *Gateway*, March 18, 1921
Seward, AK, *Gateway*, Sept. 18, 1915
Seward, AK, *Weekly Gateway*, Oct. 20, 1906
"Sharp's stories scored," San Francisco *Call*, Feb. 22, 1896
Sitka, AK, *Daily Sentinel*, Oct. 26, 2006, p. 3
Skagway, AK *Daily Alaskan*, Oct. 22, 1909
Skagway, AK, *Daily Alaskan*, Apr. 22, 1909
Skagway, AK, *Daily Alaskan*, Mar. 14, 1922, p. 2
Skagway, AK, *Daily Alaskan*, Nov. 13, 1905
Skagway, AK, *Daily Alaskan*, Nov. 23, 1909
Skagway, AK, *Daily Alaskan*, Oct. 22, 1909
Skagway, AK, *Daily Morning Alaskan*, Aug. 4, 1901
Skowhegan, ME, *Somerset Reporter*, Dec. 5, 1901, p. 6
Spokane, WA, *Press*, Sept. 11, 1906
Stamford, CT, *Daily Advocate*, July 14, 1932, p. 8
Stamford, CT, *Daily Advocate*, Nov. 5, 1900, p. 6
Stamford, CT, *Daily Advocate*, Thursday, June 23, 1927, p. 17
Staten Island, NY, *Advance*, Nov. 26, 1946, p. 7
Tacoma, WA, *Times*, Feb. 19, 1941, p. 6
Tacoma, WA, *Times*, Feb. 19, 1941, p. 7
Topeka, KS, *State Journal*, Nov. 9, 1897, p. 3
Topeka, KS, *State Journal*, Oct. 8, 1909, p. 3
Tucson, AZ, *Weekly Citizen*, Dec. 14, 1895
"Uncle Sam's seals," Holbrook, AZ, *News.*, Jan. 13, 1911
Valdez, AK, *Alaska Prospector*, Apr. 17, 1902
Valdez, AK, *Alaska Prospector,* Aug. 30, 1906
Valdez, AK, *Alaska Prospector*, Sept. 17, 1903
Valdez, AK, *Daily Prospector*, August 5, 1913
Valdez, AK, *Prospector*, Dec. 24, 1908
Vernon County, WI, *Censor*, Sept. 29, 1909, p. 7
Virginia City, MT *Madisonian*, Dec. 14, 1895
Wailuku, HI, Maui *News*, Dec. 31, 1904
Wakarusa, IN, *Tribune*, Dec. 1, 1910
Walla Walla, WA, *Evening Statesman*, Dec. 31, 1909 p. 6
Washington, D.C. *Evening Star*, Aug. 31, 1922, p. 13
Washington, D.C. *Evening Star*, Dec. 1, 1912, p. 9
Washington, D.C. *Evening Star*, Dec. 10, 1909, p. 20
Washington, D.C. *Evening Star*, Dec. 19, 1909, p. 8
Washington, D.C. *Evening Star*, Dec. 24, 1944, p. B-5
Washington, D.C. *Evening Star*, Feb.8, 1896, p. 2
Washington, D.C. *Evening Star*, Jan. 19, 1924
Washington, D.C. *Evening Star*, Jan. 3, 1909, p. 14
Washington, D.C. *Evening Star*, July 19, 1921, p. 13
Washington, D.C. *Evening Star*, July 30, 1939, p. C-12
Washington, D.C. *Evening Star*, July 8, 1939, p. A-4
Washington, D.C. *Evening Star*, June 5, 1927, p. 14
Washington, D.C. *Evening Star*, Mar. 21, 1909, p. 12
Washington, D.C. *Evening Star*, March 17, 1896
Washington, D.C. *Evening Star*, May 7, 1933, p. A-9
Washington, D.C. *Evening Star*, Nov 8, 1910, p. 2
Washington, D.C. *Evening Star*, Nov. 30, 1947, p. 29
Washington, D.C. *Times*, Feb. 2, 1927, p. 8
Washington, D.C. *Times*, Feb. 25, 1926, p. 8
Washington, D.C. *Times*, July 6, 1900, p. 7
Washington, D.C. *Times*, May 20, 1912, LAST EDITION, p. 7
Washington, D.C., *Evening Star*, Aug. 31, 1922, p. 13
Washington, D.C., *Evening Star*. Sept. 26, 1926, p. 10
Washington, D.C., *Evening Star*, July 9, 1933, p. A-2
Watauga, NC, *Democrat*, May 13, 1926
Waterbury, CT, *Democrat*, Apr. 11, 1941, p. 6
Waterbury, CT, *Democrat*, Feb. 1, 1946, p. 2
Waterbury, CT, *Democrat*, Nov. 9, 1943, p. 4
Waterbury, CT, *Evening Democrat*, July 3, 1890
Waterbury, CT, *Evening Democrat*, Sept. 22, 1890
Waterbury, CT, *Evening Democrat*, Sept. 6, 1900, p. 4
Wichita Falls, TX, *Times Record News*, Mar. 18, 1944, p. 2
Wichita, KS, *Daily Eagle*, Jan. 28, 1896, p. 7
Wichita, KS, *Daily Eagle*, Oct. 1893, p. 6
Wilmington, DE, *Evening Journal*, Dec. 8, 1890
Worcester, MA, *Daily Spy*, May 7, 1893, Worcester, MA, p. 9
Wrangell, AK, *Sentinel*, Sept. 15, 1927
Wrangell, AK, *Sentinel*, Sept. 2, 1932, p. 3
Wrangell, AK, *Sentinel*, Sept. 23, 1938, p. 3

Bibliography

Internet

https://brainyquote.com/quotes/steve_backshall_1169830
http://www.fdca.org.uk/Stephens_Whalers.html
https://en.wikipedia.org/wiki/Lady_Franklin_Bay_Expedition
https://www.history.uscg.mil/Browse-by-Topic/Assets/Water/All/Article/2082164/bear-1885/
https://alaskashipwreck.com/shipwrecks-by-area/west-central-alaska-shipwrecks-2/west-central-alaska-shipwrecks-g/
https://www.brainyquote.com/quotes/mark_twain_141733
https://www.history.uscg.mil/Browse-by-Topic/Notable-People/All/Article/1848494/captain-michael-a-healey-usrcs/ (New York Sun)
https://hakaimagazine.com/article-short/true-blue/
https://www.history.uscg.mil/Browse-by-Topic/Notable-People/All/Article/1762503/commodore-ellsworth-p-bertholf/
http://whalerswahine.com/
https://en.wikipedia.org/wiki/Last_voyage_of_the_Karluk (incident synopsis)
https://en.wikopedia.org/wiki/Hubert_Wilkins
https://abcnews.go.com/US/wireStory/coast-guard-wreck-found-atlantic-storied-cutter-Bear-80589510

Books

Bunes, Robert M. *Wind, Fire, and Ice: The Perils of a Coast Guard Icebreaker in Antarctica*. Lanham, MD: Lyons Press 2021.
Kroll, C. Douglas. *A Coast Guardsman's History of the U.S. Coast Guard*. Annapolis, MD: Naval Institute Press, 2010.
Ostrom, Thomas P. *The United States Coast Guard: 1790 to the Present*. Oakland, OR: Elderberry Press, 2004.
Walling, Michael G. *Bloodstained Sea: The U.S. Coast Guard in the Battle of the Atlantic, 1941–1944*. Wilmington, DE. International Marine/Ragged Mountain Press; 1st edition, 2004.

General

About Us | Alaska Commercial Co.—NWC
Kern, Florence & Barbara Voulgaris. *Traditions: 200 Years of History*. U.S. Coast Guard History Center. 1990. https://media.defense.gov/2018/Jan/10/2001864388/-1/-1/0/TRADITIONS.PDF
Launching USCR Cutter McCulloch: The Queen of the Revenue Marine: MCCULLOCH-LAUNCHING-Dec-1896–001.PDF (1896)
Logs of the US Revenue Cutter Service and US Coast Guard: https://www.archives.gov/research/military/logbooks/revenue-cutter-and-coast-guard
"O Captain! My Captain!" an 1865 poem by Walt Whitman about the assassination of U.S. president Abraham Lincoln.
Revenue Cutter *McCulloch* Specifications: https://media.defense.gov/2021/Dec/09/2002906425/-1/-1/0/1895_NO3-RCS-MCCULLOCH.PDF (1895)
Shelling of the Alaskan Native American Village of Angoon, October 1882. Washington, D.C.: Department of the Navy, Naval Historical Center. https://media.defense.gov/2021/Dec/15/2002909572/-1/-1/0/1882_ANGOON_ATTACK_HEALY.PDF
SRCS Officers Petition Regarding Retirement System for the RCS: https://media.defense.gov/2022/Mar/16/2002957638/-1/-1/0/1899-RCS-PETITION-001.PDF
Stika, Joseph—VADM (Retired). An oral history conducted by Chief Marine Science Technician Dennis L. Noble about the early years of Admiral Stika's remarkable career in the nation's oldest sea service (1908–1951)
United States Coast Guard (USCG) Historian's Office: https://www.history.uscg.mil https://media.defense.gov/2022/Mar/29/2002965138/-1/-1/0/

Index

Numbers in ***bold italics*** indicate pages with illustrations

Abbie M. Deering 62, 63
Adams (Coast Guard) 113
Adams (Navy) 42
Admiralty Island, Alaska 41
African-American 39
Akutan 29, 160; *see also* volcano
Alameda, California 11–12, 187
Alaska 94–95, 156
Alaska Commercial Company 33, 56, 59, 115, 117, 121, 123
alcohol 7, 28, 47, 49, 50, 54–57, 64, 83, 106–109, 111, 164, 183; aboard cutters 28, 54, 64, 83
HMS *Alert* 5
Aleutian Islands, Alaska 4, 11, 24, 29, 36, 124, 135, 138, 182
Alger, Russell A. 76
Algonquin 25, ***78***, 160
Allen, Jim 172, 173, 176
Alpha 92, 93
Amundsen, Roald 110, 155, 157, 158, 159, 160, 177
Anadyr, Siberia 19, 20
Anderson, Seaman *see* Icy Bay
Andrew Hicks 59
Angoon, Alaska 41, 42, 43
Apache 101, 109
Arctic hitchhikers 178
Army, U.S. 5, 7, 32, 66, 93, 96, 181, 186, 188
Artisall, Charlie 35
Asuncion 33
Atagh 116, 118, 119

Baker, Genevieve 1
Baker, Lucille 1
Ballinger, J.G. ***16***, 21, 22, 147, 148
Bartlett, Robert 153, 160
Bayard, Thomas 129–130; *see also* Secretary of State
Bayard, Thomas H. 143
Belvedere 85
Berate Cave 27
Berg, H.B. ***175***

Bernard, Joe 18
Berry, John G. 54–55, 83, 85, 197
Bertha 136
Bertholf, Ellsworth P. 1, 9–10, 15, 17, 65, 67, 70, 72, 83, 86, ***87***–91, 141–143, 146, 156, 197
Birke, Frederick J. 25
Bishop, Dell 158
Black Diamond 127
Blaine, James G. 127
Blum, Leon 73
Bodkin, Thomas 46
Boedecker, John 25
Bogoslaw 29; *see also* volcano
Bogosloff Island, Alaska 139
Bonanza 21
Boundy, William 48, 58, 59, 197
Boutwell ***13***–14
Bowdoin 185
Bowers, George M. 118, 119
Bristol Bay, Alaska 27, 139
Broadbent, A.L. 56
Brower, Charles D. 167
Brown, Aycock 190
Brown, Captain 32
Brown, James M. 17
Brown, Le Grand 103, 104
Bruce, Miner W. 32, 198
Bruning, F.F. 158
Buchgoldi, aviator 20
Bugby, Bessie E. 36
Bugby, John S. 36
Buhner, Albert 15, 17, 46, 48–50, 54, 56–57, 59, 62–63
Buskoe 185
Butcher, R.W. 168, 189, 190, 192
Butler, Matthew 131
Byrd, Richard 160, 187, 192–193
Byrnes, Joseph 48

Call, Samuel 83, 86, ***87***–89
Camden, B.H. 17, 197
Canada 4, 5, 8, 23, 93, 115, 126–131, 133–134, 141, 143, 151–153, 187

Cape Faukoff, Alaska 29
Cape Flattery, Alaska 49
Cape Navarina, Alaska 30
Cape Pankoff, Alaska 29
Cape Prince of Wales, Alaska 30, 69, 75, 152, 155, 160
Cape Romanzoff, Alaska 17
Cape St. John 24, 27
Cape Smyth 85, 111, 167
Carlisle, John G. 49, 61
Castle, Asst. District Attorney 22
cat 1, 120, 153
cattle round-up 101–102
Chandler 39, 41
chickenpox 194
Churchill, Frank G. 106
Clement, P.E. ***175***
Coberg 189
Cochran, Frances 162
Cochrane, C.S. 9, ***16***–18, 83, 164, 166–167, 176, 197
Coffin, Charles W. 46, 48, 57
Collector of Customs 34, 94, 103
Comanche 185
Connell, George G. 57
Cordova, Alaska 33, 170
Corwin 39, 41–53, 54–56, 71, 77, 113, 132, 136, 152–153, 157–158
Coulson, W.C. 53
court-martial 10, 17, 38–39, 41, 43–47, 49, 51–52, 63–64, 75, 83, 138; *see also* Healey, Michael
Covell, Leon Claude (L.C.) ***16***, 106, 160, 164
Craig, Donald A. 7
crime 9, 42, 45, 61–62, 95, 106–109, 111
Crossley, District Attorney 143

Daily, John K. 46
Dallas 52
Daniels, George M. 46–48, 50–51, 54, 57, 63

209

Index

Danish 181–183, 188
Dashing Wave 28
Davis Strait, Greenland 185l; *see also* Greenland; submarine
De Otte, F.N. 13, *175*
Department of Alaska 41
Department of Commerce and Labor 116, 147
Derby, Wilfred N. 25
Dexter 71–72
Dickinson, Commander 76
Dietrich, Charles 62
Dingley, Nelson, Jr. 128
Diomede Islands 19, 108, 111, 175
District of Alaska 25, 34, 36, 41
Dodge, Frank S. 104
Dodge, Frederick C. 69–70, *71*–72, 104, 160
dog 66, 69, 74, 82, 89, 117, 120, 151, 152, 153, 162, 164, 169, 188, 197
Dorothy 175
Dorry, J.E. 46, 50–51, 56, 64, 106
Dove 72
Dunberg, Herman 48
Dunwoodie, Captain 138, 139
Dutch Harbor, Alaska 11, 13, 26, 61, 71, 97, 109, 111

Eacrett 95
Eagleson, Dr. 82
East Cape, Alaska 18, 19, 158
Eastwind 188, 190
Eddy, W.M. 22
Egg Island, Alaska 97, 98
Elisif 175
Elliott, Charles 95
Emery, Howard 46, 48, 51, 54
Emma Village, Siberia 18
Ennatha 116–119
Evergreen 190

faker 154; *see also* Steffanson, Vilhjalmur
Fearless 85
Fengar, A.A. 6
Fessenlen 53
first land-plane descent onto drift ice 157
fisheries agreement 123, 125, 127–29, 130, 134
Foley, Captain 113–114
Ford, George 43
forest fire 104
Forman, Sands W. 36
Fox, Dr. 117
Fram 152
Frederich, Engineer 54–55
Freeman 85
Frothingham, Robert 15

Frye, William P. 131
Fugitive 42

Gaelic 36
Gage, Lyman 75–77
Galveston 101
gasoline pump 177
General McPherson 22
Germany 130, 186–187, 191
Gertrude 158
Glover, J.W. 106
Glover, Russell 132–133
Godthaab, Greenland 183; *see also* Greenland
Golden Gate 62
Gordon, Thomas 167
Gorman, F.J. 169, *175*
Grant 53–55
Gray, Agent 59
Great Britain 5, 8, 55, 92, 111, 115, 125–131, 133–136, 138, 143, 148, 163, 183, 186–187, 193
great mystery cruise 103
Greely, Adolphus 5–6
Greenland 1, 5–6, 13–14, 18, 181–185, 187–193
Grieve, O. 5

Haake, F.J. 113–114
Haida 25, 187
Hair Seal Cape, Alaska 28
Halifax *Recorder* 127
Hamilton, W. 106
Hamlet, H.G. 17, 197
Hamlet, Oscar C. 101–104
Hamlin, Charles Sumner 51–53, 57–58, 60–61
Hammarstrom, L.O. 170
Harrison, Benjamin 128–130
Hartley 53, 57, 62
Hayden Packing Company 80
Healey, Dick 152
Healey, Fred 36, 50
Healey, James 41
Healey, J.T. 33
Healey, Michael 1, 6–7, *9*–10, 15, 17, 24–25, 27–64, 69, 75–76, 83, 86–87, 92, 124–126, 128–130, 135–138, 152, 180, 184, 193; *see also* court-martial
Healey, Patrick 41
Healey, Sherwood 41
Hearst, George 70
Hearst, William 69
Helene 101, 103
Hemingway murder 27
Herbert, Hilary A. 63
Herschel Island, Alaska 49, 77, 80, 85, 109–110, 151, 154
Hilborn, S.G. 74
Hinser 141; *see also Kensei Maru*
Hoar, George Frisbie 128–129

Hodgson, D.B. 53
C.S. *Holmes* 159, 177–79
Honolulu, Hawaii 36, 100–105
Hooper, Captain 4, 57
Hosmer, Ralph S. 104
Hottel, James Freeman 25, 168–170, *175*
Howe, Mabel ("Charming") 47
Hudson **90**
Hutton, Patrick 55, 56

Iceland 183, 186–188
Icy Bay, Alaska 59, 157–158; *see also* Anderson, Seaman; Nelson, Seaman; Smith, Seaman
immorality 165; *see also* morality
Indian Claims Commission 42
Indian Point, Alaska 30–32
infantrymen 189
Iroquois 100, 147
Iwalani 103–104

Jackson, Dr. Sheldon 32, 86–88, 94, 98
Jacobs, William V.E. 145–147
Japan 8, 23, 37, 100, 115, 135, 137–142, 144–150, 186, 189
Jarvis, David 1, 15, 17, 21, 24–30, 32, 34–36, 70–71, 86–*87*, 88–89, 95–99, 155–156, 197
Jeannette 85, 108–110
Jessie 21
The Jewish State 193
Johjnsen, Axel 106
Johnson, J.H. 95
Johnson, Judge 34
Johnston, O.L. 25
Johnston Island, Alaska 104
Jones, Edward 19, 25, 168, 176
Jones, Engineer 51, 54
Jones, Joseph "Pig Iron" 109, 111
Judge, James 117, 145–146
Jumna 41

Kaiwo Maru 140
Kalugen, Lawrence 34; *see also* Russian Pete
Karluk 77, 151–154, 156, 160
Kensei Maru 141–142, 144; *see also Hinser*
Khabarovsk, Russia 20
Kilauea 100; *see also* volcano
King, Joseph 111
King and Wing 152–153
King's Island, Alaska 32, 135, 169, 176, 179
Klinger, Thomas S. 25
Knapp, E.J. 107
Knapp, Lyman 25, 34
Kosterometeroff, George 25

Index

Kotzebu Sound, Alaska 21, 155–156, 179
Krassin 26, 178, 179

Lady Franklin Bay Expedition 5
Landers, W.N. 107
Ledge Island, Alaska 22
Lee, Hugh 107
Legion of Merit medal 190
Levanefsky, Sigismund 19–20
Lincoln, Abraham 15, 41
Lindberg, Jatfet 152
Lindbergh, Charles 19, 157
Lindsay, R.M. 75–76
Littlefield, Charles Edgar 93
Loch Garry 5
Lodge of Workmen 37
London *Daily News* 131
London *Daily Telegraph* 131
London *Standard* 127
London *Times* 127
Long, John Davis 73–77; *see also* Secretary of the Navy
Lopez, Jerome 109, 111
Los Angeles (dirigible) 159
Loud, H.F. 74

Mackenzie Bay, Greenland 185; *see also* Greenland
Mackinac **102**
Maclean, A.J. **175**
MacMillan, Donald 159, 160
Macon, Georgia 41
Maglathlin, W.C. **175**
Maguire, James G. 74
mail 21, 25–26, 65–66, 83–84, 104, 114, 153, 164, 169–171, 175–177, 179
Makushin 29; *see also* volcano
Manning 9, 62–**63**, 92, 106, 113–114, 142, 145–146, 148
Mare Island, Washington 77
Marines, U.S. 42, 62–63
Martin, Asst. District Attorney 143
Mattern, Jimmy 19, 20
Matthews, A.C. 136
Mattie Dyer 136
Matzpen 193
Maud 158, 159, 161
Mayo, Mariano 37, 38
McArthur 92
McAuliffe, W.J.B. **175**
McCormick, Cyrus 71
McCulloch 9, 139, **140**
McGregor, A.H. 77, 151
McKenna, James 75
McKinley, William 75–78, 153
McMillan, C.C. 106
McPherson 22
Meade, E.E. 103, 106
Melville, George S. 4, 76

Merriman, E.C. 42
Mexico 135
Meyers, William C. 56
Miller, murder victim 34
Modoc 185
Mojave 25
Moore, W.C. 157; *see also* Icy Bay
morality 13, 35, 88, 108–109, 151; *see also* immorality
Morning Star 37
Morris, J.S. 22
Morris, William 42
Mount St. Elias 157
Muir, John 43
Munger, Captain 54
Murane, Judge 22
murder 21, 24–25, 27, 29, 34, 36, 62–63, 94, 109
Murphy, James 95; *see also* St. Lawrence Bay
Myers, U.S. Consul 133

Napoleon 30
Navy, U.S. 4, 5, 7, 14, 21, 42, 49, 61, 63, 66–67, 73–74, 76, 81, 83, **90**, 93, 101, 104, 122, 126, 147, 159–160, 164, 181, 186–187
Neilson, Jans B. 22
Nelson, Seaman 157; *see also* Icy Bay
New York *Herald* 83
New York *Journal* 69, 80–81
Newport 85
Newport, Rhode Island 67
Newport News, Virginia 166
Newth, E.W. 108–111
Nice, J.N. 59
1911 sealing treaty 148–49
Nome, Alaska 18–20, 22, 26, 34–35, 65–66, 92–99, 107–111, 145–146, 152–153, 156, 158–162, 164–165, 169–170, 174–179, 182, 194
Norge, dirigible 157
Norma 37
North American Commercial Company 59, 106, 122, 134
North American Transportation Company 3
North Fork 71
North Pole 65, 86, 153, 155, 157–161
North Port 188
North Star 185
Northeast Greenland Patrol 14, 185
Northeast Point 23, 114, 138, 141
Northland **150**
Northwest Trading Company 42
Norton Sound, Alaska 22, 74

Nunivak Island, Alaska 65, 69, 86, 88, 94
Nushagak, Alaska 139

Occidental Hotel 36, 49
Oduna 160
Ohio 96–98
Orca 85
Oregon 97
Orphan seals 165
Otter Island, Alaska 26
Ouyaga 183
Ozernoy 27

Pacific Whaling Company 73
Paddy, Cochran's dog 164
Paeringerhaven, Greenland 183; *see also* Greenland
Paige, Charles 12
Parker, S.V. 20, 168
Paulson, Captain 27
Peary, Robert 153, 160
pelagic sealing 115–116, 131–132, 147, 149
Perkins, George Clement 60, 74
Perry 54, 57, 112, **113**, 114, 138–139, 146, 148
Peter Bregt, Greenland 185; *see also* Greenland
Peterson, J.P. 48
HMS *Pheasant* 55–57
Phillips, Captain 54
Phillips, William 20; *see also* Secretary of State
photography 164
Piltz, George 103
Pioneer Club 22
pirate 3–4, 33–35, 66, 126, 133
Pirate Cove 27–28
poachers 6, 21–24, 60, 65, 92, 100, 108, 112, 115, 122–130, 132–133, 135–150, 192
Point Barrow, Alaska 4, 17, 21, 30–31, 35, 43, 64–65, 67–70, 73–75, 77–78, 80, 83–89, 94, 107, 109–111, 121, 151–153, 155, 157–159, 162, 164, 166–167, 169, 172, 174, 176–179
Point Belcher, Alaska 69, 177
Point Hope, Alaska 19, 21, 30, 69, 75, 109, 153, 162, 164, 170, 174, 176–177, 179
Point Lay, Alaska 177, 179
Polar Bear 151
polar bear cubs 174
Popoff Island, Alaska 27
Port Clarence, Alaska 21, 31–32, 74, 91, 111
Port Townsend, Washington 53–54, 61, 64, 94, 132–133, 136, 157
Portland 3–4
Portland, Maine 41, 112

Index

Portland, Oregon 3
Portuguese Union of San Leandro 37
Post, Wiley 19
Poten River, Siberia 18
Powell, marshal 22
Powers, Thomas 48
Premier 24, 27–28, 30–31
Pribilof Islands, Alaska 23–27, 29, 34, 65, 112–116, 123–124, 129–130, 134, 138–139, 144–145, 149–150, 164, 208
Pribylov, Gavriil 27

radio station, German 185, 188
radio station, Greenland 183
Ralph J. Lung 62
Ram 158
Randall, George M. 96, 98, 99
Rankin, Bert 11, 12, 13
Raritan 185
Reef Point, Alaska 138
Reid, Silas 143
reindeer 7, 21, 30–32, 34–35, 39, 43, 65, 69, 74–75, 86–91, 96, 106, 109, 152, 162, 165
Reynolds, R.R. 172–173
Reynolds, W.E. 53, 160
Ritchie, H.S. 143
Robinson, L.L. 157
Rogers, H.B. 53
Roosevelt, Theodore 34, 103, 138
Rosario 85
Rose, Earl G. 190
Ross, Thomas 18, 22, 155, 159, 161
Ross, Worth G. 55, 114, 119
Rossig, Seaman 22
Rush 9, *12*, *63*, 92, 127, 129–130, 132–133, 136, 139–140, 142
Russell, Isaac Cook 157
Russia 4, 8, 15, 17–20, 26–27, 40, 89, 91, 100, 114, 121, 123, 130, 134, 138, 148, 152, 175, 178, 182, 188–189
Russian American Fur Company 114
Russian Pete 28, 33–34; *see also* Kalugen, Lawrence

Safety Harbor, Alaska 22
Saiki Maru 141
Saint George Island, Alaska 26–27
St. Lawrence Bay 19, 21, 65, 95, 109, 111, 158, 162, 175, 179; *see also* Murphy, James
St. Matthew Island 32, 65, 69, 147
St. Michael, Alaska 4, 22, 26, 32, 70–71, 77, 80, 94, 96–97, 155, 174–175

St. Paul 32, 96
St. Paul Island, Alaska 26–27, 113–114, 117–118, 123, 136–141, 147
San Francisco, California 9, 12, 17, 21, 25, 27–28, 36–37, 43, 46–53, 58, 62, 69–71, 73–75, 77, 80, 84, 95–96, 100, 110, 117, 121, 123, 129–130, 142, 145, 151, 156, 163–164, 167, 170, 181, 192, 197–198
San Francisco Call 47–49, 69–70, 73–85, 130, 197
San Francisco Examiner 17, 36, 70, 80, 197
San Leandro, California 37–38
Sand Point, Alaska 28–29, 34
Santa Anna 96–98
Sausalito, California 47–48
Scammel, William K. 26, 168
Schley Winfield Scott 5, 15
Schmidt, Otto 20
Scullion, Thomas 76
Sea Horses, Alaska 177–179
seal islands 6, 114, 121, 124, 135–136
Seattle, Washington 4, 9, 22, 24–26, 29–30, 36, 63, 68–72, 80–81, 84, 94, 96–97, 99, 110, 114, 127, 132, 140, 145–146, 149, 153, 158, 160, 163, 165–166, 170, 174, 197–198
Secretary of State 40, 127, 129, 208
Secretary of the Navy 63, 73–74; *see also* Long, John D.
Secretary of the Treasury 47–49, 51, 72, 75, 92–93, 106, 128, 130, 133, 169; *see also* Sherman, John
Semper Paratus 11, 52, 92, 154
Seward, William 40, 182; *see also* Secretary of State
Sharp, Benjamin 58–59
Shaw, J.C. 71
Shenandoah, dirigible 156, 159, 160
Shepherd, L.G. 127–130
Sherman, John 128, 131; *see also* Secretary of the Treasury
Shivhaidin 29; *see also* volcano
Shoemaker, Charles F. 3–4, 45–46, 50–52, 60, 70–73, 76–77, 79, 83
Shoemaker, P.R. 106
Shoup, marshal 34
Shumagin Islands, Alaska 27, 138
Simeonoff Island, Alaska 138
Sitka, Alaska 23–25, 28–31, 34, 36, 42, 94, 125, 127–128, 132, 136, 157
smallpox 95–98

Smith, Edward H. "Iceberg" 185
Smith, H.D. 54
Smith, Mary Elisa 41
Smith, Seaman 157; *see also* Icy Bay
Society of the Nanooks 106; *see also* True Polar Bears
South Greenland Survey Expedition 184
Southwind 188, 190
Spalding, Asst. Secretary of Treasury 133
Spencer, J.W. 33–34
Spitsbergen, Norway 158, 160
Spreckels, John D. 77, 79, 83–84
Stackable, E.R. 103–104
Standon, C.A. **175**
Star Chamber 48
Steffanson, Vilhjalmur 151–152, 156–157, 167
Stephens, Alexander 5
Stephens, William 5
Stodder, L.N. 53
Stoney, George M. 74–75
Storis 186, 188–190
Straus, Oscar 147
Stromberg, William 25
submarine 157, 163, 185, 188; *see also* Davis Strait, Greenland
Sukkertoppen, Greenland 183; *see also* Greenland
Swenson, Olaf 152–153
Swift, D.S. 22

Tacoma 96
Tahoma 114, 148, 150
Taimyr 152
Talbot, Stephen P. 110, 111
Tarpley, Louis H. 24, 36
Teddy Bear 18
Teller Station, Alaska 19, 89, 92, 98, 111, 158, 175, 179
Thetis 9, 11, 39, 62–63, 110, 139, 145–147, 149–150
Thetis I 5, **6**
Thiesen, William 193, 194
Thompson, Sir John 131
Thompson, Dr. Thomas G. 172–173
Thrasher 75
Thurber, Judson 116–120
Ti'Len 42
Tilton, F. 59
Tingle, Mr. 33
Tlingit 41, 42
Todd, Clement J. 25
Tokwa Maru 138–139
Tonki Point, Alaska 113
Townsend 156
Toya Maru 140
Tozier (Captain) 54–55
Trader of Nome 178

trafficking 107–108
Treasury Department 3, 23, 25, 31, 43–44, 46, 50, 54, 60, 62, 64, 67–68, 75, 80, 83, 93, 95, 97, 101, 111, 113, 121, 128, 133, 136, 143, 145146, 148, 164, 193
Tropic Bird 36
True Polar Bears 106; *see also* Society of the Nanooks
Tunguse reindeer 89–90
Tuttle, Frank 9, 15, 17, 50, 64, 68–69, 75, 77–84, 90, 92–96, 98–99, 127, 197

Unalaska, Alaska 11, 24–27, 29, 33, 36, 49, 55–57, 59, 62–63, 65, 69, 77, 98, 106, 112, 121, 125, 142, 144, 146, 152, 160, 167
Unalga 25, 71, **150**
Underwood, W.H. 103–104
Unga, Alaska 27, 34
Urquhart, J.C. **175**

Valdez, Alaska 23, 62, 139–141, 143, 146
Vancouver, British Columbia 72, 92–93
Vanderbilt, J.M. 42
Van Ness, Violette 36–37
Viani, Peter 32
Vincent (survivor) 30, 31
Vogel, H.B. 48
volcano 29, 100

Wadsworth, Captain 54
Wainwright, Alaska 109, 159, 172, 176–179
Wales, Alaska 19, 179
walrus hunt 169–173
Walrus Island, Alaska 23, 26, 145–146
Wanderer 85
weirdest battle 186, 188
Wheeler, Bob 181, 183, 184, 185
Whitbeck, John E. 25

White, Chester M. 46–47, 51–52
White, J.W. 41
White, Stephen M. 60, 74
S.G. *Wilder* 36, 37
Wilkins, Sir Hubert 157
Wilson, Robert 58
Windom, William 130
Wolcott 54, 132, 133
Wood, H.M. 83
Wood, R.E. **175**
Woodruff, E.H. 83, 86
Woyciehowsky, S.J. **175**
Wrangell Island, Alaska 151–154, 159, 164
Wright, Dora 11, 12

Zeusler, Frederick A. 19, 65, 168, 172, 176–180, 187

www.ingramcontent.com/pod-product-compliance
Lightning Source LLC
Chambersburg PA
CBHW060342010526
44117CB00017B/2938